Faulkner and His Contemporaries
FAULKNER AND YOKNAPATAWPHA,
2002

Faulkner and His Contemporaries

FAULKNER AND YOKNAPATAWPHA, 2002

EDITED BY
JOSEPH R. URGO
AND
ANN J. ABADIE

UNIVERSITY PRESS OF MISSISSIPPI
JACKSON

www.upress.state.ms.us

Copyright © 2004 by University Press of Mississippi
All rights reserved
Manufactured in the United States of America

Paperback Edition 2010.

∞

The paper in this book meets the guidelines for permanence and durability of the Committee on Production Guidelines for Book Longevity of the Council on Library Resources

Library of Congress Cataloging-in-Publication Data

Faulkner and Yoknapatawpha Conference (29th : 2002 : University of Mississippi)
Faulkner and his contemporaries/Faulkner and Yoknapatawpha, 2002; edited by Joseph R. Urgo and Ann J. Abadie.
p. cm.
Papers originally presented at the 29th Faulkner and Yoknapatawpha Conference in 2002.
Includes bibliographical references and index.

ISBN: 978-1-60473-544-4

1. Faulkner, William, 1897–1962—Criticism and interpretation—Congresses.
2. American fiction—20th century—History and criticism—Congresses.
3. Faulkner, William, 1897–1962—Contemporaries—Congresses.
4. Modernism (Literature)—United States—Congresses.
I. Urgo, Joseph R. II. Abadie, Ann J. III. Title.

PS3511.A86Z78321174   2002
813'.52—dc22   2003027612

British Library Cataloging-in-Publication Data available

In Memoriam
James Murry "Jimmy" Faulkner
July 18, 1923–December 24, 2001

Contents

Introduction   ix
    JOSEPH R. URGO

Note on the Conference   xxvii

Tribute to Jimmy Faulkner (1923–2001)   xxxi
    DONALD M. KARTIGANER

Traveling with Faulkner: A Tale of Myth,
    Contemporaneity, and Southern Letters   3
    HOUSTON A. BAKER, JR.

William Faulkner and Other Famous Creoles   21
    W. KENNETH HOLDITCH

Cather's War and Faulkner's Peace: A Comparison of
    Two Novels, and More   40
    MERRILL MAGUIRE SKAGGS

"Getting Good at Doing Nothing": Faulkner,
    Hemingway, and the Fiction of Gesture   54
    DONALD M. KARTIGANER

The Faulkner–Hemingway Rivalry   74
    GEORGE MONTEIRO

William Faulkner and Henry Ford: Cars, Men,
    Bodies, and History as Bunk   93
    DEBORAH CLARKE

Surveying the Postage-Stamp Territory: Eudora Welty,
    Elizabeth Spencer, and Ellen Douglas   113
    PEGGY WHITMAN PRENSHAW

"Blacks and Other Very Dark Colors":
    William Faulkner and Eudora Welty   132
    DANIÈLE PITAVY-SOUQUES

Invisible Men: William Faulkner, His Contemporaries,
    and the Politics of Loving and Hating the South in the
    Civil Rights Era; or, How Does a Rebel Rebel?   155
    GRACE ELIZABETH HALE

William Faulkner and Guimarães Rosa: A Brazilian Connection   173
    M. THOMAS INGE AND DONÁRIA ROMEIRO CARVALHO INGE

Contributors   189

Index   193

Introduction

JOSEPH R. URGO

[William Faulkner] spoke of a recent trip to New York. My strong impression is that he did not care for the place; in fact, he disliked it. It appears that he had attended some rather fatuous literary parties and that he did not like them; that he had never been so tired of literary people in his life, and cared not at all for a city "where everybody talks about what they are going to write, and no one writes anything."
—Louis Cochran, 1931[1]

You know that state I seem to get into when people come to see me and I begin to visualize a kind of jail corridor of literary talk. I dont know what in hell it is, except I seem to lose all perspective and do things, like a coon in a tree. As long as they dont bother the hand full of leaves in front of his face, they can cut the whole tree down and haul it off.
—William Faulkner, 1932[2]

Strange and contrary impressions come to mind with the conference title Faulkner and His Contemporaries. Surely, he must have had some, thought he did. Some writer's names come to mind immediately. Ernest Hemingway, considered by many, then and now, to have been a rival, with whom Faulkner exchanged words in print. But only in print: the two writers never met, never seemed even to want to meet. Willa Cather is another, with whom Faulkner had a career-long intertextual dialogue, again, in print; they may have met in 1931 at a Knopf party, but there is no evidence except testimony that he was there, and that he and his companion, Dashiell Hammett, were too drunk to engage in even the most rudimentary of polite formalities. Of Hammett and Faulkner, Joseph Blotner writes, "The men continued to enjoy each other's company at the same time that they presented difficulties to others."[3] Contemporary writers and intellectuals with whom Faulkner had what may be called a social relationship (not counting working relations with editors and agents and filmmakers) were more often drinking friends, people with whom he was comfortable to go carousing in New York or Hollywood, or hunting in Mississippi, or the handful of women with whom he had love affairs—and even these were successive, secretive, and relatively speaking, monogamous. There was no charmed circle in Faulkner's world, no cohort of literary men and women whom we may identify as Faulkner's crowd, his contacts, no regular correspondents or interlocutors.

"Faulkner was shy. Faulkner was arrogant. Faulkner went barefoot on the streets of Oxford. Faulkner tore up his driveway to discourage visitors." Such is the introduction given by James Webb and A. Wigfall Green, in *William Faulkner of Oxford*, a collection of forty reminiscences by local contemporaries, "those who knew him on his home ground." What emerges there are forty distinct perspectives on a civic enigma who had become world famous. "Even to the people of Oxford, Faulkner was a kind of legend in his own lifetime."[4] While he did not accomplish his self-proclaimed "ambition to be, as a private individual, abolished and voided from history, leaving it markless, no refuse save the printed books,"[5] his reticence and his remarkable success at maintaining an exclusive existence have resulted in the scholarly need to think deeply about Faulkner's relationship to human beings who were alive at the same time he was alive, particularly with others who may have failed at leaving the world markless when they left.

It may be that one of the most important things to know about Faulkner and his contemporaries is that he did not believe himself to have any. One of his most perceptive observers—at least, one whose perceptions continue to ring true as years pass, consistent with new scholarship—was Robert Coughlan, the *Life* magazine reporter who enraged Faulkner for his success at prying personal information out of friends and acquaintances during a nine-day stay in Oxford in the early 1950s. Coughlan subsequently published the first book-length study of Faulkner, with a title that surely irritated the author, *The Private World of William Faulkner*, released as a $.50 Avon Book. Coughlan offers this portrait:

> Confident of his own genius, determined to write for himself ("I don't give a damn whether anybody reads my books," he has said) and more perceptive generations to come without reference to current taste, nurturing his private nightmare for purposes which perhaps eluded his own understanding, he had begun to regard critics and the literary world in general with indifference and contempt. . . . With his withdrawal he became increasingly anti-intellectual, drawing over himself the mantle of the simple, rough "farmer" who "happened to write sometimes."[6]

The portrait is perceptive on a number of levels. Faulkner did have contemporaries in the 1920s—people he sought out, like Sherwood Anderson and William Spratling in New Orleans. Almost as soon as his writing career was under way, as early as 1930, he began to retreat from his contemporaries, a retreat made emblematic by the purchase of Rowan Oak, and from then on came the enforced isolation, and the comments about the "jail corridor of literary talk" he felt whenever anyone wanted to talk about books and the contemporary literary scene. In the 1950s, when Faulkner emerged as a public figure, he became a kind of spokesperson for privacy, and attracted the descriptive terms Coughlan uses: the private nightmare, the anti-intellectual, the indifference and the contempt for anyone who tried to treat him as a literary peer.

Faulkner's sense of himself as being without contemporaries, the aloofness produced by a combination of shyness and arrogance, should not be understood and dismissed as egocentrism, even if Faulkner was well aware of his gifts, as Coughlan suggests. Faulkner spent a good deal of public time in the 1950s reflecting on and speculating about what he had accomplished—or what, to be more precise, he happened upon accomplishing. In 1956 Faulkner told Jean Stein, "If I had not existed, someone else would have written me," and offers as proof evidence for the existence of "about three candidates for the authorship of Shakespeare's plays." It is not important who wrote the plays, he continues, only that the plays exist. When Stein asks whether the individuality of the writer matters at all, Faulkner responded: "Very important to himself. Everybody else should be too busy with the work to care about the individuality." Inexplicably, Stein does not pursue Faulkner's dodge, but rather ingenuously asks, "And your contemporaries?" to which Faulkner replies, equally ingeniously and equally evasive, "All of us failed to match our dream of perfection." He then moves on to his familiar theory that "failure to do the impossible ... is the healthiest condition for an artist. That's why he keeps on working, trying again."[7]

Particularly provocative is the idea that the individuality of the writer should be of interest only to the writer, and not anyone else. Faulkner does not want to be asked personal questions, he says at the very start of the interview; he prefers questions about his work only. "When they are about me," he explains, "I may answer or I may not, but even if I do, if the same question is asked tomorrow, the answer may be different." Stein does not follow up on the remark (or perhaps Faulkner does not allow it, as scholars assume that he had a hand in crafting the interview), which is itself a revealing statement about Faulkner's sense of his individuality. He may well have doubted his own existence as a cohesive being, or at least one that could be adequately captured in print or by his own self-reflective speculation. Or, Faulkner, in Coughlan's words, may have eluded his own understanding. He may well have remained a mystery to himself in his lifetime, a state of mind which would account for the peculiar combination of arrogance and humility associated with his character. A person's being, the essential self, was something Faulkner had identified elsewhere as foreign, repeating the idea that in essence man is "in conflict with himself," as well as with his time and place and circumstance. The idea of the heart in conflict with itself, which Faulkner admitted was a personal credo,[8] postulates a sense of individuality which is transient and ephemeral but at the same time interlocked with something eternal, something unknowable, toward which the individual strives and with which it is often at odds.

Faulkner often referred to beings—created characters or actual people—who attempted to be better than their circumstances allowed, who strove to overcome or, in a much preferred term, to endure. "Don't bother just to be better than your contemporaries or predecessors," he told Stein. "Try to be better than yourself." These remarks can too easily be dismissed as homilies if they are not linked to similar formulations made by Faulkner when asked about his relationship to his own time and place, or when he was asked personal questions designed to elicit self-definition. The most famous response was to the Nobel Prize committee, in the opening sentence of his acceptance speech, where Faulkner claims that "this award was not made to me as a man, but to my work."[9] His work is the closest approximation he was able to create in order to give form to what Coughlan called his private nightmare, the vision of perfection which drove him to create. He could answer questions about his work because, along with anyone else, he could read it and comment on it. His personal struggle, the struggle between Faulkner and his own heart, like that between him and his family, him and his contemporaries, and the circumstances of his existence—these were matters over which he claimed no expertise and, by the evidence of the comments he did make, matters over which he had much less desire to achieve mastery. Those who were interested in such personal phenomena were intolerable to Faulkner; he simply did not recognize a correlative or significant relationship between the physical existence of the writer and the work he produced. It is a view at odds with current critical assumptions about the identity of writers and their creativity, and the association of writers with particular interests, ethnicities, or subject groups, and therefore may strike today's up-to-date critics as disingenuous. Nonetheless, when Faulkner described the Nobel Prize as something which could be "only mine in trust," the statement reflected a lifelong detachment from his work, a sense of self which possesses enormously challenging implications for his view of who or what may be considered his contemporaries.

At the end of the interview with Jean Stein, Faulkner claims as "my own theory" the idea that "time is a fluid condition which has no existence except in the momentary avatars of individual people." The theory is emblematic of a Faulknerian ontology. He subscribed to the idea of the contemporaneity of all literature, understood as a form of writing which pursued perfection and always failed because, like time, it relied upon "the momentary avatars of individual people" to experience it and to attempt to write it down. In *The Sound and the Fury*, Quentin recalls his father telling him that "clocks slay time."[10] Clocks destroy the phenomenon they are meant to measure. So too, in Faulkner's formulation, does literature, once written down, slay the writer's vision. In the same way that the individual is drawn toward something unattainable which it knows only as its self, a desire defined variously as happiness, fulfillment, or perfection, the artist is drawn, in his writing, toward what, if he could only get it right, is his imagination of perfection. The artist inevitably fails, as one always will when employing physical reality to embody transcendent vision. The view is Platonic, and it assumes the existence of eternal forms toward which physicality strives. Time, Literature, Individuality, the verities he was fond of referencing—in Faulkner's mind these were eternities without material existence, forms of absence in the physical world, but which possessed an immense pull on the physical world to approximate. The writer tries again and again to create on the page the "dream of perfection" pursued by his mind. The very definition of life is embodied in that pursuit because, as Faulkner explained to Jean Stein, if the writer should succeed in matching the work to the image, "nothing would remain but to cut his throat, jump off the other side of that pinnacle of perfection into suicide." Failure is the keystone in Faulknerian ontology, from his sense of a novel as a splendid failure, to his sense of himself as a failed poet, and to his tendency to judge other writers by what they in turn failed to accomplish. There was nothing which we might consider "personal" in these formulations; they were, rather, Faulkner's ontological speculations on the origins and existence of something which was, in his mind, worthy of being called art.

Faulkner understood that the writer, like anyone else, bears a relationship to himself which we call personal, or private. However, he understood his engagement with his own individuality as an interest that could not be shared or even appreciated by someone else. Possessing a sense of himself as the avatar of William Faulkner, Faulkner could say "If I had not existed, someone else would have written me," which is to say, if I were not me, someone else would be me—someone else would do the work demanded by the time and place and circumstance. The "I" in the statement, "if I were not me," refers to the physical man, the man who lived in Oxford; the "me" in the statement refers to the necessity, or the eternal form, of the person we know as Faulkner but who, had William Fa(u)lkner not existed, would be someone else—maybe someone in Alabama or Arizona, Mexico City or Madrid. Faulkner's sense was that he *participated* in himself; he was Faulkner only by the random chance of universal caprice, and he devoted his life to an attempt to articulate what that meant—the voices he told Malcolm Cowley that he heard, the stories in his mind which demanded aesthetic shape and form and to which he bowed his will. "I listen to the voices ... and when I put down what the voices say, it's right. Sometimes I don't like what they say, but I don't change it."[11] The sense of himself as medium, as the temporary and ephemeral location of a set of energies and ideas we call Faulkner, was at once archaic, for its Platonism, and prescient in its anticipation of postmodern critiques of identity. Once again, however, these notions of self and art set Faulkner apart not only from his own contemporaries, but from ours in the twenty-first century. One can already hear the term "schizophrenia" as a response to the voices, missing entirely Faulkner's account of himself as a fleshy creature associated with the authorship of those books.

For the purposes of the volume at hand, we begin with a sense of the complexity in Faulkner's thinking about contemporaneity and his contemporaries. After all, the magnitude of his accomplishments results in the existence of contemporaries in numerous categories. There were his local Oxford contemporaries, friends, companions, mentors; there were literary contemporaries, those in whom he was expected to have an interest because he was a writer; there were his contemporaries in Hollywood and New York and places he frequented; and there were his contemporaries who lived at the same time as he, and whose own accomplishments place their lives in inevitable juxtaposition—names like Henry Ford, Albert Einstein, anyone whose mind affected the century. Who is it we need to have Faulkner talking to? Whom do we need to know as his contemporary? Faulkner seemed not to understand why the work he did compelled him to be "a literary man." He repeatedly denied the affiliation, claiming to be a farmer, or a Mississippian, or a private citizen—anything to distance himself from others who might possess a systematic conception of literature or who might assert a claim on him by virtue of what they did for a living. The books he felt closest to, by his own claim, the works of Shakespeare, the Old Testament, Cervantes, implied that the contemporaneity he felt as a writer had little to do with the time in which he happened to live. At West Point in 1962, he was asked, "And you're simply not interested in contemporary literature, is that it?," to which he answered, "Not enough to keep up with it."[12] The response was not materially different from comments made in 1931. "Asked about the most significant literature being produced in the world today, Mr. Faulkner said very decidedly that there is none being produced."[13] Faulkner is not telling the truth; we know he read his contemporaries, and when pressed, would offer opinions about them—albeit usually in the form of canned or stock responses. Nonetheless, in his comments about contemporary writing we detect the same detachment from the associations we take for granted, aligning and entangling people by their identities, identifying people by what they do. It seems fairly clear that Faulkner fled such entanglements, struggled throughout his life to come to terms with who he was and who he had become, and struggled most heroically with the voices and the vision that possessed and drove him, the only evidence for which we have now are the books.

2

You get born and you try this and you dont know why only you keep on trying it and you are born at the same time with a lot of other people, all mixed up with them, like trying to, having to, move your arms and legs with strings only the same strings are hitched to all the other arms and legs and the others all trying and they dont know why either except that the strings are all in one another's way like five or six people all trying to make a rug on the same loom only each one wants to weave his own pattern into the rug; and it cant matter, you know that, or the Ones that set up the loom would have arranged things a little better, and yet it must matter because you keep on trying or having to keep on trying and then all of the sudden it's over.
—William Faulkner, 1936[14]

While Faulkner may have raised questions about the very idea of contemporaneity, he had no doubts about the ways in which minds influenced and struggled with one another, and about the compulsion felt by human beings to connect to others. Judith Sutpen, whose voice is quoted above, continues to assert the importance of going "to someone, the stranger the better, and give them something" that would impress them, something to "be remembered even if only from passing from one hand to another, one mind to another." *Absalom, Absalom!* is Faulkner's great study of contemporaneity. The novel expands the idea of the contemporary to encompass much more than the coincidental living generation, to include the desire of the living to be contemporaneous with the dead as well as with the alive, to blur the distinction, moreover, and to leave some evidence of having made the attempt. At key points in the novel characters in the present become contemporaries with characters and events from the past; in their imaginations, the living may inhabit the past intellectually and emotionally; as well, in their intellects and emotions, characters in the present may be visited by ghosts, alternately called heroes, demons, or saints, the dramatis personae of contemporary memory and desire.

Each of the ten essays in the volume at hand wrestles with the idea that Faulkner was contemporaneous to a specific time and a locatable space, even if our sense of who his contemporaries are differs from his. Houston Baker, Jr., in "Traveling with Faulkner: A Tale of Myth, Contemporaneity, and Southern Letters," begins by discussing Faulkner's own sense of his contemporaries—Eliot, Housman, Anderson—and speculates on Faulkner's failure to recognize, or his silence regarding, his more local contemporaries, including Wright, Hurston, and Hughes. Houston asks, "Who, then, are his contemporaries?" The question leads Baker to "The Bear," the central portion of *Go Down, Moses*, where through the McCaslin-Beauchamp plantation economy Faulkner asks the same questions about who is included in notions of community, family, and identity. "There is, then, a sense in which I think of Faulkner less as an author than as a journey, a mythic and always contemporary encounter waiting, like an interpretive stone, to mark our modernity. And mark our modernity especially with respect to what we have made of an American South and its outrageous economies of race."

Baker's journey includes an encounter with *The Sound and the Fury* during a racially charged summer in Louisville in 1957, when "the Compsons were going crazy." The experience is not clarified for years, when Baker acknowledges his need for "*a myth of my own* through which to engage the parallel time of the South" and to counter the linguistically encompassing myths created by Faulkner. The journey continued at Howard University, where Baker relates a remarkable classroom moment more significant now than imaginable at the time, and then to Paris, where a professionally savvy Professor Baker finds himself lecturing on Wash Jones's relation to Thomas Sutpen in a make-shift café classroom outside the Sorbonne, closed by student riots and guarded by Algerian marshals, vaguely reminiscent of the Senegalese soldiers in *A Fable*. And on into the 1980s, when seasoned Ivy League Professor Baker tried to convince suspicious students that Colonel Sutpen mattered to them. Finally, though a brutal replay of Faulkner's tortured racial prose in *Light in August*, Baker locates what anguishes so many of Faulkner readers, his seeming complicity in so many "prurient, disastrous myths of black blood and odor, Negro razors and bovine stupidity, white nymphomania and black-male lasciviousness, militaristic white desire sublimated into grim and unlikely castration." At the end of the journey, in a kind of cold-war moment between Baker and Faulkner, between American Black Studies and the great fact of Faulkner in American literature, emerges a strikingly adept confession, as genuine and yet as suspect as the diplomatic moment it mimics.

We do not think of Faulkner as a city boy, but in his youth he did come to know one city very well. We do not think of New Orleans as a city in Mississippi, either, but in its early history, it almost was. W. Kenneth Holditch, in "William Faulkner and Other Famous Creoles," reminds us that "when the Louisiana Purchase was divided up into states, the original plan would have used the Mississippi River as the dividing line, and

New Orleans would have been part of Mississippi." This fact accounts or documents for the affinity most Mississippians have always felt for the Louisiana city, a place too big mythically and too diverse culturally to be held by any one state, or nation. Indeed, writers have referred to the region of southern Louisiana as the northern tip of Costa Rica, a Mediterranean city, an Arab state. Cosmopolitan visitors describe it as America's only European city, sensing that in the French Quarter one is brought in spirit to Paris, Madrid, or Athens.

Faulkner was no different from many Southern (and non-Southern) writers drawn to the city's exotic charms and, perhaps most significantly, its disdain for Prohibition and other restraints and interdictions. Holditch provides accounts of numerous literary associations and stations in New Orleans. "All through the 1920s, artists and writers flocked to the city, for a variety of reasons," Holditch explains, "not the least of which involved the presence of Sherwood Anderson." John Dos Passos and Faulkner each encountered Anderson at this time; both careers may be traced to Anderson's influence. Dos Passos and Faulkner were contemporaries, and throughout Faulkner's life they "remained friends and admirers of each other's work, although they rarely met." Holditch charts Faulkner's various associations in the city, drawing on interviews with "all the Famous Creoles who were still living in New Orleans," in 1974 and 1976. An important image of Faulkner as a young man, with characteristic confidence (which, before fame, was surely read as arrogance), starting a career in the arts in one of the few American cities where an artist's vocation was considered, among Faulkner's contemporaries in the Vieux Carré, as important as it was irrelevant, maybe even more so.

It may well be that the contemporaries Faulkner never met were more important to him than those with whom he spent time in New Orleans, New York, or California. "Cather's War and Faulkner's Peace: A Comparison of Two Novels, and More" is the latest in a series of essays by Merrill Skaggs suggesting a career-long dialogue between Faulkner and Willa Cather, one which includes a portrait of Faulkner in *One of Ours* and features a string of sometimes cryptic and sometimes astounding references to one another. The Faulkner portrait is one that will arrest any Faulkner reader. In *One of Ours* appears a man with a "humming-bird moustache," possessing "an air of special personal importance," wearing a Royal Flying Corp uniform, carrying a cane, reeking of alcohol, and telling stories about flying in France. While there is no smoking gun to establish a physical connection, Cather and Faulkner were both in Greenwich Village in the summer of 1921, when this RFC-weary character is more or less what Faulkner personified. There is also a good bit of borrowing from *One of Ours* in *Soldiers' Pay*, including similarly (and uncommonly) wounded soldiers, parallel motifs and images, and a shared projection of misogyny which provides some impetus to male war volunteerism. "That's the surprise," Skaggs claims; "how much Cather's Claude loves war, and how much William Faulkner chooses to believe other soldiers do, too."

The influence Skaggs charts between these two rough contemporaries is private. It is not the shared-state neighborliness of the Welty-Faulkner connection, nor the machismo rivalry of the Hemingway-Faulkner tug of war. It is, rather, a silent, unpublic, and easily missed series of nods and exchanges never intended for critical consumption. Anyone who knows both authors as well as Skaggs does can hear the echoes, however, and suspects that these two writers read each other very carefully. "For his major work," Skaggs demonstrates, "William Faulkner mined five central Cather novels, including *One of Ours*, thoroughly." He then acknowledged and repaid the favor, by writing a Cather-bodied woman into his own fiction as one of his more memorable female characters, one with "the strength and fortitude of a man" whose name plays on Cather's own male persona, Jim Burden, emerging as Joanna Burden. Skaggs's sleuthing, and her adept intertextual eye, proves that when probing the influence of contemporary writers, we are in fact probing the workings of minds interlocked in myriad ways.

The contemporary relationship that was not private but often embarrassingly public was that between Faulkner and Ernest Hemingway. Donald M. Kartiganer, in "'Getting Good at Doing Nothing': Faulkner, Hemingway, and the Fiction of Gesture," offers the first of a pair of essays in this volume to explore the connections between two men who were contemporaries, rivals, public interlocutors—but who also never met, a nonmeeting which is, as Donald Kartiganer says, "just as well, because as writers and personalities they seemed to be completely opposite in every respect." And more, the opposition they embody seems emblematic to American literature: Hemingway's sparse and linguistically exclusive style matched by Faulkner's "art of inclusion," the accumulation of words that never quite get to be exclusively representational. Kartiganer identifies the opposition as "one of the recurring phenomena of American literature," echoing previous embodiments in Hawthorne and Melville, Dickinson and Whitman, Crane and Dreiser, Frost and Williams. In the case of Hemingway and Faulkner, the opposition is seen most clearly in the way it revolves around a shared, career-long fascination with what Kartiganer calls "gesture," defined as "an action that signals intention, a purpose, but is never completed"; or, in intellectual terms, gesture occurs "when realization appears to be impossible at the very outset." The phenomenon is known also as "failed gesture" or "empty gesture"; but such phrases are redundancies in Hemingway and Faulkner because in the fiction of both writers "gesture always fails," according to Kartiganer, and "proves in the end to be empty."

Arising from carefully selected examples is a sense of the thematic centrality of failure, a "persistent defeat of purpose" which both informs and gives rise to "the gestural mode." However, each writer gets to this thematic concern by vastly different paths, paths which would seem never to converge. "Faulknerian gesture is often ambitious to the point of arrogance," while it also "remains almost blithely indifferent to its actual outcome." In Hemingway, by comparison, gesture is "rooted in disciplined patience," where virtue is measured not in Faulknerian "flamboyant motion" but in Hemingway's signature emphasis on the "art of not saying too much." The difference may be between the gesture that surrounds failure, circling it like birds of prey, and gesture that lies at the heart of failure, the calm eye of the storm which is, in effect, no storm at all but something else. Kartiganer charts divergent aesthetics important to our understanding of these contemporaries. Faulkner once explained that to his idea of art, it is "best to take the gesture, the shadow of the branch, and let the mind create the tree"—to surround the thing, in other words, and let the reader infer its presence. Hemingway, on the other hand, sought to "make something through . . . invention that is not a representation but a whole new thing," so that the reader senses the presence of something new. The characteristic Hemingway gesture is thus "clean, straightforward," with "no tricks," and marked by simple action, according to Kartiganer, whereas the signature gesture in Faulkner is "not a program for action but a script for a posture, a stance, an attitude." Both writers, however, ended in a similar place, where art, essentially gestural, accomplishes nothing, "admits—no, boasts of—its irrelevance," in Kartiganer's words.

George Monteiro, in "The Faulkner-Hemingway Rivalry," charts the numerous public and private gestures made by each writer toward one another throughout their lives. In a thoroughly researched essay, Monteiro contributes the definitive account of "the incidents and episodes" that constitute the relationship between the two writers. These "flash points," as Monteiro accurately calls them, amount to strong evidence that the two men thought about each other often, perhaps to the point of imagining the other reading over his shoulder. Faulkner called Hemingway "the best we've got" in the 1920s, starting a series of compliments which always seemed to contain something disturbing to Hemingway—"the best we've got," for example, being quite something else besides "the best there is." Hemingway's view of Faulkner was also consistent; on the one hand, he would assess Faulkner as "damned good when good" and on the other, find him "often unnecessary."

Among the most intriguing of these interlocutions is evidence that Faulkner may have retained a 1940 essay about Hemingway by Archibald MacLeish (where Hemingway is brought to task for devaluing the "old verities") and then incorporated the sentiment into his Nobel Prize Address in 1950 where he argues that "the old verities and truths of the heart" are all that's worth writing about. The speech also contains echoes of an apology Faulkner had offered Hemingway in the past. For his part, when Hemingway had opportunity to give his own Nobel Prize Address four years after Faulkner, he used the occasion to criticize writers who turned themselves into public spokesmen—coincidentally, Faulkner was at the time on the payroll of the State Department, speaking the old verities to foreign nations deemed receptive to American cultural initiatives. The rivalry continues postmortem, and now decades after the last ding-dong clocking either man's voice has stopped, each writer's critics and biographers explore the rivalry and the pairing—Faulkner/Hemingway has emerged as among the century's major aesthetic dialectics, as evidenced by Kartiganer's essay in this volume. The match, at present, seems, to Monteiro, to be tilted in Faulkner's favor. Hemingway's champions still defend him, still explain Faulkner's error in listing Hemingway where he did on his list of the best writers, or counter Faulkner's claim that as a writer, Hemingway lacked courage. Almost no one seeks to defend Faulkner in terms of his writerly courage, but this may also be because Faulkner "discovered the exact terms by which his rivalry with Hemingway might serve him." Moreover, Monteiro establishes that the gestures made toward one another throughout their careers accomplished a great deal, and continue to influence the way critics imagine Faulkner and Hemingway and their relative positions of influence in twentieth-century American literature.

The simple fact of being contemporaneous may arrest; placing two seemingly unrelated contemporary minds in juxtaposition expands and refines what it is we mean by contemporary. Deborah Clarke's "William Faulkner and Henry Ford: Cars, Men, Bodies, and History as Bunk" is an exploration and meditation on this fact: Henry Ford and William Faulkner were contemporaries. One devoted his life to the manufacture of automobiles; the other devoted important aspects of his art to exploring what the automobile meant. Henry Ford, while revolutionizing automobile production, remarked in 1926, "we have not yet found out what the automobile means." At the same time, Faulkner was projecting realms of car-significance, including the creation of Jason Compson's emblematic (and illicitly bought) automobile, pointedly *not* a Ford, the means of both his liberation from and his entrapment within circumstances. Clarke provocatively juxtaposes Ford's various visions of the future with Faulkner's aesthetics, centering, for example, on Ford's efforts to transform the types of men who would become workers and Faulkner's interrogations into the effects of industrialization on the quality of life in northern Mississippi.

Henry Ford wanted to make the automobile within the purchase of every American, thus transforming the car from luxury to necessity. Faulkner saw the process accomplished in his lifetime, even in the poorest region of the nation, to the extent that Gavin Stevens would conclude (in *Intruder in the Dust*) that "The American really loves nothing but his automobile: not his wife his child nor country no even his bank account . . . but his motorcar." Both men were also deeply interested in continuity, especially the relationship to the past which defined community. Ford created Greenfield Village, "a recreation of his idyllic vision of the past," as Clarke describes it, a kind of reification of the communities Faulkner envisioned at stake in a novel like *Go Down, Moses*. Throughout the various juxtapositions of Ford and Faulkner, the automobile serves as the chief vehicle. Clarke explores the relationship between the car and nostalgia, gender definitions (and autosexual metaphors), criminality, and the myriad intersections among cars and speed, mechanization, and masculine identity. Ultimately, Clarke suggests we consider the relationship (and the tension) between art and industry as twin forces affecting and defining contemporary identity.

Bringing us back to Mississippi, Danièle Pitavy-Souques, in "'Blacks and Other Very Dark Colors': William Faulkner and Eudora Welty," describes the two writers as equally engaged in the socially compelling events of the late 1940s in Mississippi, though in vastly different ways. For example, while both "use the strategy of exposing the Southern infatuation with language," they do so by employing distinct methods. Faulkner's language "exposes the bombastic rhetoric of political discourse" which works to endlessly delay action, while "Welty exposes the drama and vacuity of humorous chitchat." However, as Pitavy-Souques argues, "whether staged for large audiences or restricted to the intimacy of a front porch, Southern discourse can prove a terrible weapon." Her essay then meticulously examines the emotional content of Southern discourse, its reliance on cliché and other vacuous tropes, to produce a sense of each writer's attempt to both expose and counter the language of the contemporary scene. Her texts are Faulkner's *Intruder in the Dust* (1948) and Welty's *The Ponder Heart* (1953), novels which, from the vantage point of fifty years, are contemporary texts.

One particularly engaging point of intersection between the two novels lies in their parallel employment of transgression. Drawing on the work of Georges Bataille (particularly *Literature and Evil*), Pitavy-Souques places Faulkner's Lucas Beauchamp alongside Welty's Daniel Ponder in a study of comparative transgression. Beauchamp's offense is revealed when he "refuses to act like a nigger" and acts as if his right to exist emanates from within his self, rather than from his alleged betters. Daniel Ponder, resembling "a child obstinately immerged in the present," transgresses by "subverting the establishment with his disregard for riches and social conventions." In Faulkner's novel, the transgressive acts of Beauchamp lead to "a new awareness of racial issues" in the community. Acknowledging that Welty's novel "seems to be lighter," Pitavy-Souques argues that while its plot is less consequential than Faulkner's, its ultimate significance is not easily dismissed. In *The Ponder Heart*, "the true manipulator of the plot is the uniform and deadly power of language." By probing into the abuses of language in the cold war/civil rights era, Welty's novel is as politically charged as Faulkner's, examining as it does "the contemporary fallacy" of the American response to Communism. Faulkner, in *Intruder in the Dust*, overtly invokes the cold war by naming "a fascist background against which the present situation in the South" may be evaluated. Welty, at virtually the same moment, "offers a comic version of a totalitarian regime headed by a half-wit . . . whom all will reject in the end." What Pitavy-Souques reveals is two very different Mississippi writers, close contemporaries, never rivals but responding, according to discordant aesthetics, to the same social and cultural crises.

Opening with a fact we sometimes forget, Peggy Whitman Prenshaw, in "Surveying the Postage-Stamp Territory: Eudora Welty, Elizabeth Spencer, and Ellen Douglas," reminds us that there is nothing especially significant, historically or otherwise, about the area Faulkner identified as his "postage stamp of native soil" in northern Mississippi. Prenshaw is astute to point this out. Other areas of the state of Mississippi, before Faulkner, would be certain to come to mind as containing a richer historical significance, such as Vicksburg or Natchez, or more social and cultural importance, such as the Delta area around Clarksdale. Nonetheless, the northern hill country in and around Lafayette County has tremendous significance now, of course, because of what Faulkner did with it. What happened in this area is Faulkner: Faulkner happened, and forever after, the event of Faulkner is one that subsequent writers, writing about Mississippi and the South, must confront. Prenshaw looks carefully at three writers, Welty, Spencer, and Douglas, who responded specifically to Faulkner and who, in their responses, "imagined an alternate mapping of the region, one originating in their different experience of it."

Faulkner loomed large in the imaginations of all three of his female contemporaries, all of whom were publishing in his lifetime and into the wake of his reputation. Faulkner's Yoknapatawpha "came to be not only a part of the general textual universe, but part and parcel of the imaginative universe" of these three women. At the same time they departed significantly, in part because they were women, with access to and no access to certain modes of experience. Welty, for example, "a white girl growing up in a deeply gendered and racialized society, was segregated from Faulkner's Mississippi, as from Richard Wright's Mississippi, in profound ways," the profundity of which resulted in the projection of a very different kind of Mississippi fiction, one which nonetheless cannot but know of Faulkner. Spencer's experience in Mississippi in the 1950s, after writing three Mississippi novels (with traces of Yoknapatawpha), was to sense "that the homeland she knew was disappearing" and, as a result, she left the state, eventually settling in Chapel Hill and writing novels "not anywhere near Yoknapatawpha." Ellen Douglas, finally, in her writing "demonstrates no assured sense of entitlement to appropriate the larger world of country or state or region" but, writing "the female world" which was inaccessible to Faulkner, narrates a more "modestly scaled" world, "more ephemeral in memory, more contingent upon a daily shifting reality." In all three cases, writing as women, after Faulkner, results (or perhaps compels) a reconciliation to "mortal limits," Prenshaw argues, a view that admits to "the elusiveness of originality and the constraints upon truth."

Faulkner's shadow looms very large in Grace Elizabeth Hale, "Invisible Man: William Faulkner, His Contemporaries, and the Politics of Loving and Hating the South in the Civil Rights Era; or, How Does a Rebel Rebel?" Hale juxtaposes the Southern Renaissance in literature of the 1930s and '40s with the Southern rock phenomenon in popular music of the 1970s, comparative moments of Southern ascendancy in the national imagination, both of which tended to obscure their debt to African American cultural forms. Hale centers on the figure of the "rebel," that vestige of Confederate dissent which recurs whenever white Southerners find themselves at odds with or in defiance of national policies, trends, or entertainment modes, either by active rebellion or in transcendental reverie. "The civil rights movement made it impossible to be both a Rebel in the Confederate sense, someone who defied his nation to defend his region, and a rebel in the romantic sense, a seer who defies his society to defend a greater truth." The greater truth, if recognizable, was regressive at best and unjust to most outside observers, if that truth was, as Faulkner suggested, to "go slow" toward civil rights for black citizens.

Hale attempts a line of continuity from Southern Agrarians to Southern rock musicians, with Faulkner (and, also, Shelby Foote and James Dickey) providing the bridge of a conflicted white Southern consciousness. Typical of white Southern intellectuals, these men "could no longer be romanticized outsiders within the larger American culture." What we find them doing, in response to an impossible situation, was adopting "the most traditional of American male images," rooted in a sense of exclusion, and with an uneasy relationship to violence, both ecological and domestic.

The dilemma, according to Hale, found its way into the music scene a generation later. "Southern rock provided a safe place outside of politics for white Southern men to express and romanticize their experience of loss," according to Hale, while also, we might add, turning loss into celebratory ritual in a deeper sense, a sense that tapped into the national consciousness. Like the writers of the Southern Renaissance, Southern rock musicians were heavily indebted to black cultural forms, in this case blues music. Ironically, the sense of loss emerging from the civil rights era (if not loss of personal privilege, then certainly loss of regional prestige in international terms) provided an experience approximating the *blues*, so that black music became an important resource for the expression of white angst. In this sense, Southern rock music is cultural integration, a hybrid form for what only appeared to be "white" music. "In Southern rock," Hale concludes, "the Rebel and the rebel," Confederate and transcendental alike, "merged, creating an image specific enough to be appealing and yet vague enough to symbolize whatever kind of rebel a man wanted to be." This marked the popular manifestation, one generation removed, of the conflicted white intellectual made emblematic by Faulkner's efforts, in the 1950s, to be both outsider and moral force.

From Yoknapatawpha to beyond Mississippi and beyond the borders of the United States, M. Thomas Inge and Donária Romeiro Carvalho Inge, in "William Faulkner and Guimarães Rosa: A Brazilian Connection," explore Faulkner's Latin American contemporaries. Noting the well-established links between Faulkner and Latin American writers writing in Spanish, particularly those associated with the South American "boom" era, the Inges trace an important set of parallels between Faulkner and the Brazilian author Guimarães Rosa (1908–1967). While there is no direct evidence that Rosa read Faulkner, the Inges provide convincing intertextual evidence that Faulkner's influence on Rosa, writing in Portuguese, was equal to his established influence on other South American writers of the era. Guimarães Rosa was an adventurous author who experimented with prose methods. His short stories, according to the Inges, "sometimes read more like essays or character sketches" and often lack the "basic plot structure and conflict of the traditional literary story." Rosa's subject matter is taken from "his own beloved *sertão*, or backlands," an area used much like Yoknapatawpha, "a cosmos of his own which serves at the same time as a microcosm of the larger world and society." The Inges conclude that Rosa, like writers of the Latin American boom, "probably felt liberated by the possibility of turning to his own regional world of Minas Gerais as an appropriate fictional matter for fiction."

The essays in this volume make a start on a project which will occupy Faulkner scholars in the twenty-first century: the relationship of William

Faulkner to his self, his time, and his circumstances, and the idea of Faulknerian contemporaneity. Where the lines of influence begin and where they go is as much an ontological matter as it is a biographical, critical, and intertextual issue. *"Yes. Maybe we are both Father. Maybe nothing ever happens once and is finished."*[15] Quentin Compson came to know his contemporaries to be an ever-widening circle of lives, some lived, some speculated to have lived, some never to have existed anywhere save for his personal compulsions and desires. In considering Faulkner and his contemporaries, we begin with his personal sense that he had none, to an equally outrageous suspicion that all within and without the grasp of his intellect was, in some way, contemporaneous with Faulkner. To paraphrase, contemporary is not *was*, but *is*.

NOTES

1. James W. Webb and A. Wigfall Green, eds., *William Faulkner of Oxford* (Baton Rouge: Louisiana State University Press, 1965), 106.
2. Joseph Blotner, ed., *Selected Letters of William Faulkner* (New York: Random House, 1977), 56.
3. Joseph Blotner, *Faulkner: A Biography*, 2 vols. (New York: Random House, 1974), 1: 741.
4. Ibid., vi, v.
5. *Selected Letters*, 285.
6. Robert Couglan, *The Private World of William Faulkner* (New York: Avon Books, 1954), 103–4.
7. A number of quotations in the next paragraphs are taken from "Interview with Jean Stein Vanden Heuval," *Lion in the Garden: Interviews with William Faulkner*, ed. James B. Meriwether and Michael Millgate (Lincoln: University of Nebraska, 1968), 236–57.
8. See *Faulkner at West Point*, ed. Joseph L. Fant and Robert Ashley (New York: Vintage, 1969), 64.
9. The "Address upon Receiving the Nobel Prize for Literature" is available in many volumes. See *Essays, Speeches, and Public Letters by William Faulkner*, ed. James B. Meriwether (New York: Random House, 1965), 119.
10. William Faulkner, *The Sound and the Fury* (1929; New York: Vintage Books, 1984), 85.
11. Malcolm Cowley, *The Faulkner-Cowley File: Letters and Memories, 1944–1962* (New York: Penguin Books, 1978), 114.
12. *Faulkner at West Point*, 66.
13. Interview in University of Virginia *College Topics*, in *Lion in the Garden*, 17.
14. *Absalom, Absalom!*, in *Faulkner: Novels, 1936–1940*, ed. Joseph Blotner and Noel Polk (New York: Library of America, 1990), 105.
15. Ibid., 216

Note on the Conference

The Twenty-Ninth Annual Faulkner and Yoknapatawpha Conference sponsored by the University of Mississippi in Oxford took place July 21–26, 2002, with more than two hundred of the author's admirers from around the world in attendance. Ten lectures presented at the conference are collected as essays in this volume. Brief mention is made here of other conference activities and details about special groups in attendance.

In the opening session, conference director Donald M. Kartiganer gave a tribute to Jimmy Faulkner (1923–2001) and dedicated the conference to his memory. Oxford Mayor Richard Howorth and Joseph R. Urgo, chair of the University English Department, welcomed participants, and Charles Reagan Wilson, director of the Center for the Study of Southern Culture, presented the sixteenth annual Eudora Welty Awards in Creative Writing. Kilby Allen of Indianola won first prize, $500, for his short story "An Order for Compline," entered by the Mississippi School for Math and Science in Columbus, where he is a student. Leann Peterson of Brandon won second prize, $250, for her poem "Knots-A Sestina," entered by her school, Jackson Preparatory in Jackson. Frances Patterson of Tupelo, a member of the Center Advisory Committee, established and endowed the awards, which are selected through a competition held in high schools throughout Mississippi. Donald M. Kartiganer, director of the conference, introduced Steven Stankiewicz, who read the winning entry—"The Rabbit"—of the thirteenth annual Faux Faulkner Contest, sponsored by *Hemispheres* magazine of United Airlines, the University of Mississippi, and Yoknapatawpha Press. A selection from V. P. Ferguson's "Days of Yoknapatawpha"—a memoir of the writer's relations with Faulkner during the early 1950s—was read by George Kehoe, who also joined Betty Harrington, L. W. Thomas, and Rebecca Jernigan in reading selections from Faulkner's fiction. Following a buffet supper, at the home of Dr. and Mrs. M. B. Howorth, Jr., Houston Baker gave the first lecture of the conference.

Monday's program included three lectures, Thomas S. Rankin's slide lecture about the work of Faulkner and photographer Walker Evans, and panel presentations by Eoin F. Cannon, Peter J. Ingrao, and Peter Mallios. Colby Kullman moderated the third Faulkner Fringe Festival, an open-mike evening at Southside Gallery on the Oxford Square. The event attracted a large and appreciative audience and seven presenters, among them Marianne Steinsvik, from Spain, who talked about discovering books and Faulkner, and Dr. Ralph Friedman, still a practicing physician in his ninetieth year, who spoke eloquently of growing up in Oxford and meeting Faulkner on several occasions. Beverly Carothers, wife of Faulkner scholar Jim Carothers, evoked comic and moving scenes of her family's life beginning with her husband's graduate work at the University of Virginia in the 1960s, continuing through his career as a professor at the University of Kansas, and including annual pilgrimages to Faulkner and Yoknapatawpha Conferences, first with children and now with grandchildren. Other fringe participants were Oxford residents Milly Moorhead and Mary Barres Riggs and students Kassandra McLean and Scott Siekierski, both of the University of Texas at Dallas.

Guided tours of North Mississippi and the Delta took place on Tuesday, as did an afternoon party at Tyler Place, hosted by Charles Noyes, Sarah and Allie Smith, and Colby Kullman. The day ended with Merrill Maguire Skaggs lecturing on Faulkner and Willa Cather. In addition to a lecture and two discussion sessions on Wednesday, "Faulkner in Oxford" assembled local residents Will Lewis, Jr., and Elizabeth Shiver as panelists for a discussion moderated by M. C. "Chooky" Falkner, one of the writer's nephews. Reckon Crew, a group comprised of singer-songwriters Tommy Goldsmith, Tom House, David Olney, and Karren Pell, performed their musical interpretation of Faulkner's classic novel *As I Lay Dying*. Thursday's program offered three lectures and a panel with Sean K. Kelly, Holly Hutton, and Timothy S. Sedore. On Friday were a lecture, two discussion sessions, and Arlie Herron's slide program of photographs he made during the conference over the years since its inception in 1974.

Receptions for two exhibitions took place during the conference, with *Paradox in Paradise*, mixed media artworks by Lea Barton, at the University Museums, and *Ms. Booth's Garden*, photographs by Jack Kotz, in the Gammill Gallery at Barnard Observatory. The University's John Davis Williams Library displayed Faulkner books, manuscripts, photographs, and memorabilia; and the University Press of Mississippi exhibited Faulkner books published by university presses throughout the United States. Films relating to the author's life and work were available for viewing during the week. Other events included a walk through Bailey's Woods before the annual picnic at Faulkner's home, Rowan Oak, and a closing party at Off Square Books. A highlight of the conference continued to be the special "Teaching Faulkner" sessions conducted by James B. Carothers, Robert W. Hamblin, Arlie Herron, and Charles A. Peek.

For the fourth year, high school teachers, the recipients of fellowships funded by a grant from Saks Incorporated Foundation, on behalf of McRae's, Proffitt's, and Parisian Department Stores, attended the conference and took part in special workshops led by members of the Department of English at the University. Also attending were an Elderhostel group led by Joan Popernik and two groups of students, Phyllis Bridge's from Texas Woman's University and Theresa Towner's from the University of Texas at Dallas.

The conference planners are grateful to all the individuals and organizations who support the Faulkner and Yoknapatawpha Conference annually. In addition to those mentioned above, we wish to thank Square Books, St. Peter's Episcopal Church, the City of Oxford, and the Oxford Tourism Council.

Tribute to Jimmy Faulkner
(1923–2001)

I open the Twenty-Ninth Annual Faulkner and Yoknapatawpha Conference by drawing your attention to a very large absence from it. James Murry "Jimmy" Faulkner was a central figure in the town of Oxford and at this conference for many years. Born July 18, 1923, he died this past December. He was the son of John Faulkner, himself a novelist and painter, and the nephew of William Faulkner. Those of you who have attended this conference before will recall vividly his marvelous presentation, "Knowing William Faulkner," a combination of reminiscence and slide show about the man whom he knew as "Brother Will."

William Faulkner had three brothers and two daughters, one of whom died in infancy, but he never had a son. I think Jimmy filled in as that son. For years they hunted and fished together; on at least one occasion they flew together. As Jimmy used to recall in his conference presentation, Brother Will introduced him to the gin and tonic. He was the last member of the family to see William before he died in Byhalia in 1962.

In some respects Jimmy lived out the life that his uncle had lived in fantasy: he was a Marine Corps fighter pilot in World War II and the Korean War. Whereas Faulkner's RAF plane crashes in France and Germany in World War I were wholly imaginary (he was a cadet training in Canada at the time), Jimmy had been shot down in the Pacific, near Okinawa. He earned the Distinguished Flying Cross, the World War II Victory Ribbon, and the Pacific Theater Ribbon. Faulkner once summarized Jimmy's career in the service with characteristic exaggeration: "He's got two DFCs, 5 Air Medals, and 3 Court Martials. He's a *good* boy."

Jimmy was a contractor with his own Faulkner Construction Company, the author of a number of books and essays, as well as the subject of several major interviews, the source of some of the most delightful and penetrating insights we have into William Faulkner. He was himself a wonderful storyteller and a thoroughly warm and engaging man.

As we all know, William Faulkner was a very private man. One of his biographers, Joel Williamson, wrote, "among writers of Faulkner's generation, none was so deeply unknowable. Virtually no one, it seems, ever knew the real Faulkner." I think we can say that Jimmy Faulkner knew William Faulkner, the man he called "Brother Will." And we can also say that he provided William with comfort and strength and much needed amusement. Faulkner once said of him, "Jim is the only person who likes me for what I am."

I wish to dedicate this year's conference, "Faulkner and His Contemporaries," to the memory of Jimmy Faulkner.

Donald M. Kartiganer

Faulkner and His Contemporaries
FAULKNER AND YOKNAPATAWPHA,
2002

Traveling with Faulkner: A Tale of Myth, Contemporaneity, and Southern Letters

HOUSTON A. BAKER, JR.

Analyzing William Faulkner's relationship to contemporaries is an expansive chore. His life covered more than sixty years and found him traveling abroad and cross regionally in the United States, joining convivial associates in New York, New Orleans, Paris, and Los Angeles. To ask of his contemporaries, therefore, requires selectivity. If we look to Faulkner's earlier contemporaries—or better, influences—we discover a poetical Faulkner under the tutelage of his friend and first mentor Phil Stone. At Stone's urging, Faulkner apprenticed himself to romantic and late-romantic poets such as Keats and Shelley, Aubrey Beardsley, and Algernon Swinburne. By the 1920s, however, Faulkner had taken up Conrad Aiken, A. E. Housman, James Joyce, T. S. Eliot, and other moderns. The moderns were to serve as formal guides for a good part of his career.

But in the course of his travels and in the process of settling on his own principal theme, Sherwood Anderson played a significant, regionalist role for Faulkner. Author par excellence of the psychology and affective geographies of small town America, Anderson enjoined Faulkner to concentrate his artistic labors on that "little patch of Mississippi" where he was born and reared. Anderson, thus, provided both an artistic model with his novel *Winesburg, Ohio* and a contemporary's usefully regionalist advice. He turned Faulkner's gaze and ambitions in a fruitful direction.[1]

In a sense, Anderson licensed Faulkner to be a Southern writer—not simply another partisan in the lists of the moderns and romantics. Curiously enough for a Southern writer, Faulkner can scarcely be said to have acknowledged even a single Afro-American contemporary. The stores of black authors such as Charles Chesnutt, Jean Toomer, Langston Hughes, Richard Wright, Waters Turpin, Zora Neale Hurston, and others remained an invisible marketplace to Faulkner, as they did to the literary-critical and cultural establishments that took their own sweet time recognizing even one of Faulkner's own artistic achievements. There can be little doubt, though, that when American literary-cultural establishments did "get onto" Faulkner, they heralded him as indisputably modern and inescapably Southern. I would like to suggest that T. S. Eliot's definition of the "truly new"—or in another phrasing, the truly "modern"—offers analytical possibilities for addressing the question of Faulkner and those who might be considered his contemporaries. Eliot suggests that the "really new" work of art is one that absorbs into itself and presents its own unique *agon* with a panoply of "existing monuments" that mark a creator's field of vision and endeavor as he commences his labor.[2]

Now, I am fully aware that Eliot's notions are both conservative and set in a conservative frame of critical reference. But if we extrapolate from them—as we are free to do—then we can say that Faulkner's "contemporaneity" is as contingent upon his immersion in Greek and Latin classics as it is upon the Mississippi's writer's modernist experimentation with stream-of-conscious narration. The ground on which Faulkner reads out as a traditionalist, therefore, might be thought of as a temporal plane spanning millennia, and yet, as accessible and presently available as Rowan Oak's library copy of *Ulysses*.

Holding across this temporal plane, moreover, is a formal constant drawn from our traditionalist reading of "contemporaneity" and "contemporaries." That formal constant is myth. Many of the English romantics to whom Faulkner apprenticed himself were in substantial agreement with the prophetic William Blake, whose *Los* avers: "I must Create a System, or be enslav'd to another Man's." We think of Blake's masterful creation *The Vision of the Daughters of Albion* as one installment on this resolution. Blake's romantic successors and their mythic romantic creations include Shelley's *Prometheus Unbound*, Keats's *Endymion*, and Swinburne's *Atalanta in Calydon*. Faulkner's romantic, mythic impulse yielded rich store and has a distinct bearing on his own grandly illusioned and heroically soliloquizing figures such as Thomas Sutpen, a creation fully worthy of William Blake the prophet.

Glancing to London's literary circles of the 1920s, we recall another literary-historical moment in which myth is held to be coterminous with the best designs and legacies of the artist as social visionary. Again, we look to the criticism of T. S. Eliot. In an essay titled "*Ulysses*, Order, and Myth," Eliot writes as follows:

> In using the myth [of Homer's *Odyssey*], in manipulating a continuous parallel between contemporaneity and antiquity, Mr. Joyce is pursuing a method which others must pursue after him. . . . Instead of narrative method, we may now use the mythical method. . . . It is, I seriously believe, a step toward making the modern world possible for art. . . . And only those who have won their own discipline in secret and without aid, in a world which offers very little assistance to that end, can be of any use in furthering this advance.[3]

Deploying "antiquity" to stage the modern was, of course, Eliot's game, as he demonstrated so masterfully in the richly allusive, mythical masterpiece *The Wasteland*. And Faulkner adopts from Joyce what Eliot notes as the "continuous parallel" and its possibilities for artistic modernism. Unlike Eliot, however, Faulkner has no interest in pursuing the mythical method as an ideologically conservative homage to antiquity. Faulkner and antiquity—indeed Faulkner and the past *tout court* —were not twin souls, but rather feuding, baleful, inseparable alter egos in desolate counterpoint, savagely refusing to release one another to quiet certainty . . . or even simple rest.

We have, then, for Faulkner, romantic myth as both grand, lyrical evocation and ideologically charged re-presentation of the past. We have as well myth as object lesson, prophecy—code of conduct, faith, epistemology, and decorum—in the mode of William Blake and his successors. Additionally, there is modern myth—critically encoded by Eliot to describe Joyce's continuous, formally eloquent paralleling of the past. All of these, I think, work their formal course in Faulkner's oeuvre.

Having taken up artistic residence on that "little patch of Mississippi"— what he called his own "little postage stamp of native soil"—recommended by Anderson, and drawing on "contemporaries" from romantics and moderns, Faulkner turned multiple deployments of myth to brilliant fictional advantage. Who, then, are his contemporaries?

I hazard the response that his contemporaries are all who occupy and creatively challenge the same mythical time/space that Faulkner inhabited as a Southerner and an American, a white American born into strange racial economies, a man of the "new world" who dared tally the accounts of mankind's responsibility to a holy errand "into the wilderness." Faulkner's contemporaries, one might say, are those who recognize and do what they can to emulate his own prolific labors with a Southern past, as well as his ethical and prophetic wrestlings with the state and possibilities of mankind's future. Those who share—in another common sense of "contemporary"—Faulkner's modernity do so because they, like he, dare as readers and as ethical, fair-minded contemporary interpreters to enter with him into furious contest and dreadful excavation of the past of the Americas. The McCaslins of "The Bear" know how taxing that past can be. Listen:

> "—So this land is, indubitably, of and by itself cursed": and he "Cursed:" . . . that whole edifice intricate and complex and founded upon injustice and erected by ruthless rapacity and carried on even yet with at times downright savagery not only to the human beings but the valuable animals too, yet solvent and efficient and, more than that: not only still intact but enlarged, increased; brought still intact by McCaslin, himself little more than a child

then, through and out of the debacle and chaos of twenty years ago where hardly one in ten survived.[4]

The real bond, I think, between Faulkner and those who would be contemporary with him resides in a common dedication to the well-wrought representation and honest moral judgment of the mythic encounter with the pastness of the Americas. There is, then, a sense in which I think of Faulkner less as an author than as a journey, a mythic and always contemporary encounter waiting, like an interpretive stone, to mark our modernity. And to mark our modernity especially with respect to what we have made of an American South and its outrageous economies of race.

To travel with Faulkner and engage him at every step with contemporary questions is to discover, I think, what promises of modernism we have kept and which others we have tragically broken. Arguably, only Richard Wright among our twentieth-century authors has issued a summons as profoundly relevant to such a journey through the South as William Faulkner.

Hence, in the spirit and mode of Faulkner himself, I want to set out in what follows selective contours of my own mythic journey and encounter with, through, in awe of, and, **yes**, at times, in furious repudiation of Faulkner. I write as a black American, one born in the South, and now middle-aged, academic, literary-critical. What follows, then, is a weave of mythic encounters with Faulkner. It is only myth. It is designed not to bore. It is my contemporary Southerner's tale of one of our region's most furious mythographers.

2

It was the summer of 1957 in Louisville, Kentucky, and the Compsons were going crazy.

> *Taint no luck on this place, Roskus said. The fire rose and fell behind him and Versh, sliding on his and Versh's face. Dilsey finished putting me to bed. The bed smelled like T. P. I liked it.*
> "What you know about it." Dilsey said. "What trance you been in."
> "Don't need no trance." Roskus said. "Aint the sign of it laying right there on that bed. Ain't the sign of it been here for folks to see fifteen years now."[5]

My father said: "You. You should have known better. Michael's older. But he's not from around here. It was you who should have known better."

The bicycles glinted in the sweltering day. Sweat was pouring off our faces as the man behind the counter said: "Y'all can get them here. But you can't drink 'em at the counter."

"Why?" said Michael. He was the nephew of a friend of my mother's who lived in Detroit. "Why can't we drink them here? The place is empty."

"Jes can't. We don't never serve y'all in the front, neither at the counter."

The door leading to the kitchen swung open. The colored woman walked right up behind us seated at the counter and said: "You boys know you can't drink at this counter. You boys come on with me to the back. It's cool back there. I got a table."

Michael had the money. He paid for the milkshakes. The table was an unweildy chopping block. She pulled up two sturdy chairs. She said: "You all must be crazy. There ain't no need for you to be in here. You could'a gone to Page's up on Chestnut Street if you wanted ice cream. Drink them things quick and get on out of this kitchen. It's enough that I gotta be here."

My father said: "Michael is visiting, but you live here. You should have known better than to drink in anybody's kitchen. This is the South. You should have known better. Don't ever do that again."

Then my brother came home from Fisk University. He was different from when he left. He said there were all sorts of incredible—that was his word "incredible"—things going on in the South where he had been in school all year. He said he and his friends were working with a famous man who gave the most beautiful orations—that was his word—he had ever heard. His name was King.

It was 1957, and I asked my older brother what King "orated" about, and he said freedom for colored people in the South. "What about the South?" I asked him. My older brother said: "You should know better. You live here." Then he gave me a book called *The Sound and the Fury*. "Here," he said. "Read this. Everything is changing in the South."

I didn't ride my bicycle for three days. I was going into the ninth grade in the fall. I sat on top of the long, full book cases my mother's father had built in the big room on the third floor and read this book my older brother gave me by William Faulkner. It was a crazy book. The image/feeling of Benjy the idiot "bellering" and seeming to love the smell of rain made me nauseous. Luster, and Roskus, and T. P., and Dilsey—all funny-sounding colored people—almost didn't register at all. I had no working knowledge of them. Perhaps because television was but two years old in our household, and very controlled. Perhaps because my parents were not partisans of minstrelsy. I did recognize Dilsey's church at the end of the book. I had been there. Was that grotesque of a preacher "orating" like my brother's King? I wondered. But the white people were the major players. At least I thought so, and I couldn't for the life of me figure out what muddy drawers had to do with anything, had to do with the South, or me and Michael. I should have known better. I hated

"Miss Cahline" and Jason. Quentin and Caddy's breathless, incestuous touching brought adolescent response along my pulses.

"Well, did you read it?" My brother asked. "Yes." I answered. "What's it about, then?" he asked. "Crazy people. But what's that got to do with the South?" He laughed.

I was from the "here"—the South of my father's chastisement. I should have known better. I might have known what was signified by the sound and the fury. I had seen the sign "White Waiting Room" at the train station. I was one of the colored pioneers who integrated white schools full of people who regarded us like we were Luster and T. P. and alien forever.

> "Go on." T. P. said. "Holler again. I going to holler myself. Whooey." Quentin kicked T. P. again. He kicked T. P. into the trough where the pigs ate and T. P. lay there. "Hot dog." T. P. said. "Didn't he get me then. You see that white man kick me that time. Whooey." (20)

I should have known better. But one's natal geography is so deep, so saturated in the flesh and consciousness—fitting, as the artist Zora Neale Hurston put it, "like a tight chemise." It is "here" and "home" and "our town" and "my city," but never, at least at adolescence (a well-fed, mind you, and loved and sheltered adolescence) never a territory requiring map and compass. Orations and ideology and history and race relations and plantations and slavery were not the curriculum of my boyhood. There was no burden of racial memory foisted upon me. What derived then from the South as geography early on was only the stifling fear and foreknowledge that came—usually inexplicably—when told "We don't serve y'all in the front, neither at the counter." I wish I had known better. Faulkner was no help at all.

Only years later did I learn that what I, of course, required most desperately was *a myth of my own* through which to engage the parallel time of the South (past and present) and to release me from the bondage of incomprehension before that redolent myth of another, namely Mr. Faulkner. Though there was certainly an implicit Southern dread—an actual terror yet to be discovered—in what transpired at the counter, in the newly integrated schools of Louisville, and at rallies and boycotts that my older brother was attending in Tennessee, I didn't yet know the longer story rooted in the land of my birth. Did not even have a notion that the instantaneity of impression made by a mentally ill Benjy on my adolescent consciousness was part of a grand myth made by Mr. Faulkner—one with which I would have to come to my own terms of order and understanding. Only later, then, did I recognize some clear contemporaneity with the sole proprietor of Yoknapatawpha County. In time, we might become regionalists, together.

I wish I had known better.

3

"King" was no longer a remote name when the train deposited its Louisville contingent at Washington's Union Station on a sultry August evening in 1961. "King" was elaborated and unfolding. A civil rights revolution had as leader Dr. Martin Luther King, Jr.—the Right Reverend Dr. Martin Luther King, Jr.—charismatic orator par excellence. The descendant whites of Yoknapatawpha were going completely crazy—bombs, arson, murder, beatings were standard fare in resistance to the colored thousands, those dark bodies and faces moving across landscapes and sites of old exclusion in the South, singing "And before I'll be a slave/I'll be buried in my grave/And go home to my lord/And be free."

The "campus pals" of Howard University met us and transported us to Charles Drew Hall to settle in for the larger education ahead. We boasted we were from the "Big L." We did not make claims to Southern heritage, thinking we were hiply cosmopolitan. Louisville was, after all, the largest city in Kentucky. And we all knew Cassius Clay—homeboy, Olympic champion in Rome; he had partied with us, run track against us for Central High. We drafted his account for mythic status in our first Howard University comings and goings.

Then as term began, I walked through the door of a classroom drenched in September morning sun and saw one of the most beautiful brown-skinned women I had ever seen. Seated atop the desk, gorgeous legs showing from a dark skirt, and cream-colored sweater subtly décolleté. She was my humanities teacher. Her bearing was that of an oracle.

I took up residence on the front row. Seated next to me was a thin, impatient, intense brown-skinned young man who seemed to hum with energy. His hair was roughly curly, not short, smooth, and greased down like that of boys from the "Big L."

We began. The text was William Faulkner's "The Bear."[6] I had read at the book with the kind of type-A alacrity I brought by that time to all my studies. "The Bear," a good hunting story, should have been simple for me, a lover of adventure stories who was always inventing backyard wildernesses, obstacles, challenges for myself. But the language kept getting in the way, and the characters seemed to be a single bundle—like those cartoon moments when rival forces are battling and one sees only a big cloud of dust with various arms, legs, hands, and faces pummeling about. Who was Sam Fathers? Why were he and Boon clamored into the same breath? What was Major De Spain a "major" of? What did Old Ben really symbolize?

The beautiful, appropriately histrionic, honey-voiced humanities teacher worked to help me out. She explained that this was a *bildungsroman*.

I wrote that down. A tale of the "coming of age" of a young man. "Ike McCaslin," she said, "has to journey into the wilderness hands free—no gun, no compass—in order to understand the grandeur of his heritage." She went on, saying: "Sam Fathers, the bear, the great gun-metal-blue dog Lion are forces teaching young McCaslin humility and courage before forces and powers larger than his single life." I continued writing. And then a voice broke across the honeyed stream of the teacher's speaking, demanding: "Why are we reading the work of an old cracker Southern white man anyway? Isn't this a Negro university? Aren't Negroes today doing everything they can—marching, and boycotting, and integrating schools—to get us rid of people just like this old Mississippi cracker we are paying so much attention to today? We ought to be reading Mao Tse Tung. We ought to be in the streets of Cambridge, Maryland. We ought to be helping out Dr. King!"

His voice grew more fiercely declamatory with each pronouncement. His eyes more intense. It was the young man with roughly curly hair. He was staring now at the teacher.

"Mr. Carmichael," she said (for it was Stokeley Carmichael who was seated beside me), "There are times and places—as I am certain you know and as scripture dictates—for all things. To everything there is a season. Here, in my class at Howard University, on this day, it is time for Faulkner. Besides, Mr. Carmichael, if you read *all* of 'The Bear,' you might be surprised. You might even find in it something to help you help Dr. King." The last she delivered with a smile that suggested endless possibilities.

I was enamored by Professor Morrison's response (for it was Toni Morrison who first taught me the humanities). She was a Faulkner advocate. Six years before that classroom exchange, she had written in her M.A. thesis for Cornell University, as follows: "In 'The Bear' . . . there is a description of Sam Fathers as a man who 'had learned humility through suffering and learned pride through the endurance which survived suffering.' The call for humility and endurance is familiar enough in Faulkner's works to suggest a credo, and it is precisely these qualities that Quentin does not have. Though he suffers he does not learn humility."[7]

Stokeley Carmichael was silenced. Like me, he read *all* of "The Bear." But in the bourgeois provinces of 1961 Howard University, I am not certain any of us understood the connection—the mythic solidarity—between the mere hunting story of the work's initial offering and the tale of the awful ledgers that occupies the work's closing. Comparative slavery was not on the course list for the fall term of 1961 at Howard University, the "Capstone of Negro Education." In fact, I think there were many like myself who had no idea of the holocaustal horror that was our American past. Toni Morrison did all she could to induct us into the myth of suffering, humility, guilt, and expiation that William Faulkner had crafted to illuminate America's regions of servitude. But we were so awfully young. How—even in the continuing stages of our own conscientious and ambitious efforts to redeem the land of cotton—could we make sense of the type of gigantic, horrible egos that Faulkner mythically set before us?

> "Who else," ask the McCaslins, "could have declared a war against a power with ten times the area and a hundred times the men and a thousand times the resources, except men who could believe that all necessary to conduct a successful war was not acumen nor shrewdness nor politics nor diplomacy nor money nor even integrity and simple arithmetic but just love of land and courage."[8]

Who else, indeed, but those who have corrupted a God-bequeathed and incorruptible wilderness with their possessive design, their unfeeling egos driven to make the wondrous world into *things*, to make all into a *thing*? Life becomes trivialized and disgustingly reduced to stakes in a poker game by men who do not take the wilderness to heart, but take it—saw mill and railroad girder and switch engine and razor-edged axe crashing into timber—take it, read it out as possible possession to be scratched at and scratched at until it yields currency. Such men leave ledgers, records, whole libraries of inscribed guilt to be reckoned with by subsequent generations.

Uncle Buddy had won Tomey's Terrel's wife Tennie in the poker game of 1859—"Possible Strait against three Treys in sigt Not called"— no pale sentence or paragraph scrawled in cringing fear of death by a weak and trembling hand as a last desperate sop flung backward at retribution, but a Legacy, a Thing, possessing weight to the hand and bulk to the eye and even audible.[9]

In "The Bear," the concluding journey of young Isaac—son of the fathers, bearer of the weight of countless generations, Biblical in his exchanges with his cousin McCaslin the elder—ends, as do so many sober paragraphs of Faulknerian myth, with madness: Boon and the squirrels. The scene swells with belated, screaming protection for that which is already doomed, forever dishonored by offices of Southern life.

Toni Morrison labored—against a backdrop of white Southerners' rabid resistance, rage, rape, and vilifying rhetoric against civil rights—to teach us Faulkner's use value and mythic potential for seeking our own knowledge and redemption with respect to economies that were still holding us in desperate fee.

> *"Apparently they can learn nothing save through suffering, remember nothing save when underlined in blood."* (286)

If Toni Morrison could not—as no person can—bestow upon us a myth of our own, she was still patently aware what language and moral wrestling of grand myth looks like. And she urged us—even Stokeley Carmichael—not to judge the "old Mississippian" by his fall, but by his mythically heroic prose wrestling with what man had done to man ... and to all the earth and the animals entrusted by God to his keeping.

After such knowledge, what myths of redemption and forgiveness could we forge?

4

We had lived in Paris—my wife, my infant son, and I—long enough for me to feel entirely confident about finding my way to the branch of the Sorbonne where I was scheduled to lecture to a seminar of French students on Faulkner's long short story "Wash." Professor Marie Claire Vanderest had asked, upon learning that I hailed from the American South, if I liked Faulkner. Truth to tell, since my course with Professor Morrison and a brief, disastrous encounter with *Light in August* in graduate school, I had not given the Mississippi writer a thought. I had not discovered—nor was I really concerned to discover—my "Southern contemporaneity" with him. In fact, I had labored mightily to bring about that successful affectation of accent and personal bearing that would completely disguise my "Southernness." I was a "Dr." now—a Ph.D. who had shared institutional space with Cleanth Brooks, Rene Wellek, R. W. B. Lewis, and Harold Bloom. What had I to do with the South, or the South with me? I was in my own version of Parisian exile for a year, living in Antony and riding the *Linge de Sceaux* into Paris's Luxembourg Gardens metro stop to take in the Latin Quarter, strolling about where Joyce and Wright and Hemingway and Baldwin had taken their leave. Did I like Faulkner? Well, certainly not!

But who would—especially in French exile—scruple at an invitation to speak at the Sorbonne? Not I. Of course when Professor Vanderest named the text she wished me to elucidate, I swallowed hard. Uh, "Wash." What was that? I asked her to send me a copy of the text so that I would be, as it were, "on the same page" with her students. She agreed to do so. And when the bulky sheaf of pages in photocopy arrived, I sat down immediately and commenced reading.

I was bowled over, enthralled, knocked back utterly on my literary-critical heels, astonished by the world and its inhabitants who were washing over me like some savage Mississippi flood, pulverizing deltas of provinciality. It was an ocean of passions of race and rage, miscegenation and moral innocence. I had never, never in my comings and goings among texts encountered anyone remotely akin to Colonel Thomas Sutpen, sole proprietor of Sutpen's Hundred.

The awe of the title character Wash Jones (while ethically naïve and self-destructive) in some ways expresses my own astonishment at Sutpen. Says Wash: "A fine proud man. If God Himself was to come down and ride the natural earth, that's what He would aim to look like."[10] This of Sutpen galloping on his black stallion across his hundred acres wrested from the wilderness. This of a man Wash factors as "his own lonely apotheosis" and white-supremacist "self-defense" against his own mean, poor white caste status in a South where Negroes are better spoken, clothed, fed, and cared for than Wash Jones.

By the time I encountered Colonel Sutpen, I had shared space with the exalted white academics (Bloom & Co.) at Yale aforementioned, but in New Haven my most dedicated labors (something I have already hinted) had been to the kind of self-reinvention that is archetypally "American." I had gone in a shot from tweed-coated "good Negro professor" to African Dashiki wearing "Bad Revolutionary New Black Man." The poster on my Yale office wall—purchased at Mr. Micheaux's famous 125th Street and Lenox Avenue bookstore in Harlem—had black fists raised and read: *The Ultimate Solution Is Black Revolution!*

To change the order of things we needed Black Studies. We needed Black Power. We needed Black Nationalist institutions of our own—books and journals, schools, and a literary and cultural critique of our own.

My hair was wildly roughly curly now. My eyes were always striving for intensity. Most importantly, my mind had commenced to absorb the shadows and acts, accountings and reckonings, narratives and powerful lyrics of a *black past* that had never been disappeared *tout court* by the United States, but only *invisible* in that marketplace ignored by a kind of general, white, academic gentleman's agreement.

Nothing there to buy, right?

And he: *No, nothing.*

John Hope Franklin, W. E. B. Du Bois, James Baldwin and Benjamin Quarles, Frantz Fanon, Gwendolyn Brooks, Alain Locke and Langston Hughes, Ralph Ellison, Gil Scott Heron, The Last Poets and Nina Simone, Ed Bullins, Amiri Baraka, Sonia Sanchez, James Weldon Johnson, and Arna Bontemps ... merchants and prophets and apostles and sapient sutlers of the orishas and loas all ... an African and Afro-American festival of rare and generous gifts of a transatlantic dark spirit's survival and flourishing. *When the revolution comes. When the revolution comes!* No, it won't be televised.

I read "Wash" and Colonel Sutpen against the backdrop of my mind-enhancing and spirit-expanding acquaintance with a South that had always been hiding inside my brown body, waiting to emerge. Here were Ole Sis Goose and Brer Rabbit and High John and Stackalee filling in the interstices of Faulkner's mythscapes.

No longer were there only the visible, lamentable, or laudatory whites tragically worn—nor solely the taciturn, shambling, dissembling, enduring, comic, block-headed, parodically pompous Negroes when I read "Wash."

I knew the other story, the story of those Negroes who drove Mr. Wash Jones maddeningly and buffoonishly, in a wretched triumph of "race pride," to sacrifice his own granddaughter to the "rutting" of Sutpen.

Wash Jones was less undone by a passive well-keptness of "Negroes" than by the fear of what I came to know as Afro-America's ineluctable dynamism—a brilliant black creativity (even if no more than of character and resistance) out of bare bones and spare rags. Wash realized his being as epiphenomenon—a sad secondariness to the ruthless exclusionism of his dreamed apotheosis, Colonel Thomas Sutpen. And though Wash claims an awful vengeance for his own stupidly racialized episteme, he can never quite eradicate the boomeranging outrageousness of the Colonel's brutally casual first-response to the child (the daughter) he has fathered (with Wash's total complicity) upon the granddaughter: "Well, Milly too bad you're not a mare. Then I could give you a decent stall in the stable" (535). All that scuppernong harbor *amité* between Wash and the Colonel come roaring up the poor white's esophagus like flushed bile. Time's chosen healer, Wash takes scythe in hand and slays the man who arrived in Jefferson, at his second showing, with twenty "wild niggers" and a French architect.

I was able to grasp the grandeur—and the severe limitations—of Faulkner's driving myth in that year of 1972 because I had my own necessary background of black and Southern history, a myth of my own in formation. I took up the larger story with Faulkner's majestic achievement *Absalom, Absalom!* And knowing the whole story—as Faulkner saw it—I set out by metro for the seventh arondisement of Paris to lecture to French students.

Of course, Faulkner had done Paris long before I. He was a shy writer in exile who was afraid to speak to James Joyce. But he drank the Left Bank café rounds nonetheless.

The metro offered a perfect ride and—*comme l'habitude*—was resolutely on time. I strolled the few blocks to Paris 7 rehearsing the rituals and rhetoric of the Faulknerian revelation I would bring to these French students. My grasp of the materials seemed secure, particularly buttressed by my handsomely acquired and shining new Black Studies insights.

About a block from the campus I was drawn up by scores, upon scores, upon scores, of riot-gear-clad French police troops and rings and rings of black mariahs (those awesome carriers and incarceration vans that put one strongly in mind of tumbrels—and Foucault). There had been a mini riot at Paris 7 that morning. The university was on lock-down. It was still true that the aftershocks and revoutionary and incendiary spirit of *Mai Soixante-huit* were shaking the city of Balzac and Zola. Would Faulkner have understood this continental and youth-led *"Je refuse"*—this demotic repudiation of old aristocratic arrangments of things? Perhaps. But one doubts he would have sympathized with its earlier dark-complected stirrings with Algerians, or its new millennial energies (as of today) in the vast immigrant arrivals and strivings that gave Jean Marie Le Pen such a boost from rabid whites in recent elections of France.

I found Marie Claire. She suggested we take our show to a local café. We did. The students, I am convinced, were far more serious about their steaming cups of espresso and public, café attitudes than about Mr. Wash Jones and Colonel Thomas Sutpen, whom I labored mightily—with all the mythical acumen I could muster—to bring clearly before their eyes.

"This is America," I wanted to scream at them. *"This is the America of a South I am coming to know. It is a South forever and already changed by the mind and souls of black folk. Colonel Sutpen is dead . . . and yet, never more mythically alive than at this revolutionary moment."*

I hear Wash Jones inquiring "they kilt us, but they aint whipped us yit, air they?" (539). And I don't need Sutpen or anyone else to say for me: "For *America's* sake, let us certainly hope you are whipped forever." Not through war and pillage and carnage on the field, but by our construction of an accessible path to the invisible marketplace where our voices have always been.

"Thus sadly musing." "Thus sadly musing," writes Du Bois in *The Souls of Black Folk* of his train journey back to Nashville from the "behind the mountains" place where he witnessed the demise of the beautiful black woman-child Josie's ambitions to live a larger life. My metro return to Antony was nothing so dramatic. But I did know that I was rendered by the experiences of that day forever a contestatory American contemporary of that fellow Southerner Faulkner, who was white, brilliant, male, and I know now, heroically limited.

5

In the 'eighties I taught *Absalom, Absalom!* to Ivy League students—black and white—and found such dead space as would amaze you. They so much more appreciated Mark Twain and his remarkable twins. Perhaps they were as baffled as I—way back in early days perched upon those grandfather-built bookcases—by the utter "craziness" of the families of Yoknapatawpha. It was the Reagan/Bush era. And maybe these students felt Faulkner was simply too "old school" to count, despite my feverish, moralizing, histrionic urgings to discussion and debate. "Aren't you concerned about the history of the South," I shot at them. Only to see blank stares. Of course, I now see that my failure was to register my *own* mythic discoveries as the opening gambit to teaching Faulkner. I did not share with them my journey. And—most importantly—I did not alert them that I repudiated—and repudiated utterly—the enormous failings of the author from Oxford.

Earlier, I mentioned a disastrous graduate school encounter with *Light in August*. Let me explain. I was the only black person in an American literature graduate seminar of fifty students in a palmy West Coast venue during the mid-1960s. Dr. Martin Luther King was seemingly unstoppably on the march. Civil rights and voting rights "bills" had become law of the land. My older brother was a Wall Street lawyer. My father had left Louisville and become a major player in public health in the nation's capital. I had won a prestigious fellowship for graduate study.

And then came *Light in August* with its feverish, homicidal, mad, laborious, racialized syllables of purest bizarrerie. Listen: "surrounded by the summer smell and the summer voices of invisible negroes. . . . On all sides, even within him, the bodiless fecundmellow voices of negro women murmured. It was as though he and all other manshaped life about him had been returned to the lightless hot wet primogenitive Female."[11] Listen more: "Then he told her. 'I got some nigger blood in me'" (196). Again, listen: "He now lived as man and wife with a woman who resembled an ebony carving. At night he would lie in bed beside her . . . trying to breathe into himself the dark color, the dark and inscrutable thinking and being of negroes, with each suspiration trying to expel from himself the white blood and the white thinking and being" (225–26).

And we are not—nor will we ever be—finished listening to the feverish, awful, nightmare of our Southern mythographer's disaster of a novel that is, finally, not about anything—at least not about anything real, save perhaps, prurient, disastrous myths of black blood and odor, Negro razors and bovine stupidity, white nymphomania and black-male lasciviousness, militaristic white desire sublimated into grim and unlikely castration.

O yes, and this is in a single novel that I was called upon to "explicate" for that graduate seminar of interested whites. "Mr. Faulkner," I wanted to scream, "how could you do this to me?" But I didn't even know—then—that that is what I wanted to scream. I was made ill—physically ill—by the pandering to White American Racism and deeply mentally ill fantasies that are *Light in August*. Stokeley was—at least where this novel is concerned—correct about William Faulkner being an "old Mississippi cracker."

Of course, *Light in August* is merely the most offensive of Faulkner's mythological errors. Ashley Montagu calls "race" America's "most dangerous myth."[12] And the novelist from Oxford was not always the most careful person in avoiding the pitfalls of the dangerous myth. His miscegenatory underpinnings and overlays for plot, theme, and motif are often grandiosely bereft of any known objective correlative. The sound and fury about Joe Christmas's "bloodlines" is disasterously silly, as are some of the purple prose passages rendered to Charles Bon and the Octoroons of New Orleans.

How profound a historical fact is it anyway that white men who had all power, on armed plantations, brutally raped black women slaves and gave birth to second "colored families"?

Are we shocked by this history?

Perhaps.

But we certainly can never again, I hope, be titillated or obsessed with it as was Faulkner.

The fecundity and grandeur of his myth flounders, indeed, in the prurience of his fascinations. Listen to these words about Bon from *Absalom, Absalom!*: "the white men who, when he said he was a negro, believed that he lied in order to save his skin, or worse: from sheer besotment of sexual perversion; in either case the result was the same: the man with the body and limbs almost as light and delicate as a girl's giving the first blow."[13]

Within the same economies, a shoddily characterized Joe Christmas takes it upon himself to kick the living daylights out of a Negro girl who he is complicit in gang-raping. Heavens! And with all those classics and philosophy books in his library, no less, Faulkner plays the racist pulp fictionist. Sad, really. He should have known better. In a contemporary reading, he seems only to be a victim of the rankest—and, yes, most distinctively *white male and Southern*—fantasies of white patriarchs that they have open license to the sexuality of a putatively bounden and dark "other."

In such failed moments of Faulkner as *Light in August*, it comes as pathetic explanation and sad commentary to know that he was—from an early age—a chronic alcoholic, and in later life an abuser of narcotics and alcohol who endured the horrific therapy of electroshock and wandered, rather, from sanitarium to sanitarium—cheating death by only momentary clean-and-sober intervals.

Despite the purely secular bizarrerie and pathological explanation for it of such racist slippages as *Light in August* and other Faulknerian texts, there remains—strong as ever in some instances—a white (and, yes, in these days, a truly bizarre *black*) literary critical, and culturally-critical demiurge to save Faulkner and his work from their own racial failings. It is as though Wash Jones—having discovered the mad megalomania and unfeeling indifference of Colonel Sutpen—decides not to slay the dragon, but to find a symbology—or an excuse—to proclaim everything Sutpen ever did represented a labor of indisputable greatness.

For example, there is a reading of *Light in August* that suggests the novel represents Christian allegory. Because Joe Christmas receives his name from a white orphanage when he is delivered to the orphanage's doors at Christmas, resolute critics wish to see Joe's "birth" as the resonant figuration of (can it really be?) the Virgin Birth of Jesus Christ. Given Christ's genealogy and the utterly "unorphaned" state of His birth, where do such critical postulates about "Christmas" come from? Does a strange critical impulse to find in the novel's substitution of a seasonal nominative for "Doe" produce the confusion?

Again, when salvation-of-Faulknerian-greatness criticism attempts to read Joe's last days as a figuration of Christ's Passion—which is sacramentally characterized by conviviality, discipleship, generosity, outgoing acceptance of the world and of His fate to redeem it—what are they thinking? Joe, in his last days, is mentally distraught (ill?), hermetic in extremis, wearing "Negro shoes," from which (in perhaps one of the novel's most outrageous moments) he seems to absorb an essentialist, Negro "racial essence." (This is not, of course, unlike Lena Grove in her "men's shoes." And of course, Lena is the novel's real, sympathetic protagonist—even in all the misogyny of the narrator's commentary on "woman." Lena's story is certainly more compellingly, artistically, and authentically told than Joe's.) Christ perishes in resounding redemption of a sinful world—with a free willingness and a barely comprehensible sacrifice. By contrast, Joe forever reminds us of the South's most brutish moral obtuseness. He is victim to that dread practice of Southern spectacle lynching. He represents, in one view, certainly *not* Christ, but the most heinous of Southern sins for which *only* Christ's mercy might atone.

Light in August is not a powerful, or successful, or redeemable allegory that artistically brings together the lives of Christ and Joe Christmas. I think only a radically ham-fisted salvation-of-greatness weds Joe and Jesus. *Light in August* is, perhaps, a racist parody from the pen of a Southern author who suffered tremens of self-medication all his life. But it is not an artistic or achieved allegory, at least where race in America is concerned. The question then abides: "Mr. Faulkner how could you do this to us?"

6

So how then do we sum up an Afro-American "contemporaneity" with the sage of Yoknapatawpha?

We say, I think, that he is always the Cerebus at the gateway of a Southern landscape without who we can not experience and encounter mythic *America*. He is also the avatar and mythic craftsman of so many "undead" ghosts of our national imaginings. "What did you do?" we ask. "What did you do to enable yourselves exclusively to be called the only true *Americans*, further to deem yourselves speakers and possessors of the land's only *native* language and natural wonders? What did you—all locked, as you are, into the consensus of *whiteness*—do to assume the *rights* of denying and incarcerating, flaying, raping, and murdering with a flattering word all who do not look like you?"

Faulkner's mythic answer—despite his aberrant radio interview remarks about "shooting Negroes" and making them wait 200 years for "civilization"—is perhaps as closely akin to my own—and to a just contemporary assessment of matters—as one can get. Such brutal exclusivity as represented by the imperious "you" of the question is purchased, in Faulkner's Yoknapatawpha economies, only at the price of the most catastrophic betrayal of that possible "refuge and sanctuary of liberty and freedom from . . . the old world's worthless evening."[14] Abundance and rich possibility is what the imperious "you" has turned into a tawdry possessiveness of the sick ego intent on a "pureblooded" ownership.

While my own contemporary Black Studies mythography would suggest that Faulkner's vision of expatiation and redemption for such flagrantly uncharitable possessiveness accords too much passivity to "the Negro," still my own emerging myth of origins and new Southern promise suggest that Faulkner got his agents right. He knew Afro-Americans provided not only the music of Southern spheres, but also the complicating energies of those spheres' revolutions.

Richard Wright proclaimed that "the Negro is America's metaphor."[15] The mythic Faulkner proclaimed possibilities of modal salvation from black Americans because of that ineffable ability to endure—in humility and courage and self-understanding and outgoing embrace of humanity's awful incumbencies.

Faulkner knew Afro-Americans possessed "what they got not only not from white people but not even despite white people because they had it already from the old free fathers a longer time free than us because we have never been free" (295). Thus speaks Ike McCaslin near the conclusion of "The Bear."

Would it not be delightful to have the Toni Morrison of *Playing in the Dark* and William Faulkner of that great wilderness short story in the same room discussing the merits of the Mississippian's prophesied relief for momumental American moral failures?

I think so.

But such a prospect of two so-removed geniuses in conversation in the same academic rooms carries us out of myth and into fantasy. It is time to stop with a French paraphrase of an American Presidential moment long past.

If asked—even in the hot dread of his ranting Southern lucubrations—if I was, indeed of the party of the old Mississippian, I would have to answer—with all the complexity of my black, Southern being: *Moi, Je suis un Faulknerian!*

NOTES

1. Stephen B. Oates, *William Faulkner: The Man and the Artist* (New York: Harper and Row, 1987). For Faulkner biography, I have relied almost exclusively on this source. Joseph Blotner's magnificent, two-volume biography is, of course, the comprehensive biographical source for the specialist.

2. T. S. Eliot, "Tradition and the Individual Talent," in *Selected Essays* (New York: Harcourt, Brace and Company, 1950). For all references to Eliot's classic essay, I have relied upon this edition.

3. T. S. Eliot, "*Ulysses*, Order, and Myth," *The Dial* 75 (November, 1923): 480–83. All citations are to this version of the review-essay.

4. William Faulkner, "The Bear," in *Go Down, Moses* (New York: Vintage Books, 1973), 298. All citations refer to this edition.

5. William Faulkner, *The Sound and the Fury* (New York: Vintage International, 1990). All citations refer to this edition.

6. "The Bear," 191–331.

7. Chloe Ardellia Wofford (Toni Morrison), "Virginia Woolf's and William Faulkner's Treatment of the Alienated," (master's thesis, Cornell University, 1955).

8. "The Bear," 288–89.

9. Ibid., 271.

10. William Faulkner, "Wash," in *Collected Stories* (New York: Vintage International, 1995), 538. The longer version of this story in Malcolm Cowley's famous *Portable Faulkner* is the one I read in our Antony apartment in France.

11. William Faulkner, *Light in August* (New York: Vintage International, 1990), 114–15. All citations are to this edition and are hereafter marked by page numbers in parentheses.

12. Ashley Montagu, *Man's Most Dangerous Myth: The Fallacy of Race* (New York: Columbia University Press, 1942).

13. William Faulkner, *Absalom, Absalom!* (New York: Vintage International, 1990), 167.

14. "The Bear," 283.

15. Richard Wright, *White Man, Listen!* (New York: Doubleday, Anchor Books, 1964), 72.

William Faulkner and Other Famous Creoles

W. Kenneth Holditch

Please pardon the repetition if you who have heard this anecdote before, but I cannot indeed forbear. When in 1958 I was at the point of concluding my graduate course work in the English department at Ole Miss and began to consider a dissertation subject, my thoughts turned quite naturally to William Faulkner. He had been, after all, very much a presence in my life: I was born six miles from his birthplace, had always known members of his family, and had read everything he had published up to that point. That reading had been done first on my own, then under the guidance of Harry Modean Campbell, who with Ruel Foster wrote the first critical study of Faulkner and taught the first Faulkner seminar at Ole Miss. In those early years of Faulkner study, however, it was not clear to the English department that Faulkner alone was worthy of a course, and as a consequence, he was yoked with his contemporary, Ernest Hemingway! My proposal to write about Faulkner, was rejected because—and I quote—he "had been done." At that point, there were, I believe, only three book-length critical studies of his work, hard as that is to believe with forty years of hindsight.

Because I was far from as brash then as I would later become—after I had taught a few years and found it expedient to put on the armor necessary for survival in the academic world—I acquiesced to the professorial decision and set about searching for another topic. My second choice was John Dos Passos, a writer who at first thought might strike one as being totally unlike Faulkner in his themes and style. I had stumbled on Dos Passos by accident in my hometown library one summer and selected him for a very strange reason—because I *liked* to read him. I say *strange* because given today's academic climate in too many English departments in too many universities, merely *liking* an author's work is deemed to be of little consequence, paling in significance to other presumably more contemporarily popular reasons for studying novels and poems and plays, reasons entangled with such arcane words as *deconstruction* and *post-structuralism*, and *historicity* and so forth. Merely *liking* the works of an author may, indeed, be considered reactionary and may count as a strike against the student, who has not yet learned the hard lesson of contemporary criticism.

My choice of Dos Passos as subject was accepted with a certain amount of scepticism, and after two years I produced a dissertation of 468 pages. It may seem odd to some that I have never done anything with that dissertation, other than publish a couple of articles and deliver a few papers at those philological conferences the "publish or perish" philosophy forced me into. But after spending all that time and work—remember that what would later be Xerox was yet to come and I had to type four copies using carbon paper and I had only eight days in which to do it. Granted it was an electric typewriter, but there were no erase keys in those prehistoric days.

After all that, I simply lacked the stomach to revise the entire work into any publishable form. When Linda Wagner finished her book on Dos Passos, she asked me why those of us who had been early laborers in the Dos Passos vineyards had left the work of publication to her and others, and I hardly had an answer. However, let it be known that my devotion to Dos Passos as a great writer has never wavered and I share Faulkner's evaluation of his significance to twentieth-century literature and Modernism. Forget for the moment the fact that the judgment was probably not meant for public consumption and that Faulkner was not above making outrageous remarks to create an aura of drama about himself, the question remains: why did Faulkner classify Dos Passos as the third best author of his generation? I think I know the answer to that question, and will be happy to share it with you on some other occasion, but that is not part of the intention of this paper. It is clear, however, that the two of them were perhaps the most daring experimenters among the major novelists of their generation.

Having finished my dissertation and received the first Ph.D. in English at the University of Mississippi, I floundered about for three years at a job in a Catholic college I did not like—and do not wish to discuss—before I wound up at the University of New Orleans, where I was to spend the next thirty-two years. I don't have to explain to any Mississippian *why* I took a teaching position in New Orleans, since as late as my generation, at least, we believed—even prayed—that when we died we would go to that Creole city to drink and dine on fare fit for the gods. Finally my wishes and prayers were answered. At the time, I was far from being aware that the conjunction of the two dissertation topics—the one I had first desired and the one I settled for—had occurred in the mid-1920s, when a significant group of American authors converged on the Vieux Carré in New Orleans, drawn there by rumors—which proved to be true—of great and inexpensive food, cheap rents, and free-flowing liquor, in a city oblivious to the Prohibition which was the bane of the rest of the United States. It was here that Dos Passos and Faulkner first met and became friends, along with other authors, some of them still read, others faded into what John Pilkington in his courses at Ole Miss used to call "the undergrowth of American literature."

What is it about New Orleans that has made it an enchantress not only for Mississippians but writers and artists from all over the country—a "courtesan," Faulkner wrote—enticing them to migrate there, remain to soak up the atmosphere, and then move on? I remember one long meal at Galatoire's a few years ago, complemented by Old-Fashioneds and Sazeracs, during which Willie Morris and Philip Carter, Hodding and Betty Carter's son, devised a plan to annex the city to their native state of Mississippi, where they felt it had belonged all along. (Indeed, when the Louisiana Purchase was divided up into states, the original plan would have used the Mississippi River as the dividing line, and New Orleans would have been part of Mississippi.)

The city itself has not, as Walker Percy pointed out, produced any native writers of the highest order—Lillian Hellman and Truman Capote are good but not of the first rank—and yet it has provided a home or haven as well as an inspiration to thousands of writers from William Makepeace Thackeray and Walt Whitman to Richard Ford. What the attractions of the city have been for the creative seem to involve not just the accessibility of liquor in a dry time or the Romantic atmosphere, but a degree of freedom from moral and other restrictions, a rejection of the Calvinistic work ethic, a *joie de vivre* that seems almost part of the humid air itself, a degree of tolerance for the different, even the bizarre, unmatched anywhere else in the country. In an interview with Don Lee Keith in the 1970s, Tennessee Williams observed that "in New York, eccentrics, authentic ones, are ignored. In Los Angeles, they're arrested. Only in New Orleans are they permitted to develop their eccentricities into art."[1] Finally, in New Orleans we find a tendency to leave people alone to do whatever they want—there is an old saying in New Orleans that people don't care what you do; they want to know about it, but they don't care.

New Orleans has been, since before the Louisiana Purchase, an anamoly in the United States, a part of the Union and yet perversely separated from it. Why? For one thing because of its unique population, including French and Spanish and West Indian, and because of its stubborn resistance to any sort of amalgamation or fusion into the American mix. Writers and other outsiders have from the beginning not only been aware of that distinction and contrast but even fascinated by it. A. J. Leibling referred to South Louisiana as the strange northern tip of Costa Rica, "within the orbit of a Hellenistic world that never touched the North Atlantic . . . one more city of the Grecia Maxima that rims the Mediterranean" and the "westernmost Arab State."[2] That view has long been widely accepted by outsiders—and by insiders, who will do almost anything to assert their uniqueness and discourage any change imposed by the dread Americans, as they still sometimes identify those from other parts of the country.

One of the earliest startled reactions to the city recorded in writing was that of Rachel, wife of Andrew Jackson, the "savior" of New Orleans, on her visits to the city. She wrote to Robert Hays of the surprise she experienced there. "I have seen more already than in all my life past it is the finest Country for the Eye of a Strainger but a Little while he tirs of the Disipation." In 1821, when she and her husband returned for a tribute the city had arranged for him, she wrote to Eliza Kingsley, "Great Babylon is come before me. Oh, the wickedness, the idolatry of this place! unspeakable riches and splendor." Of the honors bestowed upon the general, including his being crowned with a laurel wreath, she expressed Protestant indignation, "The Lord has promised his humble followers a crown that fadeth not away; the present one is already withered the leaves falling off.... Oh, farewell! Pray for your sister in a heathen land."[3]

By the 1920s, however, that contrast, shocking as it had been to Mrs. Jackson, was one of those things much to be desired in New Orleans by the outsiders. What Mrs. Jackson found too pagan for her taste, Sherwood Anderson relished. Having fled Ohio in full rebellion against the Puritan ethic of his background and childhood, he found in New Orleans what he thought the best attitude toward life in the United States, the perfect amalgam of two cultures, the French and the African American. Romantically, Anderson's idealized version of the New Orleans mystique, as expressed in his story "A Meeting South," involved what he termed the "Latin" quality of the Vieux Carré, the laziness and sensuousness of its inhabitants, and the "French influence, ... a sort of matter-of-factness about life."[4] The well-known sexual license of the city, which in 1920 was more at odds with the attitudes of the rest of the country than in the twenty-first century, clearly delighted many of the authors. In the 1920s, prostitution was still rampant in the Vieux Carré,[5] and in a 1926 sketch, Edmund Wilson, one of the many literary guests who found shelter in the Andersons' apartment, has a character observe, after a monkey creates havoc by escaping from an organ grinder and scampering into a brothel, "What a jolly place New Orleans is, ... where the policemen reassure the whores! It's a real Catholic city!"[6]

An earlier visitor, French artist Edgar Degas, who spent a few months in the city in 1872 and 1873 with his mother's family, obviously shared Rachel Jackson's revulsion at the torpor of the people and the "suffocating languor" of the atmosphere—the French can at times be every bit as Puritanical as any Anglo-Saxon. Degas wrote to a friend in France, "One does nothing here, it lies in the climate."[7] Joseph Hilton Smyth, a lesser known member of the Anderson-Faulkner circle, found the city "a pleasant place to dream in, as good as any other to recover from an abortive love affair, a relaxing place to drink in. It was conducive to everything, in fact, but work. There were always excuses. New Orleans' *tomorrow* became in time as insidious as the *mañana* of Central America." Smyth found it amazing therefore that "a sizeable amount of solid literary work came out of New Orleans during those years."[8]

By the time Faulkner visited New Orleans in December 1924, Anderson was already ensconced with his wife in what he called "the most civilized city in America—because fact had not submerged the imagination"—and had made it his own. In his essay on the *Double-Dealer* he stressed, like many another writer before him and after him, the foreign quality of the place: "sailors from many foreign lands come up from the water's edge and idle on streetcorners, in the evening, soft voices, speaking strange tongues, come drifting to you out of the street."[9] Anderson was an exotic, dressed according to a letter Faulkner wrote to his mother, in loud colored clothes and moving among other exotics, determined to express his individuality in a city where he felt that such an act was more possible than elsewhere in the United States. All the elements that made the city, particularly the Quarter, unique—the foreignness, the tolerance of different life styles, the freedom from the Puritanism he had fought much of his mature life—had produced, he believed, "the greatest field for the writer in the United States"(126). Another positive element for struggling writers was the fact that the impoverished Quarter had inexpensive rent, food, and drink, for as Oliver LaFarge wrote in his novel *The Copper Pot*, " it's a good place to be poor in."[10]

Opinions about *la vie de Boheme* in the French Quarter in the 1920s from those who were part of it, the "Famous Creoles" circle and others are diverse and often even contradictory. Natives of the city such as Hamilton Basso and James K. Feibleman tended to take a somewhat jaundiced view of the scene, even though they were part of it. Basso, who had been born over his father's shoe shop on lower Decatur Street, was inclined, like most New Orleanians, to love with no reservations his hometown, which he described in a letter to Malcolm Cowley as the last Southern place "where people know how to have fun" in contrast to the rest the South, which he saw as "too joylessly Anglo-Saxon."[11] That contrast between the two cultures was a note that has been sounded over and over by writer after writer for the past two centuries. Basso seems to have feared contamination of the pure Latin lifestyle of the city by the influx of artists and writers, but he ultimately concluded in his 1939 novel *Days before Lent* that "the Quarter managed to absorb all its invaders and come off relatively unscarred."[12] Basso's wife, Etolia, recalled in later years his stressing the fact that the writers living in the Quarter in the 1920s were not a united group "and God knows we were not a school."[13] Similarly, Roark Bradford, a popular author of the time who wrote books and stories in black dialect (some critics of the era and later even list him among African American writers), recalled the influx of "country boys and girls . . . coming in to be

Bohemians" and complained that as a result, even the immorality of the Quarter had lost "that calm professional dignity it once had."[14] However, Cathy Chance Harvey in her dissertation on Lyle Saxon quotes Faulkner as calling the relationship between the writers in the Quarter "a fellowship of art," and says that Oliver LaFarge insisted that "when one of us achieved anything at all, however slight, the others were delighted and I think everyone took new courage."[15]

Philosopher James K. Feibleman alternated between admiration for the Bohemianism of the Vieux Carré and a cynical dismissal of what he saw as dilletantish posing. He described the city as "a better place than most from which to be heard," since the benefits for the creative spirit in the Quarter were that it was "a sleepy old place full of warmth and charm" where "life could be good at the sensual level."[16] There one was living "*in* the times but not *of* them," as if it were "some remote post of empire" where the writer or artist could be free of "literary and intellectual fashions"(157). Like Sherwood Anderson, Feibleman recognized that one of the magnetic charms that attracted writers and artists to New Orleans was the fact that it had thus far escaped the commercialization, industrialization, and "the self-regimentation of conformity"(272) that had afflicted the other American cities. It was "an oasis where the sensual life was free and could be combined with contemplation undisturbed against a sleepy background of hot humid days, and sultry nights. Life was to be enjoyed for its own sake and not for any other end, a rare enough thing in the United States"(272). In retrospect, Feibleman identified the primary advantage he had gained from being part of that circle as "an intense dislike of Puritanism," for his generation was not, he insisted, "lost" but was certainly "free"(329). The Vieux Carré shared with Paris and Greenwich Village, Feibleman wrote, a "socially tolerant atmosphere" where people were "happy to be left alone just to be themselves"(271). In addition, he argued that both the climate and the Latin population "contributed to the leisurely pace" necessary for creativity, and that the area had developed, "not by any design but by accident" into "something of a literary center"(271). He stressed, however, that the authors and artists constituted only a small part of the population of the Quarter, and that the newcomers "did not color" that crowded multiethnic region, but rather "it colored them"(272).

Yet Feibleman could be scathing in his satirical jabs at the artistic life of the Vieux Carré, which he viewed as a weak imitation of the lifestyles of other "outposts of Bohemia," to use Tennessee Williams's phrase. What passed for *la vie de Boheme* in his hometown, Feibleman saw as merely a shadow of the life of the artist earlier in France, an ersatz copy that had evolved into "a charming, weak and mechanical life that had not the vividity and strength and vitality of novelty"(262). He criticized the gatherings of artists and writers, which he nevertheless often attended as "imitation Greenwich Village parties." However, he did grant that his native city provided a "neutral background" so that the writers who came there from elsewhere—Anderson, Faulkner, and others—"did not write about New Orleans but from New Orleans, and it was not hard to see why"(262).

By the 1920s, the existence of the literary journal called the *Double-Dealer*, to which Faulkner would contribute, was a further incentive to the production of art. In addition, the *Times-Picayune* was then, as it alas no longer is, not only a good newspaper but also an outlet for creative efforts. Faulkner became a contributor, thanks to the agency of Roark Bradford, an editor with a certain amount of discretionary money to spend every week. Among the "Famous Creoles," those contained in Spratling and Faulkner's book of caricatures as well as those who although part of the circle were omitted, several stand out. Lyle Saxon, a native Louisianian, became a friend of Sherwood Anderson in 1922 and, unlike many of the others in the group, continued to look up to the older writer (Thomas 41). Saxon was a newspaperman, an author of fiction and nonfiction works, and a character so well known in the old district where he was acquainted with almost everyone that he earned the soubriquet "Mr. French Quarter." Many feel that Saxon almost alone was responsible for the salvation of the Vieux Carré, which came close to being destroyed in the early decades of the twentieth century, and he was certainly a moving force in the establishment of a literary colony there.

By 1919, Saxon was holding a literary salon and predicting that more authors would come and "soon we would boast of our own Place D'Armes as New York does her Washington Square" (qtd. by Lake 40). By the early 1920s, his prediction was realized, for the Quarter had become a Greenwich Village South. Even Sherwood Anderson and others who saw Saxon as "old-maidish" and too much devoted to the magnolia and crinoline myth of the Old South recognized his importance (Anderson's "old-maidish," I think, is his code word for "gay"). In an article in the July 10, 1937, *Newsweek*, the writer called Saxon "the adviser, comforter, and financial ally of bitter poverty-pinched young writers" in the city.[17] Saxon and Roark Bradford both supported young authors, offering encouragement and as well as a place to stay. Saxon's support of writers continued after he moved for a while to New York City in the late 1920s and his Greenwich Village apartment became, according to James W. Thomas, a "clearing house" for authors from the South, Faulkner among them, and was nicknamed the "Southern Protective Association"(81). It is worth noting that the tolerance exhibited in the Quarter in the 1920s and later toward those who were somehow outside the mainstream seems to have been exhibited as well by Faulkner, who numbered among his close friends two gay men, Lyle Saxon and William Spratling. An interesting footnote on Saxon's career is that when the New Deal's Writers' Project was inaugurated in 1935, he was appointed to head the group that produced the *Louisiana State Guide* and the *New Orleans City Guide*. (It was the hope of getting a position working on this guide that would bring Tennessee Williams to New Orleans in 1938.)

This then was the milieu into which the young aspiring writers came, John Dos Passos first, then Faulkner. All through the 1920s, artists and writers flocked to the city, for a variety of reasons, not the least of which involved the presence of Sherwood Anderson. John Dos Passos, fleeing the cold northern winter, arrived in New Orleans in February 1924, hoping, Townsend Ludington says, to meet Anderson and to be able to work undistracted.[18] He rented a room in a dilapidated three-story townhouse at 510 Esplanade and in later years recalled one hilarious episode in which he climbed up on the steep roof to rescue the parrot of his Central American landlady, a precarious endeavor at best, made all the more so because Dos Passos always suffered from poor eyesight. Although at first he professed to be very lonely in the strange and exotic environment, he soon made friends of a literary bent, including Sherwood Anderson, Lyle Saxon, and William Faulkner. They often gathered at such restaurants as the Original Tivoli on Chartres Street, which had been opened by an Italian American couple, the Turcis, when the opera company of which they were members went broke and they were stranded in the city. Later Dos Passos would use the Original Tivoli in *The 42nd Parallel* (Ludington 232). When in the 1970s I interviewed Harold Levy, the former music director of Le Petit Theatre, New Orleans's little theatre, who had been at Harvard with Dos Passos, he recalled having taken him and Faulkner to Victor's restaurant, a favorite of the Bohemian crowd, for lunch.

Dos Passos was fascinated by the melange of cultures and architecture in New Orleans and wrote to his friend Rumsey Marvin that he loved the "streets of scaling crumbling houses with broad wrought iron verandahs painted in Caribbean blues and greens," the waterfront with hundreds of ships (New Orleans was still a major port in the 1920s), and a multitude of smells, including molasses. He walked along the levees for exercise, taking note of the odd characters, black and white. In the introduction to *USA*, in which he describes the travels of the anonymous protagonist, a sort of American Everyman of the times, he includes a description of a "bed full of fleas in New Orleans"—writers from the beginning have complained about the wide variety and persistence of insects and vermin that infest the subtropical seaport. In *The 42nd Parallel*, one of the characters, Charley Anderson, drives to New Orleans with a new Italian American friend named Grassi just before the First World War hoping to find a job and see

Mardi Gras. For three dollars a week, they rent a room near the levee from a Panamanian woman, who has a parrot that stays on the balcony. Looking for jobs, they walk through the streets of the Vieux Carré, smelling molasses and gardens and "garlic and pepper and oil cookery."[19] There seemed to be no jobs, and no one talked about anything except Carnival, which was the following week. Charley observes the infamous "shutter girl" prostitutes, and one night he picks up a woman, who complains that during Carnival the police gather up all the prostitutes and ship them to Memphis, where they "turn 'em loose . . . aint a jail in the state would hold all the floozies in this town" (343). The section is filled with local color elements from the French Quarter: "mulatto women in bandanas . . . moving around in the courtyards," the French Market, where early in the morning the vendors were displaying their fresh produce, the smell of absinthe from bars, the ever-present and often-cited smell of molasses from sugar refineries, and "the heavy damp air" that New Orleans residents learn to live with—or move away. During Carnival Charley observes the "crowds everywhere and lights and floats and parades and bands and girls running around in fancy dress." Shortly thereafter, he catches a steamer named the *Momus* (interestingly, the name of one of the oldest Carnival krewes) and heads for New York, "looking down on the roofs and streets and trolleycars of New Orleans" as the steamer heads South, passing between the "Eads Jetties" and into the Gulf of Mexico (347). After that initial visit, Dos Passos returned to New Orleans for short stays and several times refers to the city in his masterpiece, the great trilogy *USA*.

From those Bohemian days until Faulkner's death, he and Dos Passos remained friends and admirers of each other's work, although they rarely met. Dos Passos told Edie Shay in 1951, "You can say everything in the world against Faulkner, but I think he's still our greatest living novelist in the flamboyant Dickens-Dostoevsky line (with a touch of pure pulp of a Wilkie Collins sort")" (qtd Ludington 450). In 1956, Faulkner issued an appeal to Dos Passos for a writer's conference to encourage support from foreign authors, and Dos Passos, who had moved far beyond his earlier liberalism, only half-heartedly agreed, because he was discouraged that most foreign writers he met were communist-inclined and hated the United States. Both authors continued to correspond on the matter and both stood behind Faulkner's assertion in the questionnaire that "Writers shouldn't be organized, must be free"(Ludington 469).When Dos Passos was awarded the 1957 Gold Medal for Eminence in Fiction from the National Institute of Arts and Letters, Faulkner sat next to Elizabeth Dos Passos, who kept him supplied him with wine as the proceedings, meal and talk, dragged on and on. When the time came for Faulkner to present the medal, he handed it to Dos Passos and with his typical terseness said, with a double meaning, "Nobody deserved it more or had to wait for it longer" (qtd. in Ludington 471).

When Faulkner arrived in New Orleans in 1924, he probably knew of Sherwood Anderson's devotion to the city, where he and his wife, Elizabeth, a friend of Faulkner's, had taken up residence, and he certainly wanted to meet Anderson. It seems, however, that what kept the younger writer in New Orleans was the charm of the Vieux Carré, with its crumbling old townhouses and bizarre residents of several nationalities, with its easy-going lifestyle in which people might gaze curiously at human weaknesses of the flesh but did not condemn, as was the case in the Calvinistic culture in which he had been reared. One has only to remember Mr. Compson's idea of the shock Henry Sutpen must have experienced when first he saw (or did not see) the French Quarter: "I can imagine him with his puritan heritage—that heritage peculiarly Anglo-Saxon—of fierce proud mysticism and that ability to be ashamed of ignorance and inexperience in that city foreign and paradoxical, with its atmosphere at once fatal and languourous, at once feminine and steel-hard—this grim humourourless yokel out of a granite heritage where even the houses, let alone clothing and conduct, are built in the image of a jealous and sadistic Jehovah, put suddenly down in a place created for and by voluptuousness, the abashless and unabashed senses."[20] Faulkner had written short pieces of fiction before coming to New Orleans—one of them had been published in the Ole Miss newspaper. Carvel Collins states that Faulkner had told Phil Stone and others that he intended to concentrate on poetry, but he stayed on in the French Quarter longer than he had intended. Why? Several reasons present themselves: the literary scene in the Vieux Carré, where the aspiring writer turned his attention toward fiction, surely in large part because of the influence of Sherwood Anderson; and of course the presence of Helen Baird, a young and unique woman with whom Faulkner seems to have fallen in love immediately on their first meeting.[21]

It was probably 1 November 1924, when Faulkner presented himself at the apartment of his former employer, Elizabeth, while the Andersons were having a dinner for young writers, as they often did. Hamilton Basso, an aspiring novelist who was present that evening, would comment almost forty years later in his obituary of Faulkner that what Sherwood Anderson provided for beginning authors there was not just inspiration for their work but benevolence, a commitment to sharing with developing artists what he had gained. Basso remembered being impressed not only by Faulkner's "beautiful manners, his soft speech," but also by "his astonishing capacity for hard drink." Basso professed, with honest insight, to having felt inferior to Faulkner when it came to the grasp of great literature, especially that of the Modernist movement. In the obituary, he commented on the difference in their backgrounds: he a product of essentially Mediterranean and Catholic culture and Faulkner from a region "much less diluted, *sui generis* Anglo-Saxon, Protestant, and, as it were, more land-locked, turned inward upon itself." Within that contrast, of course, lies much of the attraction that brought writers from other parts of the country to the Big Easy and gave them subject matter and inspiration. Faulkner and Basso walked along the river, explored the Quarter, Basso pointing out the sites and impressions that he had grown up with—he once wrote that he had never wanted to become an expatriate in Paris because "I had Paris in my own backyard." They even went flying together with a group of stunt aviators, the Gates Flying Circus.[22]

Faulkner and Anderson seem to have become friends on their first encounter, and within a week Anderson had written the short story "A Meeting South," which details a visit an older writer and his young companion make to the home of a retired madam. Anderson had already become friends with Aunt Rose Arnold, who had retired after Storyville was closed, and the scene of the story is clearly her house on Chartres Street, half a block from Jackson Square. David, the young writer in the story, has a metal plate in his head and must drink large quantities of liquor to ease the constant pain. How long it took the Andersons to realize that Faulkner was lying about his physical condition—among other things—is not clear, but they seem not to have held it against him. The letters Faulkner wrote to his mother attest to the fact that Elizabeth Anderson not only housed him in their apartment early in 1925 but also took over management of his meagre funds. Elizabeth was one of several strong women—Miss Maud Faulkner, Aunt Bama, and others, upon whom Faulkner was dependent in those early years. Faulkner shared a room with Robert, Sherwood's son, in the Andersons' apartment in the Upper Pontalba building on Jackson Square, until the older author returned from a speaking tour.

Whatever one may think of Sherwood Anderson—and God knows he came in for more than his share of criticism from enemies *and* friends—he was always supportive of young authors, and Faulkner was not the only member of his generation who benefited from the kindness of Anderson and Elizabeth. Others included Anita Loos, who was already successful not only as a novelist but as a screenwriter, Basso, Carl Sandburg, and Edmund Wilson. Years later Wilson repaid that kindness by claiming that Anderson had kept a "mulatto mistress" in New Orleans—there is, it should be noted, no corroborating evidence of this fact—and with scornful though perhaps somewhat accurate criticism that Anderson's "ideal of literature seemed partly to have been derived from his training as a composer of advertising copy; he liked to make simple statements and to emphasize them by repetition—often to the ennui of his readers" (127). Sherwood Anderson was all too often ill-served by the disciples who had sought him out and benefited from his largess and advice.

When Faulkner moved out of the Anderson apartment, he had determined that he wanted to stay in the Quarter for a while, and he settled into three downstairs rooms in a townhouse on Orleans Alley (now known as Pirate's Alley as a nod to the tourist business) that he shared with a newspaperman, Louis Piper. William Spratling, an artist, architect, and author, who became perhaps Faulkner's best friend in New Orleans, lived upstairs. Another tenant was Joseph Hilton Smyth, who had been hired by John McClure, a neighbor on Orleans Alley, who was editor of the bookpage of the *Times-Picayune* and a founder of the *Double-Dealer*, to work in the editorial and advertising departments of the newspaper. Smyth in his memoirs, *To Nowhere and Return: The Autobiography of a Puritan*, remembered the 1920s as "the time that young writers and artists through the country discovered that the old French quarter of New Orleans was an inexpensive and pleasant place to live" and as a result "in a comparatively short period it produced a fairly important group of artists . . . a group that during the next decade was to have a definite effect as well as place in the history of American literature." At the same time, he noted, wealthy New Orleanians began to discover "that intangible something known as 'charm'" and the preservation and restoration of the region had commenced in earnest (147).

Smyth recalled that at 624 Orleans Alley "in the apartment beneath mine there lived a boy named Bill from Mississippi, who had been injured flying in the war and who now devoted his time to corn licker and the writing of poetry." One day Bill came up to Smyth's apartment very excited about what he called "the best God-damned book he had ever read," Norman Douglas's *South Wind*. It was "a source book," he said, that "Ronald Firbank and Van Vechten and those birds got their stuff from," and expressed the desire to "write a book like that." Soon Faulkner was at work on his own novel and would take what he had written each day around to Sherwood Anderson. The book, first called *May Day*, Smyth remembered, "was completed in a remarkably few weeks"(148–49). Smyth, by the way, was one of the most unusual characters in the French Quarter group. In the 1920s, he was an unknown, but later, in 1940, he purchased the *North American Review* and *Scribner's Magazine*. However, after it was discovered that the money for the purchase came from the Japanese government—remember, that was 1940—Smyth was charged as a foreign agent and the magazines ceased publication. In the 1960s, he wrote spy novels and other pulp fiction, and copublished the *Saturday Review of Literature*.

Other observations of Faulkner from what he called in a letter to his mother "my New Orleans gang" are too abundant to be included in their entirety, but a couple of them will suffice to indicate the impression that he made. Oliver LaFarge, who taught ethnology at Tulane and wrote fiction, lived with Keith Temple in an apartment they called the Wigwam because of LaFarge's interest in the Navajos. (Later a few critics would suggest that Faulkner derived material from him about the Indians for use in his own work, but I do not see any evidence of that connection.) In a long story published in 1935 in a collection called *All the Young Men*, LaFarge describes life among the artists and writers in the French Quarter before World War II. One of the characters, Jimmy Donovan, seems to reflect Faulkner. Jimmy is described as "a small wasted-looking man," a heavy drinker who had been injured when he was thrown from a horse. Jimmy's friend Frances says of him that "They had to put silver plates in his bones to hold him together; he's got one in his head, one in his right arm, and one in his left leg."[23] A painter from Oklahoma, Jimmy often "seemed to be drunk but was well under control as was common with him" (237).

The eighteen-year-old James K. Feibleman recalled sitting in the *Double-Dealer* office in 1923 with a group of authors, all of whom thought they'd be famous, he said, but satirically added that of course time would prove them wrong. He wondered at the time, however, if there was "one genius" there, and if so, which one was it? (268–69) "In one corner there was a little man with a well-shaped head, a small moustache and a slightly receding chin. He sat on the floor out of preference (there was an unoccupied chair near him) and preserved his silence with the aid of a bottle of whiskey, which he held over his head and tipped into his mouth from time to time. I had the impression more of nursing than of drinking." The "little man" only made one remark all during the gathering when the conversation turned to Shakespeare: "I could write a play like *Hamlet* if I wanted to." Feibleman admitted that he did not believe the young Faulkner and indeed deemed him "an amiable, though dull, fellow" but ironically, Faulkner would prove to be the "genius" of the group, as even the grudging Feibleman later acknowledged (270). Indeed, there were two geniuses among the young disciples of Sherwood Anderson in the French Quarter in the 1920s, Faulkner and John Dos Passos, and for Faulkner, that period of his life was a very significant contributor to his future career, although the same does not seem to have been true of John Dos Passos.

Faulkner's six-month stay in Orleans Alley, where he met Helen Baird at a party, is well chronicled in his letters to his mother. He and Bill Spratling left the city to go to Europe and when they returned, Spratling took a fourth-floor apartment around the corner, which Faulkner soon moved in to share with him. It was there that they entertained themselves by shooting an air rifle at people who were passing in the alley below, keeping a score card of their individual achievements. However, they also worked,

Spratling on his book, *Little Mexico*, and Faulkner on *Mosquitoes*, among other things, while the two collaborated on the book of caricatures called *Sherwood Anderson and Other Creoles*. It was to be Faulkner's last residence in the city, and any time he returned for visits between the end of 1926 and his death, he would stay in hotels or with Roark and Mary Rose Bradford in their Creole cottage on Toulouse, where they entertained a distinguished series of houseguests through the years—Sinclair Lewis, John Steinbeck, and Tennessee Williams among then.

Between 1974 and 1976, I interviewed all the Famous Creoles who were still living in New Orleans, including Genevieve Pitot, Marc Antony, Harold Levy, Keith Temple, Caroline Durieux, and Louis Fischer, as well as Albert Goldstein and George Healy. The latter two were not included among Spratling's drawings in *Sherwood Anderson and Other Famous Creoles*, but they were very much a part of the circle. Previously, Healy had known Faulkner at Ole Miss when he was postmaster, and Goldstein was a founder and editor of the *Double-Dealer*.

Fifty years after those halcyon Bohemian days in the French Quarter, most of those people were still charming, witty, and possessed of a considerable amount of information about Faulkner and the French Quarter of the 1920s. What I especially wanted to know from them, of course, was what Faulkner had been like, what he had done, and what he had said. Only Keith Temple, who had become a cartoonist for a New Orleans newspaper and was, at the time I spoke to him, suffering from an incurable disease that would soon claim his life, was bitter, recalling the man who had once been his good friend as "just a drunk lying in a gutter. That is my most indelible impression of Faulkner."

"Why?" I asked—as if a Mississippian had to ask such a question—"Why was alcohol so important?"

"It was that horrible thing of 'You can't do this,'" Genevieve Pitot insisted—she was, for me the most interesting of the Famous Creoles (and, indeed, one of the few real Creoles, that is, a person descended by birth from French settlers). "We drank because they told us we couldn't." Keith Temple said much the same thing: "We did not know whether or not we would be able to get a drink tomorrow or ever again, so we drank whatever came to hand."

None of the others corroborated Keith Temple's cynical view of the young writer as the drunk in the gutter, which is of course contradicted by the amazing output of work Faulkner produced, but they all admitted, often with pride, that alcohol had been very much a part of their lives. However, several of them did recall the dinner party Faulkner gave at Galatoire's after he had received a small advance for *Mosquitoes*, his second novel. None of the Famous Creoles who gathered at the famous

Bourbon Street bistro had read the novel in manuscript, apparently, so they toasted their host's success in a very convivial celebration. A few months later, the book appeared, and fifty years later, I encountered vituperative remarks from several of those who felt that they had been unkindly portrayed. Marc Antony laughingly recalled that Lillian Marcus, one of the "angels" behind the *Double-Dealer*, would rage against Faulkner for his portrayal of her, although she always insisted that she had never read the novel. (An interesting footnote to the *Mosquitoes* story is that playwright Lillian Hellman, a native of New Orleans, claimed that she has been working as a reader at Boni and Liveright when the manuscript came in and insisted that it be accepted. In fact, she did not work for the publishing company until a few years later.)

Despite the perhaps understandable rancor of a few of the Famous Creoles, who cited the fact that after Faulkner left New Orleans, he seemed to have forgotten his old friends, most still spoke proudly of having known him. Harold Levy loved to tell the story of the night when Sherwood Anderson and Faulkner came by his apartment in the Lower Pontalba. Faulkner said he was having trouble with a poem and Levy suggested a line to solve the problem. Faulkner incorporated the change and acknowledged Levy's assistance by inscribing the published poem "to H. L." Several of the group remembered that they would meet for lunch at Levy's apartment on Jackson Square and one of them would read aloud from a copy of James Joyce's *Ulysses* that had been smuggled into the United States. Genevieve Pitot, who after a few years went on to New York and became a celebrity as a composer of dance music for more than twenty Broadway musicals, including *Milk and Honey, Kismet, L'il Abner*, and *Kiss Me, Kate*, recalled with humorous affection that when she became pregnant before she was married, Faulkner and Keith Temple, who were visiting New York, came by to see her and urged her *not* to put the baby up for adoption. "We will raise the baby," they assured her—and fifty years later, when I interviewed her, she was still laughing about the prospect of Faulkner and Temple's rearing a child.

George Healy's most indelible memory of Faulkner in the French Quarter involved one of the Beaux Art balls given by the Arts and Crafts Club. They were patterned on the art parties on the Left Bank in Paris and, like those, designed to shock. The Quarter balls were held every year at the American Legion Hall on Royal Street. Almost all of the guests, Healy recalled, were dressed exotically as pirates or mendicant monks or nuns or whatever came to mind and behaved in a way designed to outrage the "local gentry"; Genevieve Pitot, for example, once came as Salome and did the Dance of the Seven Veils, much to the chagrin of her uptown Creole family. Only Faulkner, Healy said, was not in costume, but wearing his usual tattered tweed coat, sitting in the corner on the floor and drinking from a bottle in a paper bag. "He only spoke," Healy recalled, "if spoken to, but he seemed to be taking it all in." All of the others I interviewed verified Healy's memory of the evenings.

By the end of the 1920s, most members of the Anderson-Faulkner circle had scattered, and the few who stayed, Oliver LaFarge among them, were caught up a decade later in the Second World War and left those halcyon days in the Vieux Carré behind them. In his story significantly entitled "No More Bohemia," LaFarge has his protagonist remark as he prepares to leave the Quarter that the artists and writers had migrated there because it was "romantic" and remained "caught in a backwater, and bound, also, by the charm of the place." Departing, he thinks that he loves the Vieux Carré and feels "a funny sadness. I'm saying a kind of goodbye to it. I'll go on seeing it, of course; all my life, perhaps, but pretty soon I won't be right in it and belonging to it any longer" (216, 234). Nevertheless, there was still room for the artists and writers to spread their wings and find themselves, and in 1938, a young Mississippian named Tom, who would become known to the world in a few years as Tennessee Williams, arrived in the city, found a freedom that he professed to have long needed, and adopted the Vieux Carré as his "spiritual home."

It has always struck me as remarkable that William Faulkner and Tennessee Williams, two Mississippians and major American literary figures, transplanted to the French Quarter, should have produced works there that were significant in their lives and careers only half a block apart, albeit separated in time by two decades. Faulkner wrote his first novel on Orleans Alley, and Tennessee Williams wrote the final draft of *A Streetcar Named Desire* half a block away on St. Peter Street, where he could hear that "rattletrap old streetcar" rumbling along Rue Royale and thus find the appropriate title for his most famous work. Faulkner and Williams, born within one hundred miles of each other, seem only to have met twice, and both times it was more or less in passing, but certainly there was an affinity between them in terms of their subject matter and the devotion both felt to the state of Mississippi.

In 1935, Williams visited Oxford, Mississippi, and saw the home of William Faulkner, of whom he observed at the time that despite the novelist's reputation in his hometown, he was not "stuck-up," but rather, "just absent-minded, like me and other great writers."[24] After he became an established playwright, Williams acknowledged the affinity between his work and that of Faulkner and praised the novelist as honest and "a Southern gentleman." He was one of the few readers on record who at the time of its publication recognized what Faulkner had accomplished in *The Wild Palms*. Williams wrote in his journal that it is "such a mad book—by distortion, by outrageous exaggeration he seems to get an effect closer to reality (or my idea of it) than strict realists get in their exact representations. You can say that while reading 'This is delirium' but the after-effect is a close approximation of the actual" (218n). For his part, Faulkner also recognized the value of one of Williams's most difficult and unappreciated dramas. He told a friend that while he found *Cat on a Hot Tin Roof* to be unsatisfactory, because it should have concentrated on Big Daddy and not the children, he did like *Camino Real*,[25] a play which at the time it was first produced was not well received, despite the fact that Williams considered it one of his best. It is an interesting footnote that both these experimental works—*The Wild Palms* and *Camino Real*—owe part of their inspiration and setting to the city of New Orleans.

Forty years after Sherwood Anderson's romanticizing of the life of the Vieux Carré, Walker Percy became perhaps the most articulate spokesman of what makes New Orleans unique in relation to the rest of the country. Percy cites first the city's islandlike quality, "cut adrift not only from the South but from the rest of Louisiana," surrounded by river and lake and swamp, which has turned it into a cultural island separated from rest of South and nation: "It is as if Marseilles had been plucked up off the Midi, monkeyed with by Robert Moses and Hugh Hefner, and set down off John O'Groats in Scotland." Comparing it to the French cathedral of Mont-St. Michel, he describes it as set down in a "watery waste"; it seems "a proper enough American city," and yet the tourist "is apt to see more nuns and naked women than he ever saw before."[26] Percy always argued, in essays, lectures, and interviews, that much of his work resulted from "the encounter of the two cultures." He chose to live in Covington, Louisiana, which sits squarely on the line that separates the Protestant, Calvinist South from Catholic New Orleans. Percy saw New Orleans as a place whose soul exists "in a kind of comfortable Catholic limbo somewhere between the outer circle of hell, where sexual sinners don't have it all that bad, and the inner circle of purgatory, where things are even better." For him, the major paradox in that very paradoxical city was that sex and death are "treated unseriously and money seriously," and as a result, the cemeteries are more cheerful than the hotels. Percy wonders whimsically "why two thousand dead Creoles should be more alive than two thousand Buick dealers."[27] Echoing the earlier writers in their praise of the lifestyle of the city, he humorously insists that "If you fall ill on the streets of New York, people grumble about having to step over you or around you. In New Orleans there is still a chance, diminishing perhaps, that somebody will drag you into the neighborhood bar and pay the inn-keeper for a shot of Early Times" (*Signposts* 10).

As the previous descriptions may suggest, New Orleans has always been a city in which the flesh took precedence over anything ethereal or ideal, but in contrast, Cleanth Brooks once remarked that New Orleans has become a city of the mind and is therefore immortal. It is then, finally, a combination, a sensuous and sensual place which exudes much creative energy and inspires the artistic imagination. A hundred years ago Charles Dudley Warner summed up the attraction of New Orleans for writers and others: "I suppose we are all wrongly made up and have a fallen nature; else why is it that the most thrifty and neat and orderly city only wins our approval, and perhaps gratifies us intellectually, and such a thriftless, battered and stained, and lazy old place as the French Quarter of New Orleans takes our hearts?"[28]

NOTES

1. Unpublished interview, Don Lee Keith with Tennessee Williams, 1970s.
2. A. J. Liebling, *The Earl of Louisiana* (Baton Rouge: Louisiana State University Press, reprint, 1970), 221, 227.
3. Rachel Jackson, quoted in Marquis James, *Andrew Jackson: The Border Captain* (Indianapolis: The Bobbs-Merrill Company, 1933), 280, 337–38.
4. Sherwood Anderson, "A Meeting South," in *The World from Jackson Square*, ed. Etolia Basso (New York: Farrar, Straus and Company, 1948), 350.
5. Numerous of the authors in the 1920s and 1930s, from Faulkner to Tennessee Williams, testified to the fact that the Quarter was an open area of prostitution.
6. Edmund Wilson, *American Earthquake: A Documentary of the Twenties and Thirties* (Garden City, N.Y. : Doubleday and Co., 1958), 131.
7. Qtd in Christopher Benfey, *Degas in New Orleans* (New York: Alfred A. Knopf, 1997).
8. Joseph Hilton Smyth, *From Nowhere and Return: The Autobiography of a Puritan* (New York: Carrick and Evans, Inc., 1940), 151–52.
9. Sherwood Anderson, "New Orleans, The Double Dealer, and the Modern Movement in America," *Double Dealer* 3 (March 1922), 126.
10. Oliver La Farge, *The Copper Pot* (Boston: Houghton Mifflin Company, 1942), 257.
11. Hamilton Basso to Malcolm Cowley, 29 April 1940, in Cowley Collection, Newberry Library.
12. Hamilton Basso, *Days before Lent* (New York: Charles Scribner's Sons, 1939), 257.
13. Qtd. in Inez Lake Hollander, "Paris in My Own Backyard: Hamilton Basso," *Literary New Orleans in the Modern Age*, ed. Richard S. Kennedy (Baton Rouge: Louisiana State University Press, 1998), 42.
14. Quoted in James W. Thomas, *Lyle Saxon: A Critical Biography* (Birmingham: Summa Publications), 1991, 32.
15. Cathy Chance Harvey, "Lyle Saxon: A Portrait in Letters, 1917–1945" (Ph.D. diss., Tulane University, 1980).
16. James K. Feibleman, *The Way of a Man: An Autobiography* (New York: Horizon Press, 1969), 271.
17. "Lyle Saxon," *Newsweek* (20 June 1937), 20.
18. Townsend Ludington, *John Dos Passos: Twentieth-Century Odyssey* (New York: E. P. Dutton, 1980), 230.
19. John Dos Passos, *The 42nd Parallel* in USA, ed. Daniel Aaron and Townsend Ludington (New York: The Library of America, 1996), 232, 342.
20. William Faulkner, *Absalom, Absalom!* (New York: Random House, 1936), 108–9.
21. Carvel Collins, Introductory Essay with Joseph Blotner, *Helen: A Courtship* (Oxford, Miss., and New Orleans: Yoknapatawpha Press and Tulane University Press, 1981), 80.

22. Hamilton Basso, "William Faulkner, Man and Writer," *Saturday Review*, 28 July 1962, 12–1.

23. Oliver La Farge, *All the Young Men* (Boston: Houghton Mifflin, 1935), 234.

24. *The Selected Letters of Tennessee Williams, Volume I: 1920–1945*, ed. Albert J. Devlin and Nancy M. Tischler (New York: New Directions, 2000), 76.

25. Joseph Blotner, *Faulkner: A Biography* (New York: Random House, 1974), 2: 1529–30.

26. Walker Percy, *Signposts in a Strange Land* (New York: Farrar, Straus, and Giroux, 1991), 12.

27. Walker Percy, *Lancelot* (New York: Farrar, Straus, and Giroux, 1977), 249.

28. Charles Dudley Warner, "Sui Generis," in *The World from Jackson Square: A New Orleans Reader*, ed. Etolia Basso (New York: Farrar, Straus and Company, 1948), 308.

Cather's War and Faulkner's Peace:
A Comparison of Two Novels, and More

Merrill Maguire Skaggs

After Judith Wittenberg first published the facts about Faulkner's several acknowledgments of Willa Cather,[1] I myself analyzed specific literary loans she made to him. For example, Faulkner's second novel, *Mosquitoes*, recycles numerous items from Cather's *The Professor's House*,[2] while details from *My Ántonia* reappear many times in Faulkner's major fiction,[3] and *Death Comes for the Archbishop* enjoys a resurrection almost immediately in *The Sound and the Fury*.[4] Cather, in turn, seemed to address Faulkner directly in her last published story.[5] In this essay, however, I want to confront the much more challenging question of where it all started. Granted that Faulkner read everyone and everything,[6] why did he pay any particular attention to Willa Cather? To ask that harder question, I must begin where my questions first started—when I first spotted an affinity so unexpected and unsettling that it made me gasp.

It happened the first time I was about halfway through Willa Cather's Pulitzer Prize-winning war novel, *One of Ours*. Suddenly on the page before me—like an infamous, awful printshop error—was a passage that looked to me like Faulkner, signature Faulkner.[7] It described mules and read like this:

> But wasn't it just like him to be dragged into matrimony by a pair of mules!
> He laughed as he looked at them. "You old devils, you're strong enough to play such tricks on green fellows for years to come. You're chock full of meanness!"
> One of the animals wagged an ear and cleared his throat threateningly. Mules are capable of strong affections, but they hate snobs, are the enemies of caste, and this pair had always seemed to detect in Claude what his father used to call his "false pride."[8] When he was a young lad they had been a source of humiliation to him, braying and balking in public places, trying to show off at the lumber yard or in front of the postoffice.[9]

Since the vocabulary here is appropriate to the character thinking these thoughts, I could reassure myself that Cather must certainly have controlled the recording pencil. But the inventive brain and the malevolent mules[10] seemed so Faulkneresque that I had to recheck my facts. Sure enough, this Cather novel appeared in 1922, when Faulkner had published outside Mississippi only one poem in the *New Republic*: and "L'Apres-Midi d'un Faune" didn't sound mulish. Willa apparently beat Bill to the typesetter in mentioning mulish barnyard tricks. I was shaken by these forbidden thoughts—that Cather had a Faulknerian streak and that Faulkner might have learned a trick or two from her. So I read on through *One of Ours* with furrowed brow and eyes alert for other such disturbances. Thus I was awake when in the last section of Cather's novel, set in wartime France, I spotted the central figure and controlling plot device of Faulkner's first novel, *Soldiers' Pay*.

The character of the maimed American amnesiac soldier, whom women love and experts find worth recording, is described this way by a doctor in Cather's French military hospital:

> "Oh, yes! He's a star patient here, a psychopathic case. I had just been talking to one of the doctors about him, when I came out and saw you with him. He was shot in the neck at Cantigny, where he lost his arm. The wound healed, but his memory is affected; some nerve cut, I suppose, that connects with that part of his brain. This psychopath,[11] Phillips, takes a great interest in him and keeps him here to observe him. He's writing a book about him. He says the fellow has forgotten almost everything about his life before he came to France. The queer thing is, it's his recollection of women that is most affected. He can remember his father, but not his mother; doesn't know if he has sisters or not,—can remember seeing girls about the house, but thinks they may have been cousins. His photographs and belongings were lost when he was hurt, all except a bunch of letters he had in his pocket. They are from a girl he's engaged to, and he declares he can't remember her at all: doesn't know what she looks like or anything about her, and can't remember getting engaged. The doctor has the letters. They seem to be from a nice girl in his own town who is very ambitious for him to make the most of himself. He deserted soon after he was sent to this hospital, ran away. He was found on a farm out in the country here, where the sons had been killed and the people had sort of adopted him. He'd quit his uniform and was wearing the clothes of one of the dead sons. He'd probably have got away with it, if he hadn't had that wry neck. Some one saw him in the fields and recognized him and reported him. I guess nobody cared much but this psychopathic doctor; he wanted to get his pet patient back. They call him 'the lost American' here." (287)

Faulkner found several details in this passage useful when he constructed his collage of a lost generation. They include the soldier's terrible scarring or wounding; a hand he has lost use of; his amnesia which especially covers women, sweethearts, and fiancée; his lost papers as well as a recovered letter from the girl back home; his good family background; his engagement to a "nice" girl who wants the soldier to shine in the community;

concerned helpers who surround him; and most especially, his centrality to an unpublished book. Faulkner's lost American, symbolically named Lieutenant Donald Mahon,[12] also corresponds to Cather's protagonist, Lieutenant Claude Wheeler, who experiences war as euphoria until the wheel of fortune spins him round. Claude gets a war which he loves in spite of his "chump" (*Ours* 17) and "sissy" first name (*Ours* 279). His wife pronounces it *clod* (114, 179) and Faulkner uses it as the generic name of a railroad porter (*Pay* 24).[13]

Faulkner's novel begins where Cather's leaves off—with soldiers returning from the war. That fact helps obscure dozens of interesting overlaps in these works, the first, the use of a train as a linear vehicle paradoxically suggesting life's circularity. Cather had used this device first in *My Ántonia* to start her novel twice, and in *One of Ours* to start her *war* twice.[14] Faulkner reverses this train journey to bring his soldier home at his beginning, and to take Margaret Powers away at his conclusion. When Cather's Claude returns by train for a brief home furlough before shipping out, he recognizes the anti-German violence rife in the American midwest; in moving by train toward his tall ship, he discovers the frustrating delays of troop movements. And when Faulkner's soldiers start home on a train, the scene is even more frustrating and chaotic; his men are drunk and disorderly. But they, too, are in significant transit, already hopelessly trying to circle back to home places into which they cannot fit—a humiliation Claude Wheeler is explicitly spared. Claude dies suddenly, believing life had turned out well for him (*Ours* 349). All this jerky transportation dramatizes the opposite of easy riding, and in it, one can see the ironic beginnings and the endings of these destinies. Faulkner's one caring woman rolls away from the helpless men she leaves behind; in Cather's ending the remnants of Wheeler's men are left at sea, while a dimwitted Wheeler housemaid prays in the last sentence to a God hovering just above her kitchen stove (391).

Before discussing significantly similar themes developed in these two novels, I'd like to pay a tribute to Faulkner's shrewd eye and swift assimilation of useable material, whenever he read Cather.[15] *To reive* or steal is a verb he not only ended his career underscoring. He also uses it three times in *Soldiers' Pay* (*Pay* 58, 70, 291). And the quality of the reiving in this first novel is auspicious. It must have impressed Willa Cather, too, for she contrived to pay an unprecedented tribute to a living author, even against her own expressed principle.[16] In her charming essay "148 Charles Street" (1936), she quotes an eponymous schoolboy who writes from his educational trenches, "D. H. Lawrence is rather rated a back-number here, but Faulkner keeps his end up."[17] Obviously Faulkner is not the only one in this odd couple who has a good eye and a sharp pencil.

In any case, both clever writers disrupted Aristotle's "unities" in their fictions about World War I, thus sharing a technique. Both saw that disruption is fitting when one is writing about carnage. In both fictions settings dissolve, names change, characters suddenly appear and disappear, platitudes are contradicted by experience, and all strings are not tied. Judged from an Aristotelian point of view, both show that fiction about war is hell.

But one startling similarity between the two is their assertion that war itself can be heaven, even preferable to peace. On his rich Nebraska farm Cather's Claude Wheeler feels "weak and broken" (134), promises to become "one of those dead people that moved about the streets" (179), recognizes another's description of life as "a sleeping sickness" or "death in life" (262), and "didn't find this kind of life worth the trouble of getting up every morning" (89). He feels "driven into the ground like a post, or like those Chinese criminals who are planted upright in the earth, with only their heads left out for birds to peck at and insects to sting" (243). His Nebraska is so dull that even the theatrical events are *tableaux vivants*— living pictures in which the players freeze (108). Everything about the drama of war seems better than Nebraska. This everything includes Claude's responsibility to care for his men during a flu epidemic on shipboard, or his repeated risk of his life in France, or even his final dramatic dismemberment by a German land mine: all better. Since he's from Frankfort, a German-sounding Nebraska hometown, the war is almost like home, only a lot happier. In fact, he's most at home when at war. Or perhaps, the enemy *is* home.[18]

Faulkner recognizes in *Soldiers' Pay* that Cather has earned the Pulitzer by fictionalizing these suspicions. "We heard you was dead, or in the piano business or something," one of Faulkner's returning soldiers says impertinently to a civilian (*Pay* 16). Faulkner's Cadet Julian Lowe feels overpowering envy when he considers grotesquely scarred Lieutenant Mahon, who is going blind as he lies dying: "How the man managed to circumvent him at every turn! As if it were not enough to have wings and a scar. But to die!" For "what was death to Cadet Lowe, except something true and grand and sad. . . . What more could one ask of Fate?" (52). Both novels patronize this romantic peevishness. Within her novel, however, Cather uses three of her five "books" to explain how such love of war can possibly exist; Faulkner just starts by assuming it. But both novelists ask a reader to remember that it's supposed to be a "blockhead" view.[19] Ironically, the insulting German epithet *boche* also means blockhead. Again, the enemy we fight hardest may be ourselves, may be found in our own homes.[20]

Blockhead or not, the love of war comes first in the hearts of these country men. Faulkner's drunken dischargees label America the foreign country and add, "Listen, think of having to go to work again when you get home. Ain't war hell? I would of been a corporal at least, if she had just hung on another year" (10). The train conductor can see, "My God.... If we ever have another peace I don't know what the railroads will do. I thought war was bad, but my God" (12). Somehow these Faulkner lines fail to surprise. What surprises is that Cather tells the same story first. Hearing of the slaughter along the Marne Claude knows "he was not the only farmer boy who wished himself tonight beside the Marne" (148). Knowing the danger he also knows, "There was nothing on earth he would so gladly be as an atom in that wall of flesh and blood" (149). Once he gets on board a ship and away from home, Claude thinks, "in this massing and movement of men there was nothing mean or common; he was sure of that" (243). Once in uniform, he knows who he is, what he should do with his life, and what happiness feels like. Like most of his men, he's eager to get into action as soon as possible, and thinks of the front as "the big show" (305). He finds "reassuring signs" in dead trees, charred landscapes, wrecked trucks (305). That's the surprise—how much Cather's Claude loves war, and how much William Faulkner chooses to believe other soldiers do, too.

Cather spends 60 percent of her novel explaining why: Claude is a discontented, poorly educated, frustrated, bitter young man who doesn't enjoy farmwork. He is eager to escape the farm and see some action in France. No wonder basically *un*original Claude is so proud of what he's doing, and so ready to believe "It was worth having lived in this world to have known such men" (303). War is his calling, his vocation, and he responds to it with religious zeal and zest. Faulkner's veteran does not quarrel with any part of Cather's picture. He quarrels with history for leaving him out.

In both novels, however, a common sense explanation for the way these soldiers got—or get—so unhappy at home seems to be the women. Cather's Enid, the competent home manager who was meant for business or the missionary life, but whose very father warns that she's not designed for a wife, is the model for these disappointing women. Enid does all her housework dressed in white—like a professional nurse. Claude thinks of marrying her after his mules have run him into a barbed wire fence and he has developed erysipelas. Once he's immobilized in bandages, Enid comes unselfconsciously into his bedroom to cheer him up by playing chess.[21] Enid's problem is explained by Cather succinctly: "Everything about a man's embrace was distasteful to Enid; something inflicted upon women, like the pain of childbirth,—for Eve's transgression, perhaps" (180).

What is interesting to me is the extent to which Faulkner takes Enid as his coverall prototype. His dislike for the hometown flirt Cecily Saunders, Mahon's forgotten fiancée, is unremitting; she is never described positively.

Mrs. Powers, his young war widow who chooses to use her husband's life insurance to finance her taking care of totally needy Mahon, would seem to be different. Yet Margaret Powers, who hardly remembers her husband, thinks; "How ugly men are, naked" (182); and mutters repeatedly when he crosses her mind, "dear, ugly, dead Dick" (184). She asks, "Am I cold by nature, or have I spent all my emotional coppers, that I don't seem to feel things like others? Dick, Dick. Ugly and dead" (39). Mrs. Powers marries Mahon only as an act of charity when he is nearly dead and already blind, and after all the other females she has proposed sacrificial marriage to, have refused it. After Mahon dies she refuses to marry the devoted Joe Gilligan, who acts as Mahon's body servant and orderly, because she just can't tolerate his name. In Cather's just-liberated Beaufort, French women show an American squadron a good time, but that's only after they've been locked away from occupying Germans, and with no men, for four stressful years. Mostly, in both novels, mother love is the best a man ever gets and that's basically what Mrs. Powers offers Donald Mahon. Making the same point, the most passionate kiss in *One of Ours* is between Claude and his mother (225).

Perhaps one reason Willa Cather and William Faulkner have sounded discordant, when put in the same sentence, has to do with Faulkner's abundant and mordant humor and the assumption that Cather doesn't have any. Without leaping outside this war novel for barricades from which to fight this tone-deaf opinion, I'd suggest that *One of Ours* has plenty of humor, much of it at Claude's expense. For example, when Claude and Sergeant Hicks are returning from field headquarters to their squad at the front, they hear of a short cut they may use once night falls. So they take their daylight time getting to it. Cather story proceeds:

> When they struck the road they came upon a big Highlander sitting in the end of an empty supply wagon, smoking a pipe and rubbing the dried mud out of his kilts.... The Americans hadn't happened to meet with any Highlanders before.... This one must be a good fighter, they thought; a brawny giant with a bulldog jaw, and a face as red and knobby as his knees. More because he admired the looks of the man than because he needed information, Hicks went up and asked him if he had noticed a military cemetery on the road back. The kiltie nodded.
> "About how far back would you say it was?"
> "I wouldn't say at all. I take no account of their kilometers," he said drily, rubbing away at his skirt as if he had it in a washtub.
> "Well, about how long will it take us to walk it?"
> "That I couln't say. A Scotsman would do it in an hour."
> "I guess a Yankee can do it as quick as a Scotchman, can't he?" Hicks asked jovially.

"That I couldn't say. You've been four years gettin' this far, I know verra well." Hicks blinked as if he had been hit. "Oh, if that's the way you talk—"

"That's the way I do," said the other sourly.

Claude put out a warning hand. "Come on, Hicks. You'll get nothing by it." They went up the road very much disconcerted. Hicks kept thinking of things he might have said. (334–35)

While speed-readers also associate Cather with blandness, she models for Faulkner literary horror as well as humor in *One of Ours*. The worst horror in both these novels occurs in a trench. When Claude's men first occupy trenches the Germans have just vacated, they must deal not only with gunfire ahead and shells bursting nearby. They must also man guns placed amid inadequately buried German bodies. First a black hand keeps reappearing with its fingers splayed out as if grabbing or beckoning them. Then a boot reappears, though they repeatedly try to bury these body parts. Reappearing dead limbs are chilling portents of what will soon happen to the Americans. The trench has been mined by retreating Germans in whose preplanned return they will blow Americans apart.

A strong link between the two novels, however, is the association of the trenches with lethal gas attacks. In Faulkner's riff, when Mahon's local squadmates were green recruits, they were sent to such a trench, led by Margaret Powers's bridegroom Richard. Mistakenly deducing that Richard has led them to sure death by gas, one soldier shoots him in the face as he approaches with words of cheer.

No matter how many dozens of similar details, themes, and characters one compiles between these two books, however—and there are many to compare—, they do not explain sufficiently the link between these two writers. As I have shown, a dialogue runs between their works which lasts through Cather's last posthumously published story. Each writer seems to talk at the other directly. So we must ask, *Why* does Faulkner, when he writes his first novel, so uncharacteristically and thoroughly trust her, when half the male writers since Homer might have taught him how to write a war novel?

I want now to take a look at a very bizarre coincidence. In the middle of Cather's novel is a character who matches the real Bill Faulkner as he was inventing himself *at this time*. We can recognize him because we've seen his photograph,[22] nattily dressed in RAF uniform, sporting a cane, and reportedly posing as a walking war-wounded. But first, hear how Blotner describes Faulkner during a short interval in the crucial late summer and autumn of 1921, when Cather was polishing *One of Ours*, and Faulkner was living in Greenwich Village, in closest proximity to 5 Bank Street and Washington Square. At this time, Blotner tells us, Faulkner tended to drop in at dinner time on a couple called the Joices. Mrs. Joice recalls,

> "He was just back from the war and, in fact, he had a cane and walked with a limp. He was dressed in a light beige mackintosh, a dusty dark brown hat and a pipe. He was generally nice looking with dark brown eyes[23] and hair. . . . [He] had just been released from the hospital and had a metal disc close to his hip. . . . [H]e did nothing to dispel my illusion that he was a wounded hero returning from France." [When he finally removed the mackintosh] he wore a drab gray suit which gave off an odor she took to be a combination of alcohol and perspiration. [Yet he was] "so mystique" that . . . her interest cooled . . . when he asked . . . for a loan until he received some money from home, which was "a Southern plantation." (1:324)

Blotner summarizes, "the persona of the wounded pilot had made another appearance, as it would sometimes do when Faulkner found himself in a new environment. He had created an impression partly through his fictitious story and partly through assumptions he allowed his hearers to make" (1:324–25). After Faulkner returned South, Blotner quotes from James K. Feibleman's description of him in New Orleans that winter as "a little man with a well-shaped head, a small moustache and a slightly receding chin," who held himself aloof and apart until he had something he wanted to say, such as, "I could write a play like *Hamlet* if I wanted to" (1:330).

Now visualize the character in *One of Ours* whom Cather names Victor Morse—a code name for a hero, if there ever was one. Cather's physical description matches the Bill Faulkner who wrote home about learning Morse code during his aeronautical training (Blotner, 1:213). She also captures his evolving tall tales. Victor Morse climbs aboard Claude Wheeler's ship having come straight by taxi from New York's St. Regis Hotel:

> When Claude and Fanning and Lieutenant Bird were undressing in their narrow quarters that night, the fourth berth was still unclaimed. They were in their bunks and almost asleep, when the missing man came in and unceremoniously turned on the light. They were astonished to see that he wore the uniform of the Royal Flying Corps and carried a cane. He seemed very young, but the three who peeped out at him felt that he must be a person of consequence. He took off his coat with the spread wings on the collar, wound his watch, and brushed his teeth with an air of special personal importance. Soon after he had turned out the light and climbed into the berth over Lieutenant Bird, a heavy smell of rum spread in the close air. (236–37)

Throughout the next day, reports reach Claude about their new cabinmate. Finally, he can't stand the suspense any longer:

> Claude was curious, and went down to the cabin. As he entered, the air-man, lying half-dressed in his upper berth, raised himself on one elbow and looked

down at him. His blue eyes were contracted and hard, his curly hair disordered, but his cheeks were as pink as a girl's, and the little yellow humming-bird moustache on his upper lip was twisted sharp. . . .

He drew a bottle from under his pillow. "Have a nip?"

"I don't mind if I do," Claude put out his hand.

The other laughed and sank back on his pillow, drawling lazily, "Brave boy! Go ahead; drink to the Kaiser."

"Why to him in particular?"

"It's not particular. Drink to Hindenburg, or the High Command, or anything else that got you out of the cornfield. That's where they did get you, didn't they?"

"Well, it's a good guess, anyhow. Where did they get you?"

"Crystal Lake, Iowa. . . ." He yawned and folded his hands over his stomach.

"Why, we thought you were an Englishman."

"Not quite. I've served in His Majesty's army two years, though."

"Have you been flying in France?"

"Yes. I've been back and forth all the time, England and France. Now I've wasted two months at Fort Worth. Instructor. That's not my line. . . ."

All the same, Claude wanted to find out how a youth from Crystal Lake ever became a member of the Royal Flying Corps. Already, from among the hundreds of strangers, half-a-dozen stood out as men he was determined to know better. (239–40)

I suspect that Victor Morse is from Crystal Lake, Iowa, because Cather thinks she can see straight through him. But in any case, soon after, Victor Morse mentions that he hopes to report to London first:

He continued to gaze off at the painted ships.[24] Claude noticed that in standing he held his chin very high. His eyes, now that he was quite sober, were brilliantly young and daring; they seemed scornful of things about him. He held himself conspicuously apart, as if he were not among his own kind. Claude had seen a captured crane, tied by its leg to a hencoop, behave exactly like that . . . hold its wings to its sides, and move its head about quickly and glare. (245)

Soon Morse is telling gullible Claude Wheeler about his London mistress,[25] who has given him a photograph with "Á mon aigle!"—to my eagle—scrawled across it (262). Most striking of all, however, is the fact that Willa Cather gives her coded Victor Morse the death William Faulkner would most have preferred at this time. Claude Wheeler is later told: "Morse the American ace? Hadn't he heard? Why, that got into the London papers. Morse was shot down inside the Hun line three weeks ago. It was a brilliant affair. He was chased by eight Boche planes, brought down three of them, put the rest to flight, and was making for base, when they turned and got him. His machine came down in flames and he jumped, fell a thousand feet or more" (318–19). Claude thinks mournfully,

"He had really liked Victor. There was something about that fellow . . . a sort of debauched baby, he was, who went seeking his enemy in the clouds.[26] What other age could have produced such a figure? That was one of the things about this war: it took a little fellow from a little town, gave him an air and a swagger, a life like a movie-film,—and then a death like the rebel angels" (319).

If we add to this comparison Faulkner's third novel, *Sartoris*, we can find a match for every detail in this portrait. For example, young Bayard Sartoris returns to Memphis in the middle of the war to teach aviators in a flying school (54); he is said to have "knocked two teeth out of an Australian captain that just tried to speak to a girl he was with in a London dive two years ago" (360); he is associated with eagles, through the epitaph on his brother John's grave (374) and the Sartoris burial plot that seems "the eyrie of an eagle" (375); he tries to emulate that brother's cocky death like the rebel angels (321); the news of each death is conveyed by a newspaper, and in Johnny's case, a "limey paper" (319) spotted by Buddy MacCallum; and John's jaunty death is reported by Bayard, who at the crucial moment was airborne and trying to protect his brother John from the pursuing Hun (43).

These duplications force our answer, I think. Unless we are willing to concede that Willa Cather triggered or generated the earliest Faulkner fictions and the Yoknapatawpha saga, then we must concede that while they were in the same neighborhood, William Faulkner must have told vividly his current stories to Willa Cather, who liked them and promptly used them. Recognizing himself in her fiction, he thereafter felt free to plunder her work thoroughly, if indeed he needed any such excuse. But he trusted her to give him work worth plundering for two good reasons: one, because she had *liked* him first—all of him, the real him, as well as the one he conjured, plus the one who told the tall tales about a life like the rebel angels, to her satisfaction. The second reason, of course, was that she had done it to him first, in the late summer and early autumn of 1921, when Faulkner worked in New York City[27] in Doubleday's bookstore and lived in Greenwich Village, close to Washington Square where she loved to walk.[28]

For his major work William Faulkner mined five central Cather novels, including *One of Ours*, thoroughly. But I don't think this was necessarily a genial pingpong game played for recreation. I don't overlook the fact that when he quickly grew tired and testy, Faulkner took the name of Cather's most famous and clearly autobiographical character, Jim Burden, and turned it into Joanna Burden. He gave that name *Burden* to the two unnamed Yankee carpetbaggers he had repeatedly mentioned in *Sartoris*, whom the Old Colonel killed. Then he described Willa Cather back.

First, she has "a face quiet, grave, utterly unalarmed"[29] and "a voice calm, a little deep, quite cold" (218). Then she "told him she was forty, which means forty-one or forty-nine"[30]; she accepts her male lover with "hard, untearful and unselfpitying and almost manlike yielding . . . [and] surrender" (221), while she "shows the strength and fortitude of a man" (221), after which "soon she more than shocked him: she astonished and bewildered him" (224). Her lover believes she "spent a certain portion of each day sitting tranquilly at a desk writing tranquilly" (224), but finds "she revealed an unexpected and infallible instinct for intrigue" (245) and that "she began to corrupt him. He began to be afraid" (246). When he realizes she intends to kill him, he slits her throat.

What I wish to stress here is that Faulkner published *Light in August* with this reverberant sketch of Catheresque Joanna Burden in 1932. When Cather replied to *Light in August* she used an addendum which she *tacked on to* the "148 Charles Street" essay first published in 1922. Her text can therefore stress that her add-on was written in 1936. She goes to these measures to highlight the date *after* she has had four years to think about *Light in August*. Then she publishes "148 Charles Street" in a book she calls *Not Under Forty*, stressing in her title the age Joanna Burden was thought falsely to claim. After *Not Under Forty* appeared, Faulkner acknowledged her publicly and repeatedly.

They both ended saluting each other, these two. Cather's last published story concerns a little man from the law firm of Grenfell and Saunders, *Saunders* being Cecily's last name in *Soldiers' Pay*. That man must gaze dry-eyed at the planet Venus, cross a stream rushing with sound and fury, salute a fallen tree as *grandfather* (like Ike McCaslin's great snake); climb to a clearing with a bushy rowan tree, and experience there a vision of youthful pluck that restores his hearty appetites, before a reader gets to Cather's last published sentence in which she shows those with eyes to see what it looks like to get it all between one cap and one period, in four lines: "Anyhow, when that first amphibious frog-toad found his waterhole dried up behind him, and jumped out to hop along till he could find another—well, he started on a long hop."[31] Thereafter, when the State Department sent Faulkner to Japan, Faulkner said of his literary influences, "[Of] the ones that I was impressed with and that probably influenced me to an extent that I still like to read—one a woman, Willa Cather—I think she is known in Japan."[32]

At the beginning and end of *One of Ours* Cather describes Claude Wheeler as a man whose overriding emotion was his fear of being fooled (47, 344). I think many an American literary scholar may share that fear, as well as its consequences—a timid willingness to stick to safe, easy-to-document and limited conclusions, and to resist the impulse to trust oneself or others. I'd like to suggest that in considering this pair of geniuses—the Faulkner and Cather Joseph Urgo has called "the horizontal and vertical axes in American literature"[33]—we trust the evidence their work provides. They knew that all is fair in love, war, and fiction. They recognized the finest literary and imaginative quality in each other's work. They had the shrewd judgment and ample self-confidence to trust their instincts on this one. They hailed each other with admiration and respect—as the master snakes they knew they were: oleh, chief, grandmother.

NOTES

1. Judith Wittenberg, "Faulkner and Women Writers," in *Faulkner and Women*, ed. Doreen Fowler and Ann J. Abadie (Jackson: University Press of Mississippi, 1986), 287–93.
2. Merrill Maguire Skaggs, "Thefts and Conversation: Cather and Faulkner," *Cather Studies 3*, ed. Susan J. Rosowski (Lincoln: University of Nebraska Press, 1996), 115–36.
3. Merrill Maguire Skaggs, "Cather and Faulkner," *A Faulkner Encyclopedia*, ed. Robert W. Hamblin and Charles A. Peek (Westport, Conn.: Greenwood Press, 1999), 62–64.
4. Merrill Maguire Skaggs, "Willa Cather's *Death Comes for the Archbishop* and William Faulkner's *The Sound and the Fury*," *Faulkner Journal*, 13: 1 & 2 (Fall 1997/Spring 1998): 89–100.
5. "Thefts and Conversation."
6. "Stone also supplied an unceasing flow of books, avant-garde works as well as classics." Joseph Blotner, *Faulkner: A Biography*, 2 vols. (New York: Random House, 1974), 1:170.
7. Faulkner's "great mule trope" occurs in *Sartoris* (1929; New York, Random House, 1956), 278–79.
8. "Pride, false pride" is a family trait in *Sartoris* (74).
9. Willa Cather, *One of Ours* (New York: Alfred A. Knopf, 1922), 215.
10. As malevolent mules, for example: "Father and mother he does not resemble, sons and daughters he will never have; vindictive and patient (it is a known fact that he will labor ten years willingly and patiently for you, for the privilege of kicking you once); solitary but without pride, . . . his voice is his own derision" (*Sartoris* 278).
11. The word clearly means *psychiatric doctor* here.
12. I hear a *duck* (Donald) and a *man* (Mahon in a Southern drawl) in this name combining slang and the portentous.
13. William Faulkner, *Soldiers' Pay* (1926; New York: Boni & Liveright, 1954). The second novel Faulkner planned, but never completed, played on the same kind of chump name: *Elmer*. One can wonder whether his own middle name—*Cuthbert*—helped to stop him.
14. Cather loves to double beginnings and endings and does so in *My Ántonia, Death Comes for the Archbishop, Shadows on the Rock*, and *Sapphira and the Slave Girl. One of Ours* illustrates the usefulness of this doubling device when she must show something two ways in the middle of her book. Claude's war starts first when he has a last leave before shipping overseas, goes home on the train, proves himself responsible by halting hooligan harassment of a good German lunchcounter cook, and then is given a hero's welcome by his family and townsfolk. Later he successfully controls his men on a troop train stalled near Hoboken. Both incidents on a train show him in transition, but moving steadily toward more capable leadership of his men. Thus, by Faulknerian standards, he deserves his hero's death, but still gets to enjoy a hero's glory and applause first.
15. *Soldiers' Pay* is actually an homage to several Cather novels. Faulkner incorporates details from *My Ántonia, The Professor's House*, and *A Lost Lady*. He even gratuitously throws in the name *Oswald*, prominent in *My Mortal Enemy*, which is published in the same

year his first novel appears (*Pay* 93). For further explorations of Faulkner's assimilated Cather materials, see my three essays cited above.

16. "In a letter to Ferris Greenslet dated January 21, 1928, Cather said she would not comment in print on another writer's book. . . . [She] proclaimed in a letter of February 6, 1930, that she would never comment on a living writer's work." Nancy Chinn, "'My Six Books Would Be': The Cather-Hurston Connection," *Willa Cather Pioneer Memorial Newsletter and Review*, 45, 3 (2002): n. 7, 72.

17. Willa Cather, *Not Under Forty* (1936; Lincoln: University of Nebraska Press, 1988), 74.

18. All Faulkner's Sartoris men seem to think of war as "a holiday" (*Sartoris* 10). When at home, young Bayard feels as if "he was a trapped beast" (203).

19. Claude is identified as a blockhead quickly (*Ours* 17), and Cather stresses the word: "He especially hated his head—so big that he had trouble in buying his hats, and uncompromisingly square in shape; a perfect block-head."

20. According to Webster's *New World Dictionary* of 1960, *boche* is French slang first used about 1865; it's short for *caboche*, hard head. It was next found in printer's argot as *tête carrée (d'Allemand)*, or literally, the square head (of a German). Later shortened to *boche*, the term is always hostile.

21. In *Sartoris*, Narcissa Benbow comes into young Bayard's bedroom to read to him, once his chest is crushed. As Claude does, Bayard thereafter marries this inappropriate bride. Narcissa speaks of him as "the beast, the beast" (155).

22. Blotner, 1:200.

23. Blotner identifies the eyes as hazel (1:211). Cather says blue.

24. Cather's analogy of ships to designed artworks may also be intended to suggest Homer, which name Faulkner uses in his fiction for such characters as Homer Barron of "A Rose for Emily".

25. To this day, anybody in Washington Square or the northeast who mentions a tarnished sweetheart back home in Oxford will be heard to be talking of England. I, at least, mentioned several times in New Jersey, in 2002, that I was going to a Faulkner conference in Oxford, and was repeatedly rumored to be going abroad or asked how long I'd be overseas.

26. In this context it might be well to recall that William Faulkner and Willa Cather shared a love of Yeats, as well as Keats and A. E. Housman.

27. By relying on Woodress's biography of Cather we can locate the time in which they could encounter each other rather precisely. Cather returned to New York from nearly five months' stay with Jan and Isabelle Hambourg, having completed her draft of the novel *One of Ours*, in August 1921. In the momentary relief following that completed task, in late August and early September, she could relax after four arduous years' work. She is back in New York both catching her breath and also preparing for a long trip back to Nebraska. By early October she's in Red Cloud when she gets a congratulatory telegram from Alfred A. Knopf, who has just received and eagerly read her novel, and has admired it. Cather, thereafter, is lionized in Nebraska and then on her way home through Chicago. She gets back to New York in early November, exhausted enough to go to bed for a week and afflicted with a "misbehaving colon." Soon thereafter she's sent to a Pennsylvania sanatorium. Thus, the only possible "window" for this encounter seems to me the last days of August or the first of early September, when Faulkner may also have been momentarily expansive with his pleasurable escape to New York. That's also when weather usually encourages sauntering slowly around Washington Square. James Woodress, *Willa Cather* (Lincoln: University of Nebraska Press, 1987), 318–21.

28. We find these pertinent comments in a 1925 essay on Cather by an acquaintance of hers, who purports to have gotten the information from his friend the author: "Miss Cather has had the courage to stroll on eggshells" (27); "She walks a good deal in Washington Square where ashcans are prevalent" (30). Thomas Beer, "Miss Cather," *Borzoi Books*, 1925 (New York: Knopf, 1925).

29. William Faulkner, *Light in August* (New York: Modern Library, 1932), 218.

30. In early autumn of 1921 Cather was forty-seven, claiming to be forty-four.

31. Willa Cather, "Before Breakfast," *The Old Beauty and Others* (New York: Alfred A. Knopf, 1948).

32. *Lion in the Garden: Interviews with William Faulkner, 1926–1962*, ed. James B. Meriwether and Michael Millgate (New York: Random House, 1968), 167–68.

33. Joseph Urgo, "An Interview with Joseph Urgo," *Willa Cather and the Myth of American Migration* (Urbana: University of Illinois Press, 1995). Karl Rosenquist, interviewer, *Willa Cather Pioneer Memorial Newsletter*, 61:1 (1997): 16–21.

"Getting Good at Doing Nothing": Faulkner, Hemingway, and the Fiction of Gesture

Donald M. Kartiganer

But walking down the stairs feeling each stair carefully and holding to the banister he thought, I must get her away and get her away as soon as I can without hurting her. Because I am not doing too well at this. That I can promise you. But what else can you do? Nothing, he thought. There's nothing you can do. But maybe, as you go along, you will get good at it.
—Hemingway, "Get a Seeing-Eyed Dog"[1]

They never met, which is probably just as well, because as writers and as personalities they seemed to be completely opposite in almost every respect. As literary stylists they created the two most distinctive and influential forms of prose fiction in America in the first half of the twentieth century. Hemingway perfected an art of exclusion. The right words were the rarest currency, their value secured by their survival of the writer's ruthless stripping away of all the words that would not work. His essential tool was the blue pencil that signaled "cut"; his essential gift what he referred to as the "built-in, shock-proof, shit detector"; his essential task to tell the truth that is left when everything false is winnowed away.[2] Faulkner's was the art of inclusion. Since words could never be rid of their inherent lack, their state as refugees from exact reference, all a writer could do is marshal them together, clause upon clause, adjective upon adjective, through sheer mass and motion not so much to corner the Real as to surround it, not to name flatly its essence but to infer the complete range of its possibilities.

The stylistic difference is one of the recurring phenomena of American literature: Hawthorne and Melville, Dickinson and Whitman, Crane and Dreiser, Frost and Williams—each pairing manifests a comparable clash of rhetorical spareness and rhetorical profusion. In Hemingway and Faulkner the difference reverses in their subject matter and in their lives. In his life Hemingway excluded very little. He wrote in and of a dozen countries, saw and reported on four wars, hunted big game in Africa, fished for marlin in the Caribbean, watched hundreds of bull fights in Spain, married four times and fathered three sons—all the time filling his fiction with an expansiveness of event and experience that did not belie its lean prose, but became part of that knowledge, common or specialized, on which he prided himself but did not have to allude to directly. It was the knowledge making up the hidden seven-eighths of the iceberg that, "if the writer is writing truly enough," gives the reader "a feeling of those things as strongly as though the writer had stated them."[3]

Faulkner, unlike many of the high modernists, who made a principle of exile, spent his entire life in the little town in Mississippi where he grew up. He made occasional forays into the world, partly perhaps out of a sense of paying his dues to the expatriate fad—in 1925 spending six months in New Orleans and six months in Europe—and partly in later years as a way of paying his bills by doing screen-writing in Hollywood. By and large, however, he made his home in Oxford with his one wife and single surviving daughter, away from all literary coteries and salons, away from writers and critics, wholly absorbed in and apparently fulfilled by what he called his postage stamp of native soil.

Despite these differences, my purpose is to try to identify a common ground, and that is their career-long fascination with the act of what I call "gesture." Their emphasis is on gesture as an action that signals an intention, a purpose, but is never completed: what we normally call failed gesture, or—when realization appears to be impossible at the very outset—"empty" gesture. In the fiction of Hemingway and Faulkner gesture always fails, proves in the end to be empty. Particularly interesting are those instances when the maker of gesture is wholly aware of its emptiness, the gesture seeming to draw a kind of power from the fact of failure it not only cannot alter but has no hope of altering.

Let me give a couple of examples.

In Hemingway's story "In Another Country," a major in the Italian army in World War I has been wounded in the hand and is receiving therapy. The therapy is being administered by what are called simply "machines" that presumably will enable the major—once, we are told, "the greatest fencer in Italy"—to regain the full use of his hand.[4] The major, however, is convinced they will achieve nothing. Nevertheless, he cheerfully continues to come regularly to the hospital for treatment. He engages in conversation with the narrator, a wounded American, who has learned some Italian. Upon being complimented by the major on his Italian, the American confesses that he finds the Italian language so easy, he cannot take much interest in it—at which point the major asks, "Why, then, do you not take up the use of grammar?" (270). Ah yes, grammar. Grammar is one of the keys to the story: the form that is at once unnecessary for basic communication and yet warranted on the grounds of stylistic propriety, the established formalities of sound and sequence.

The major is one of Hemingway's worldly cynics: he does not believe in the machines, he does not believe in bravery or the medals that presumably signify it, he does not believe in theory. He believes in the ceremony of grammar and in the ceremony, if not the content, of therapy, as if therapy were nothing more, but assuredly nothing less, than a correct decorum when one is injured. It turns out, however, that the major is not cynical enough. For in fact he has preserved a center of content in the midst of the various forms he carries out so gracefully. This content is his marriage. Carefully waiting until he has been invalided out of the war so as not to risk making a wife a widow, he has recently married, believing that he has found something "he cannot lose," believing he has finessed the danger of war (271). In some personal calculation of his own, he has given his hand in exchange for the life he has preserved to offer as a husband.

But for all the major's careful execution, there is no effective caution in Hemingway, no possible foresight that circumvents disaster. Shortly after the major begins his therapy, his wife takes ill of pneumonia and soon dies. Now the major has a wound deeper than his withered hand:

> He looked straight past me and out through the window. Then he began to cry. "I am utterly unable to resign myself," he said and choked. And then crying, his head up looking at nothing, carrying himself straight and soldierly, with tears on both his cheeks and biting his lips, he walked past the machines and out the door. (272)

After a three-day absence the major returns to use the machines, although it is clear he still has no faith in their curative power. Now, however, the pointless routine has changed its meaning, lifting to the level of pure illusion: gesture, a style poised against the darkness the major has discovered at last. "The photographs [of hands completely restored] did not make much difference to the major because he only looked out of the window"—good at doing nothing, speaking grammatically, as it were, the language of his loss.

For Faulkner, we turn to a scene from *Absalom, Absalom!* The elegant French architect whom Thomas Sutpen has hired to design the great house at Sutpen's Hundred has finally had enough of the primitive conditions, of Sutpen and his crew of Haitian slaves, and runs off into the river bottom. He is pursued by Sutpen and the slaves, as well as by a group of Sutpen's white guests, including Quentin Compson's grandfather. After a two-day hunt, during which Sutpen has told grandfather much of the story of how he came to Mississippi, the architect is found:

> "hauled . . . out of his cave under the river bank: a little man with one sleeve missing from his frock coat and his flowered vest ruined by water and mud where he had fallen in the river and one pants leg ripped down so they could see where he

had tied up his leg with a piece of his shirt tail and the rag bloody and the leg swollen, and his hat was completely gone.... a little harried wild-faced man with a two-days' stubble of beard, who came out of the cave fighting like a wildcat, hurt leg and all ... not scared worth a damn either, just panting a little and Grandfather said a little sick in the face where the niggers had mishandled his leg in the heat of the capture, and making them a speech in French, a long one and so fast that Grandfather said probably another Frenchman could not have understood all of it. But it sounded fine; Grandfather said even he—all of them—could tell that the architect was not apologising; it was fine, Grandfather said, and he said how Sutpen turned toward him but he (Grandfather) was already approaching the architect, holding out the bottle of whiskey already uncorked. And Grandfather saw the eyes in the gaunt face, the eyes desperate and hopeless but indomitable too, invincible too, not beaten yet by a damn sight Grandfather said, and all that fifty-odd hours of dark and swamp and sleeplessness and fatigue and no grub and nowhere to go and no hope of getting there: just a will to endure and a foreknowing of defeat but not beat yet by a damn sight: and he took the bottle in one of his little dirty coon-like hands and raised the other hand and even fumbled about his head for a second before he remembered that the hat was gone, then flung the hand up in a gesture that Grandfather said you simply could not describe, that seemed to gather all misfortune and defeat that the human race ever suffered into a little pinch in his fingers like dust and fling it backward over his head, and raised the bottle and bowed first to Grandfather then to all the other men sitting their horses in a circle and looking at him, and then he took not only the first drink of neat whiskey he ever took in his life but the drink of it that he could no more have conceived himself taking than the Brahmin can believe that that situation can conceivably arise in which he will eat dog."[5]

The scene and sentence are vintage Faulkner, an excess of prose to match the excess of gesture epitomized in the French architect's majestic toss of the hat he is no longer wearing. Hemingway's brutally concise account of human vulnerability—the punishment of the body, death as the resolution of love, the meticulous performance of the meaningless, mundane act—it all seems a far cry from the stirring, and stirringly described, flamboyance of the architect. Nevertheless, however grand Faulknerian gesture may be, it is still gesture, still an exercise in artful futility, the act that, like the major's, accomplishes nothing.

Most of the fiction of both writers is a chronicle of effort issuing in failure: failure to complete a mission or the promise of a relationship, failure to execute a design or to find the peace one spends a lifetime seeking, failure to redeem the sins of a heritage or to stop a war, failure to bring back intact the giant fish. What I want to do now is to survey briefly the careers of both writers in terms of this persistent defeat of purpose and the gestural mode that often accompanies it, and then analyze one text of each in greater detail by way of exemplifying that mode in its most mature form.

I begin with Hemingway. *In Our Time*, the collection of short stories and vignettes published in 1925, offers the darkest vision its author would ever have: an unremitting account of strenuous yet pointless human action. The prevailing tone of the volume is set in its opening story, "Indian Camp," with its characteristic Hemingway combination of humiliation and horror. A vacationing physician has to perform a cesarean section with a jack knife and fishing leaders and without anesthetic, only to discover at the end of his resourceful if brutal procedure that the mother's husband, who has been lying in a bunk listening to her screams, has slit his throat. The upshot of this harrowing tale is the oldest obstetrical joke: the doctor who delivers the baby, expertly sews up the mother, and loses the father.

The only apt behavior in this world of nightmare, in which skill and boldness are ultimately undone, is demonstrated in the last story of the volume, "Big Two-Hearted River," in the figure of Nick Adams, the physically and psychically wounded man who achieves at least a temporary equilibrium through his manic attention to detail. Going on a fishing trip alone, Nick transforms the entire experience of finding and making camp, cooking and eating food, preparing to fish and the fishing itself, into an obsessively controlled activity, honing these mundane acts into a series of rituals whose precise execution, graphically described, are as important to Nick as their practical benefit. Nick's intention is not so much to enjoy a restful weekend in the woods as to perform an elaborate gesture designed at once to impede thought and to build a protective magic against the psychic demons—the nature of which we never learn—that trouble him.[6] This is gesture as pathology, gesture as neurosis. Like any neurotic symptom, it simultaneously hides and discloses its secret source, in this case the unspecified terrors that Nick can reveal only in the armored form of his gesturing. The gesture feeds on its hidden terror and vice versa. The cost, as Freud claimed, is the great energy expended in the complex act of rigorously allaying fears whose existence one refuses consciously to acknowledge.

Hemingway's development as a writer is marked by his representation of a gestural mode that is fully aware of the underlying terror *and* its own irrelevance—a mode that hides nothing, that refuses, in Hemingway's terms, to engage in "tricks" or "faking." The first Hemingway character to demonstrate what it might mean to be good at doing nothing, and know it, is Jake Barnes in *The Sun Also Rises*. Jake's tireless reiteration of his daily routine of busywork, eating and drinking, social engagements—itemizing every street and bar, every dish and drink consumed—is a style that knows its own emptiness, in terms of either significant journalistic or literary output. "Significance" is, in fact, the temptation to which Robert Cohn falls prey: the illusions of love, honor, and professional achievement that Jake has expelled from his studied routine.

To be "one of us," in the novel's terse distinction between those who know and those who do not, is to understand the folly of significance, of meaning itself. One of Cohn's grave errors, for example, is to refuse to accept the fact that his weekend with Brett Ashley at San Sebastion "didn't mean anything."[7] The kind of significance Cohn pursues resides only in the figure of Pedro Romero, whose role as the matador is the performance of a ceremony confirmed by a communal tradition. Unlike Nick Adams or Jake Barnes, who must either invent their routines or invest existing ones with ritual resonance, Romero is the priest of a fully developed liturgy, grounded solidly in the Spanish past. The threat of death has nothing of the dread that inspires Jake's carefully constructed gestures; it is fully, spectacularly present in the figure of the bull. That threat is itself the power that is defeated as the climax of what Hemingway called "the tragedy of the bullfight."[8] "Death" is destroyed, subsumed into the intelligible choreography of the *corrida*, as the matador both proves his own "immortality" and "gives [it] to the spectators" (213).

At times Jake Barnes, unlike Romero, fails to fulfill his disciplined routine, especially during the fiesta in Pamplona. As Jake admits, given "the proper chance . . . [e]verybody behaves badly" (181). The importance of *The Sun Also Rises*, however, is its suggestion that Jake's self-valorized gestures may finally eclipse Romero's communally authorized ones precisely because the former function in a world in which all traditional meaning has been lost, because they claim nothing other than their own efficiency and whatever gratification that efficiency can bring.

But it is in the short stories of the decade that follows *The Sun Also Rises* that I think we find Hemingway's finest work, marked by his creation of characters, more disciplined, more self-knowing than Jake, who fashion gestural modes of survival, strategies that gather their value from the combination of skill and intensity with which they are carried out and the candor with which they reveal their limited relevance. We see this in the major's habit of "going to the machines" in "In Another Country"; or in the gambler Cayetano, in "The Gambler, the Nun, and the Radio," who enacts a code of honor in order to protect the "fool" who shot him;[9] or the need for light and cleanness and order in "A Clean Well-Lighted Place" that does not alter the nature of the nothingness, the nada, but only realigns its elements, sweeps the floor, arranges the furniture, and suffuses the whole in an artificial glow.

There is the great artistry of Wilson, the professional hunter of "The Short Happy Life of Francis Macomber," dispensing his wisdom to the novice Macomber: how to deal with a wounded wild animal, when and how to shoot, how much to talk, how much to tip, how to respond to a failure and how not. Barely beneath the perfectly executed forms is the shoddy life of a self-confessed hypocrite who plays the prostitute, figuratively and literally, to the clients he admits he abhors. Whatever Wilson's mastery of the forms of his profession, he knows quite well just how fragile the forms are, how much they must be protected by verbal restraint. He says to Macomber, who, suddenly freed of his cowardice, is relishing the looming encounter with a wounded buffalo, "Doesn't do to talk too much about all this. Talk the whole thing away."[10] He knows that only a few too many words will reveal this form, implemented with such skill and resourcefulness and courage, to be not altogether removed from the "rot" Margot Macomber recognizes it to be; that a flagrant gap remains between the rule-bound hunt and a life in which, as he admits, "We all take a beating every day . . . one way or another" (6).

In "The Snows of Kilimanjaro" we have something like a climax and culmination of the theme of gesture. As in "The Short Happy Life of Francis Macomber," there is the jarring coexistence of a life steeped in hypocrisy and dishonesty and the devotion to and skillful creation of a form, an aesthetic pattern. Harry Walden has become the writer who does not write, who has squandered his talent for the pleasures the rich can offer, and, if anything, deepens his guilt by the confession of contempt for the very people who have provided those pleasures. Now, dying in characteristic Hemingway indignity, from a thorn cut received while trying to photograph (unsuccessfully) a herd of waterbuck, Harry summarizes and relives all the poison of his wasted life by spewing it out once again, primarily at the expense of the woman whose only crime seems to be an ample supply of money and a puzzling capacity to love him.

In the midst of this painful account of a man who knows exactly what he is, a form gradually emerges: not a studied recourse to a set of conventions such as the hunt, but a last return to the discipline of writing. The five italicized reminiscences of Harry are the "writing"—purely in his mind—of the last hours of his life. It is important to note that what Harry is *not* doing at this time is praying or exploring the "meaning" of the bizarre series of circumstances that will result in his death, the answer to the metaphysical question Helen raises: "What have we done to have that happen to us?"[11] And as the writing continues, so too the abuse and acrimony lessen, as Harry turns at last from the unpleasantness of his life to the difficult, painstaking representation of that life into prose.

The italicized portions of the story are a series of sketches, settings for potential stories that Harry has always meant to write but hasn't, gradually moving toward the shaping of a plot, then a brief but whole fiction: "There wasn't time, of course, although it seemed as though it telescoped so that you might put it all into one paragraph if you could get it right" (68). First a group of memories linked together by the common subject of snow, like an exercise assigned by a writing instructor: "write me something having to do with snow"; then the entanglements of marriage, the quarrels, the infidelity, whoring and fighting in Constantinople, a scene from the Greco-Turkish war: none of it, however, coalescing into a story. Then the emergence of possible plots: grandfather's loss of all his guns in a fire, *"and he never bought any others"* (68); the hotel proprietor in Triberg ruined by inflation who hanged himself—followed by the crucial memory of the time in Paris when life had become story: *"And in that poverty, and in that quarter across the street from a Boucherie Chevaline and a wine co-operative he had written the start of all he was to do"* (69–70).

Finally, the two concluding pieces, the briefest and yet the most complete of the memories: the story of the half-wit chore boy and the story of Williamson dying in battle—the last being Harry's attempt at the "one paragraph if you could get it right":

> *He remembered long ago when Williamson, the bombing officer, had been hit by a stick bomb some one in a German patrol had thrown as he was coming in through the wire that night and, screaming, had begged every one to kill him. He was a fat man, very brave, and a good officer, although addicted to fantastic shows. But that night he was caught in the wire, with a flare lighting him up and his bowels spilled out into the wire, so when they brought him in, alive, they had to cut him loose. Shoot me, Harry. For Christ sake shoot me. They had had an argument one time about our Lord never sending you anything you could not bear and some one's theory had been that meant that at a certain time the pain passed you out automatically. But he had always remembered Williamson, that night. Nothing passed out Williamson until he gave him all his morphine tablets that he had always saved to use himself and then they did not work right away.* (73)

The skill and aptness of this vignette is its use and transference of Harry's current situation into a scene from his past now recalled into a wholeness of fiction. Helen's platitude, "You can't die if you don't give up" (53), becomes the unsupported belief that the Lord will send nothing you cannot bear; the absence of pain once Harry's gangrene sets in becomes Williamson's intolerable pain; Harry's conviction that "He could beat anything" (72) becomes a man begging for his death. Finally, Harry's regret over his failure to put into language all the experiences *"he had saved to write"* (72) becomes the morphine tablets *"he had always saved to use himself"* and which he now gives up in order to relieve the agony of Williamson.

Following this series of memories, Harry says to Helen, without a trace of irony, "I've been writing . . . [b]ut I got tired" (74).

This is the gesture of "The Snows of Kilimanjaro"—gesture because Harry's "writing" is no more substantial than any of the other styles

Hemingway has permitted his characters to perform. These reminiscenses are not only not published; they are not written or even spoken. They do not possess the solidity of a breath or the thickness of ink on paper. In the real world of the writer they are the stories that cannot possibly matter, and yet they are the achievement of Harry's life: the unread, unheard journey toward mastery that concludes his abortive career.

At the end of the story, in what must be the most astonishing scene in Hemingway's fiction, Harry is rewarded for that achievement. The story sends him a rescue plane: "Old Compton in slacks, a tweed jacket and a brown felt hat" (75). The flight they take, however, is not to the nearest hospital but to the mountain, Kilimanjaro, the house of God. This concluding fantasy—and whose fantasy is it? Harry's? the narrator's? Hemingway's?—is a version of Harry's last stories: the fantasy that *cannot* conclude the fiction, certainly not a Hemingway fiction, becomes the brilliant replica of the stories that never get written, *cannot* get written. The final paragraphs describing what really happens in "The Snows of Kilimanjaro"—Harry dead, his gangrenous leg now hanging down from the sheets before Helen's face—do not deflate or reduce to irony Harry's unreal redemption. Rather they deepen it with the power of their own inescapable reality, the black background against which the fantasy soars, the supreme gesture, doing nothing.

In Faulkner, gesture is invariably "grand" gesture, the gallant, flamboyant motion: the French architect of *Absalom, Absalom!* gathering "all misfortune and defeat" and hurling it from him, without a trace of regret—rather, with pride compounded—in his discovery that his hand is empty. Grand not merely in the bravado with which one can mime the tossing of a hat, Faulknerian gesture is often ambitious to the point of arrogance, bent on shaking the pillars of the world even as it remains almost blithely indifferent to its actual outcome. This is a far cry from Hemingway gesture, rooted in disciplined patience, *holding on*, virtues appropriate to an art of not saying too much.

Before moving to a closer look at some specific examples of Faulknerian gesture, I want to pause over this difference in the sheer scope and breadth of gesture in both writers, and speculate on the particular representations Faulkner and Hemingway arrived at and how they may have gotten there. One large "high cultural" source for both writers is undoubtedly the movement in late nineteenth-century European literature and thought that placed an increasingly high premium on the art object and the devoted, isolated figure who made it. There is no need—and certainly no time—to rehearse this movement now, except to note the paradoxical nature of what became its dual allegiances: on the one hand to foster an art in pursuit of "a radiant truth out of space and time," and on the other hand to declare art perfectly useless.[12] The poet, according to Mallarmé, ignores what is palpably *there* in order to pursue something more beautiful and truer: "the one flower absent from all bouquets."[13] To demand anything useful of art, however—in Stephen Dedalus's terms, to want art to be "kinetic" as opposed to "aesthetic"—is to reduce it to pornography or didacticism.

Writing in 1927, in the midst of the modernism that succeeded *fin de siècle* aestheticism, Paul Valery expounds on these dual allegiances by comparing the difference between prose and poetry to that between walking and dancing: the first is the "act directed *toward* some object that we aim to reach," while the second is the act "whose end is in [itself]. It goes nowhere." Poetry does have an object, but an "ideal" one— "a state, a delight, the phantom of a flower, or some transport out of oneself, an extreme of life, a summit, a supreme point of being"—whereas the object of prose is of far more mundane value. One crucial aspect of the difference is the fate of the means each form of movement employs to its ends. The language of prose, of walking, "vanishes once it has *arrived*.... It is entirely and definitively replaced by its *meaning*," whereas the language of poetry, of dancing, "does not die for having been of use; it is purposely made to be reborn from its ashes and perpetually to become what it has been."[14]

For Hemingway and Faulkner, the difference between prose and poetry is the difference between ordinary language and the language of literature; the difference between walking and dancing is the difference between effective action in the world and gesture. The deepest truth is what one reaches only after moving beyond the available here and now— presumably the bread and butter of the novelist. At the 1955 Nagano seminars, Faulkner may well have been recalling Mallarmé's credo, as translated by Arthur Symons, that one must ignore "the intrinsic, dense wood of the trees" in order to reach "the horror of the forest, or the silent thunder afloat in the leaves."[15] Asked about his "ideal woman," Faulkner replied, "once she is described, then somehow she vanishes.... And it's best to take the gesture, the shadow of the branch, and let the mind [that is, the reader's mind] create the tree."[16] In a 1958 *Paris Review* interview with George Plimpton, Hemingway was even more forthright in the distinction between reality and truth: "From things that have happened and from things as they exist and from all things that you know and all those you cannot know, you make something through your invention that is not a representation but a whole new thing truer than anything true and alive, and you make it alive, and if you make it well enough, you give it immortality."[17] On the basis of such principles, Hemingway and Faulkner create fictional characters (not literally artists—Harry Walden being a significant exception) whose achievement consists of the performance of gestures, coupled with the conscious abandonment of the hope of utilitarian result.

Although similarly influenced by these modernist attitudes, Hemingway and Faulkner are as different from each other as we would expect in their choice of a specific fictional action and imagery of gesture. Hemingway relies heavily on a culture of conflict and violence, in its own way as "international" as the life he lived, finding its concrete representations in places and actions ranging from hunting in Africa to war in Spain to serious wounds incurred in Montana. Faulkner turns to his north Mississippi locale and history and a Southern emphasis less on action than attitude, a stance to the world constructed of memory of a past that is no longer quite relevant, yet of utmost importance.

Warfare was the epitome of the action Hemingway seems always to have craved. Referring to Tolstoy, he once commented on "what an advantage an experience of war was to a writer . . . and those writers who had not seen it were always very jealous and tried to make it seem unimportant, or abnormal, or a disease as a subject, while, really, it was just something quite irreplaceable that they had missed."[18] Given his limited experience in combat, however—he was wounded a month after beginning service with a Red Cross unit in Italy—he shifted to what he regarded as its nearest equivalents in sport: big-game hunting, bullfighting, boxing, all of which he could either participate in or study to the point of becoming aficionado.[19] When successfully performed, they all culminate either in death or bodily damage, and yet Hemingway's great emphasis in writing about them or employing their imagery is on the skill of the performer, virtually independent of the result that such skill will likely produce. It is the aesthetic of the hunt, rather than the actual kill, that is its essential criterion of value: "I did not mind killing anything, any animal, if I killed it cleanly."[20]

None of these sports can be considered mundane, yet Hemingway's use of them is completely consistent with his general aesthetic of rhetorical restraint and the theme of restraint that results from it. In *Death in the Afternoon* Hemingway's emphasis is on the skill that is demonstrated when one operates within the established rules. The measure of the matador is his willingness to risk danger, but only *"within the rules provided for his protection."* To risk danger through ignorance or "through disregard of the fundamental rules . . . [is] blind folly" (21). As distasteful to Hemingway as folly is fakery: the matador who pretends to be in greater danger than he really is, who "substitute[s] a series of graceful tricks . . . for . . . sincere danger" (215).

Even in an event as spectacular as the bullfight, Hemingway is watching for what he calls "sincerity" as opposed to trickery, for a knowledge of and obedience to the rules as opposed to ignorant innovation, for the "clean" rather than the gaudy kill. This sense of the minimum, of the clarity rather than the complexity of a movement, the straightforward adherence to rules laid down, carries over to Hemingway's comments on good writing, whose essence, like that of Madrid, "can be in a plain glass bottle" (51). Writing must be clear and straight, without tricks, without fakery. Mystification in writing, like the matador who executes his dazzling cape work at a safe distance from the bull, reveals only "the necessity to fake to cover lack of knowledge or the inability to state clearly.... Remember this too: all bad writers are in love with the epic" (54). Hence the characteristic Hemingway gesture: clean, straight-forward, no tricks: a man walking carefully down the stairs, or sitting quietly at the "machines," staring out the window, or silently writing sentences in his head as he waits to die.

Faulkner's gestures are invariably "epic." One of the keys to both his need for gesture and the specific gestures he selects is the fact of his growing up in the South during a period in which what we refer to as the Lost Cause mentality was widespread. That mentality—the preoccupation of many Southerners with the antebellum South and the defense of it in the War between the States—was fundamentally a gestural mode: not a program for action but the script for a posture, a stance, an attitude. Faulkner became familiar at an early age with this Southern fascination with gesture, with the difference between a real present and consciousness of a legendary past that contradicts it.

One Southern commentator, a woman named L. H. Harris writing in 1906, describes the psychic condition of Southern white males, portraying a figure torn between fact and fantasy, and needing to believe in the latter despite the unmistakable presence of the former. Every Southern white male, she writes, is "himself and his favorite forefather at the same time"; he inhabits "two characters ... one which condemns [him], more or less downtrodden by facts to the days of [his] own years, and one in which [he] tread[s] a perpetual minuet of past glories."[21]

One result of this psychic split is the elevation of gesture to paramount position. There is a mode of existence contradicted by the current situation, a contradiction the Southerner is perfectly aware of, and yet that existence acquires beauty and significance. It becomes the embodiment of meaning: the "truth" that matters most. According to Harris, the Southerner must be the master of gesture, adopting a "pose [behind which] he sits and watches the effects of his own mannerisms with all the shrewdness of a dramatic critic.... [H]e feels the part, sees himself in the eyes of the other and enjoys the performance as much as if he were himself observing a good actor. And he is always a good actor; every Southern man and woman must be that." And yet he always knows the difference between the gesture and the fact: "we carry our sword next to our manners, not literally, but figuratively—we have been compelled to substitute much that is figurative for what was once literal in our conduct."[22]

The first great gesturer of Faulkner's major fiction is Quentin Compson in *The Sound and the Fury*, the young man entrapped in the Lost Cause mode I have just described. Although Faulkner was dependent on that mode throughout his career as a model of gestural extravagance, his literal uses of it, first in Quentin, then Horace Benbow of *Sanctuary*, then Gail Hightower in *Light in August*, represent it as fundamentally pathological. Quentin Compson's mental aberrations in *The Sound and the Fury*, interestingly enough, echo those of Nick Adams, who is Hemingway's first example of the gestural mode. There are important differences, of course, but in both cases we see traumatized young men, deeply disturbed by destructive parenting, by what they regard as social corruption, and by the unexpected complexities of sexual engagement. They protect themselves by turning to familiar forms: for one, the habits of camping and fishing, for the other the conventions of an earlier era.

Quentin so absorbs himself in retrospect, the backward look, that he quickly heightens gesture into theater, performing acts that, half unwittingly, he has emptied of any intention they might have once had.[23] He initiates fights he cannot hope to win, assumes the protection of women he cannot protect and who in any event neither need nor want his protection, pretends to a sexual identity and desire that in fact appall him. His pathology—unlike the case of Harris's actor, who always knows the difference between the literal and the figurative—lies in his divided condition of simultaneously knowing and not knowing what he is about, taking satisfaction in gestures correctly if ineffectively performed and yet perpetually dismayed over the fact that the real world does not conform to his gestural conception of it. He knows and does not know the bankruptcy of his Southern code as well as his own inadequate defense of it.

Quentin's deepest moment of self-awareness comes in the closing pages of his monologue, when he finally recognizes the life of total gesture, and its implications, that he really desires. In a conversation with his father, which he may only be imagining, he admits that it is the fantasy of incest, not its literal reality, that he has desired with his sister Caddy: "i was afraid to [make her do it] i was afraid she might and then it wouldnt have done any good but if i could tell you we did it would have been so and then the others wouldnt be so and then the world would roar away" (177). This substitution of "telling" for "doing" is followed by Quentin's corollary claim that he is considering suicide—that is, leaping into the pure irrelevance of death, in which gesture is no longer the confrontation with "all misfortune and defeat" but the abandonment of it. It is as if he would say of the real world what he says earlier of sexuality: "O That That's Chinese I don't know Chinese" (116).

Soon enough, Faulkner would move beyond Lost Cause versions of gesture, but his major characters would all remain epic actors, taking grand attitudes, heroic stances, even as—unlike Quentin Compson—they know perfectly well that their goals are not only impossible, but that the grandeur of the stance depends on the fact of its lost relevance. By way of example I will refer to three of these figures, all of whom take as their direct model the figure of Jesus Christ, who, at least for them, is essentially a master of gesture—that is, a master of the great act that accomplishes nothing.

The epic actors I have in mind come from three distinct periods in Faulkner's career: Joe Christmas in *Light in August*, Ike McCaslin in *Go Down, Moses*, and the Corporal in *A Fable*. I begin with Ike McCaslin, whose grand gesture—and that is all it is, and all it is intended to be—is the forfeiture of his vast inheritance, the McCaslin plantation. His act of relinquishment in "The Bear" is nothing less than his response to human sin and corruption: the enslavement of a people, the possession and violation of the land. Nevertheless, Ike is perfectly aware that the gap between his gesture and the content over which it hovers will remain as secure as ever. The land will still be possessed by whites, the McCaslin plantation simply shifting into Edmonds hands; and African Americans will still toil on it as the servants of white masters. For Ike none of this diminishes the value and validity of his symbolic act: "Yes. Binding them for a while yet, a little while yet. Through and beyond that life and maybe through and beyond the life of that life's sons and maybe even through and beyond that of the sons of those sons. But not always, because they will endure. They will outlast us."[24] And again: "It will be long. I have never said otherwise. But it will be all right because they will endure" (286).

Ike's cousin, Edmonds, responds, "And anyway you will be free"— free not only of the relinquished land but free of the need to live in the new time, the time to come when whites and blacks will live together as equals. A half-century later, in the story "Delta Autumn," the nearly eighty-year-old Ike is confronted with the miscegenative offspring that will be part of the new age, and thinks, "*Maybe in a thousand or two thousand years in America.... But not now! Not now!*" (344).

Were it not for Ike's sustained, impassioned commitment to the need for at least a symbolic redemptive act, we might think we were in another version of Swift's "Modest Proposal." But Ike's seriousness persuades us of his sincerity, if not the consistency of his thinking, and possibly the absence of at least conscious hypocrisy, particularly when he adopts as a model for his earthly occupation—now that he will not be running a plantation—a master of gesture: "because if the Nazarene had found carpentering good for the life and ends He had assumed and elected to serve, it would be all right too for Isaac McCaslin" (295). Ike distinguishes himself from the Nazarene in that his own ends "were and would be incomprehensible to him," and his life—the life of relinquishment—is one, "not being the Nazarene . . . he would not have chosen" (295–96). Apparently forgetting that in the Garden of Gethsemane Jesus also acknowledges that this life of impending relinquishment is not the one he would have chosen, Ike does make it clear that he at least is not sure of just what it is he is trying to accomplish. Nevertheless, he makes the great symbolic gesture and pays the price, giving up his land, his wife, the son he hoped to father, and the respect of most of his community—not to mention, after the fictional fact, even the respect of his creator.[25]

This condition of clear, irreversible choice of action, for ends impossible of achievement except at some remote, unassignable date—and *known* to be impossible—reminds us of another appearance of the Nazarene in Faulkner's late fiction, the Corporal of *A Fable*. One of the effects of this novel is that its grim sense of the "nothing" that gesture can be so good at threatens to feed back into *Go Down, Moses* and especially "The Bear," troubling a text that seems to have been intended to at least propose an image of social progress, if not its actual fulfillment. With *A Fable* as our context we may find "The Bear" reading more as a complacent acceptance of the status quo glossed over by impotent gesture.

In the retelling of the Passion in *A Fable*, all is gesture, every act a more or less conscious reenactment of a previous act, all of them bound together by the repeated failure of their final ends. The initial mutiny led by the Corporal brings combat on the Western Front in World War I to a temporary halt. French troops refuse to mount an ordered attack. Later we learn that the aborted attack was *itself* gestural, an attack calculated to fail, a sacrifice to some undisclosed military expediency. The second mutiny, led now by the Sentry, the Runner, and the Reverend Sutterfield, is also gestural. The Runner knows beforehand what the outcome will be if British and German troops begin running toward each other, unarmed, over the space of no-man's land: "Don't you see? That's it, that's the risk: if some of the Germans do come out. Then they will shoot at us, both of them, their side and ours too—put a barrage down on all of us. They'll have to. There wont be anything else for them to do."[26] And of course that is indeed the outcome.

The role of gesture in this later fiction—with *Go Down, Moses* as the novel on the cusp, threatening to begin that last phase—suggests a sense of human futility, despite the grandest ambitions, that may outstrip even that of Hemingway. In comparing the large scope of Ike McCaslin's and the Corporal's designs—their fulfillment not so much doomed at the outset as simply disregarded as unthinkable—with the aims, say, of Harry Walden or Wilson or the Major of "In Another Country," we sense an emptiness of gesture that borders on nihilism: here is a good at doing nothing that only confirms the nothingness of nothing.

But now let us turn to one more text, and see another side of Faulknerian gesture. Joe Christmas is another secular Jesus who, like his model, will come to realize the enormity of his purpose, indeed its impossibility of fulfillment in the real world, yet he will prefer what he regards as the validity, even the moral beauty, of that purpose to any available life on earth. To summarize some work I have already done on this novel, my understanding of Joe Christmas is that he has translated the agony of his possible but by no means assured black-white division into the fundamental binary of all culture—black and white, male and female, natural and civilized—and refused to accept its accuracy or its necessity. He will not submit to the black-white divisions of the South, he will neither be black nor white according to the social and cultural meaning of those terms. In effect he seeks a nonbinary existence, with all that implies, but he eventually comes to understand that such an existence is intolerable to the world. As one character in the novel puts it, "He never acted like either a nigger or a white man. That was it. That was what made the folks so mad."[27] His model is Jesus Christ, whose message to the world is that he too is the confluence of two presumably opposed realms of existence, the human and the divine. According to his Testament, that's what made the folks so mad.

The climax of the novel, the pursuit, capture, escape, and execution of Joe Christmas, is his Passion, and in enacting it he becomes the complete representative of the gestural mode in Faulkner. Clearly Joe need not be caught by his pursuers. When he wishes to, he easily evades them, and he obviously could leave the area entirely, were that his desire. Ultimately, he neither escapes nor offers himself up to capture; he is simply *there* in Mottstown, where someone can finally "arrest" him. Later, he repeats this act that is no act. He runs from the sheriff and from Percy Grimm but does not really seem bent on getting away; as the town later collectively concludes, "It was as though he had set out and made his plans to passively commit suicide" (443). He acquires a gun, with which he could easily shoot Grimm when the latter bursts into Hightower's house, but he does not fire; he does not really resist. In other words, he refuses to come down from the Cross of his gesture.

The purpose of the last week of his life is nothing other than the representation of the healed binary that the world must destroy. That the world will not heed, will not accept his gift of the healed life, is by this time known perfectly to Joe Christmas. The rigid divisions of the world are graphically rehearsed for us by Gavin Stevens in his long account of what he reads as the stark divisions in Joe, the black and the white. In the eyes of the world, these divisions must never be unified, an insistence Christmas ultimately accepts as the necessary contradiction to his now fully gestural dream.

Such is Faulkner's version of gesture, in what Hemingway might call the "epic" mode. It is not Harry Walden laboriously writing the sculpted prose that will die with him, not the old waiter waiting patiently for the old widower to finish his drink in a clean place bathed in light. But, if they were reading rightly, Hemingway and Faulkner would see that, in the end, they were truly contemporaries.[28]

And so, what does it mean, this writing that celebrates getting good at doing nothing? That glorifies the gesture whose greatest virtue is the candor with which it admits—no, boasts of—its irrelevance? The current literary and critical climate is hardly receptive to gesture, to artful ineffectuality. Is gesture simply another term for high-modernist elitism, a valorization of artfulness while millions starve and the dishonest world continues toward its annihilation—whether of the mind or the soul or the body? A "good" that accomplishes "nothing" is not what many of us these days believe we require.

As it turns out, we didn't require it in 1932 either, when both Hemingway and Faulkner were already being attacked on the grounds that their work was insufficiently concerned with social, political, and economic issues. Faulkner does not seem to have registered a response (if he had one), but Hemingway did not hesitate. At the end of *Death in the Afternoon*, a whole book on bullfighting of all things, he writes: "Let those who want to save the world if you can get to see it clear and as a whole. Then any part you make will represent the whole if it's made truly. The thing to do is work and learn to make it" (278). In *The Green Hills of Africa*—if anything, worse, a whole book on big-game hunting—he poses "art" against "economics" and makes his position clear: "A thousand years makes economics silly and a work of art endures forever, but it is very difficult to do, and now it is not fashionable. People do not want to do it any more because they will be out of fashion and the lice who crawl on literature will not praise them. Also it is very hard to do" (109).

But then, what is art for? Particularly an art that not only bears the burden of its inherent remoteness from real things, but places at its center an act of willful futility. For Hemingway, literature may be "hard to do," but it has an inestimable value, is "an end in itself" (26). And why? "If you serve time for society, democracy, and the other things quite young, and declining any further enlistment make yourself responsible only to yourself, you exchange the pleasant, comforting stench of comrades for something you can never feel in any other way than by yourself. That something I cannot yet define completely but the feeling comes when you write well and truly of something" (148).

What is that feeling? And what do we as readers, desperate for something, a truth, the possibility of knowing who we are, the possibility, as Faulkner put it, of being better than we are—what do we glean from the writer's writing well and truly? Or from fictional characters' impotent gesturing?

What is it that the onlookers at Joe Christmas's terrible death glean from that: from the final enactment of a gesture they do not understand? "The man seemed to rise soaring into their memories forever and ever. They are not to lose it, in whatever peaceful valleys, beside whatever placid and reassuring streams of old age, in the mirroring faces of whatever children they will contemplate old disasters and newer hopes. It will be there, musing, quiet, steadfast, not fading and not particularly threatful, but of itself alone serene, of itself alone triumphant" (465).

They are not to lose it. Lose what?

NOTES

1. "Get a Seeing-Eyed Dog," *The Complete Short Stories of Ernest Hemingway, The Finca Vigia Edition* (New York: Charles Scribner's Sons, 1987), 491.
2. *Writers at Work: The Paris Review Interviews, Second Series* (New York: Viking Press, 1963), 239.
3. *Death in the Afternoon* (New York: Charles Scribner's Son, 1932), 192.
4. "In Another Country," *The Short Stories of Ernest Hemingway* (New York: Charles Scribner's Sons, 1938), 268.
5. *Absalom, Absalom!* The Corrected Text (New York: Vintage International, 1990), 206–7.
6. For an early, classic statement of the theme of ritual in Hemingway, see Malcolm Cowley, "Nightmare and Ritual in Hemingway" [1945] in *Hemingway: A Collection of Critical Essays*, ed. Robert P. Weeks (Englewood Cliffs, N.J.: Prentice-Hall, 1962), 40–51.
7. *The Sun Also Rises* (New York: Charles Scribner's Sons, 1926), 181.
8. *Death in the Afternoon*, 98.
9. "The Gambler, the Nun, and the Radio," *The Short Stories of Ernest Hemingway*, 483.
10. "The Short Happy Life of Francis Macomber," *The Short Stories of Ernest Hemingway*, 33.
11. "The Snows of Kilimanjaro," *The Short Stories of Ernest Hemingway*, 55.
12. The quote is from Frank Kermode, *Romantic Image* (New York: Vintage Books, 1964), 2. A classic statement on the uselessness of art is Oscar Wilde's preface to *The Picture of Dorian Gray*.
13. Quoted in Arthur Symons, *The Symbolist Movement in Literature* (New York: Dutton, 1919), 199.
14. *The Art of Poetry*, trans. Denise Folliot (New York: Vintage Books, 1961), 206–9.
15. *The Symbolist Movement in Literature*, 196.
16. *Lion in the Garden: Interviews with William Faulkner, 1926–1962*, ed. James B. Meriwether and Michael Millgate (New York: Random House, 1968), 127–28.
17. *Writers at Work*, 239.

18. *Green Hills of Africa* (New York: Charles Scribner's Sons, 1935), 70. Hemingway's respect for Tolstoy is clear in his various comments (using one of his favorite metaphors) on which writers he has gotten into the ring with: "I started out very quiet and I beat Mr. Turgenev. Then I trained hard and I beat Mr. de Maupassant. I've fought two draws with Mr. Stendahl, and I think I had an edge in the last one. But nobody's going to get me in any ring with Mr. Tolstoy unless I'm crazy or I keep getting better," "How Do You Like it Now, Gentlemen," interview with Lillian Ross, in *Hemingway: A Collection of Critical Essays*, 23.

19. Although Hemingway was seriously wounded in World War I, whereas Faulkner wholly fantasized his war wounds, they both indulged in considerable exaggeration regarding their war experiences. Faulkner had more creative ground to cover, given that as a cadet in the Canadian RAF he probably never got actual flight training before the war ended, let alone (as he claimed) crashing twice in Europe while serving with the British RAF. But Hemingway let it be known that he was wounded while serving with the Italian Army rather than a Red Cross unit attached to it, a fiction still fostered by the latest Scribner's paperback reissue of *A Farewell to Arms*. Both writers sported uniforms they were not qualified to wear around their home towns, Hemingway an "Italian officer's cape, with its silkish lining" and Sam Browne belt—not quite the outfit of Red Cross volunteers, Faulkner an RFC (renamed RAF in July, 1918) uniform, wings, and garrison cap, indicating he had served overseas. See Michael Reynolds, *The Young Hemingway* (Oxford: Basil Blackwell, 1986), 17; Jeffrey Meyers, *Hemingway: A Biography* (New York: Harper, 1985), 39; John Faulkner, *My Brother Bill: An Affectionate Reminiscence* (New York: Trident Press, 1963), 138–39; James G. Watson, *William Faulkner: Self-Presentation and Performance* (Austin: University of Texas Press, 2000), 17–32.

20. *Green Hills of Africa*, 272. John Gaggin writes, "Hemingway's emphasis on clean killing echoes art-for-art's-sake notions in that its thrust is largely aesthetic rather than practical; the accomplishment of the task is meaningless unless the craft is pure," *Hemingway and Nineteenth-Century Aestheticism* (Ann Arbor: UMI Research Press, 1988), 68.

21. L. H. Harris, "Southern Manners," *The Independent* (August 1906): 321–25.

22. For full discussion of the background of gesture in Faulkner, see my "'So I, Who Had Never Had a War': William Faulkner, War, and the Modern Imagination," *Modern Fiction Studies* 44 (1998): 619–45, and "Modernism as Gesture: Faulkner's Missing Facts," *Renaissance and Modern Studies*, 41 (1998): 13–28.

23. Herbert Head, during his discussion with Quentin over the former's cheating at Harvard, comments, "We're better than a play you must have made the Dramat," *The Sound and the Fury*, The Corrected Text (New York: Vintage International, 1990), 108.

24. *Go Down, Moses* (New York: Vintage International, 1990), 281.

25. See, for example, *Faulkner in the University*, ed. Frederick L. Gwynn and Joseph L. Blotner (New York: Vintage, 1965), 245–46, and *Lion in the Garden*, 225. Theresa M. Towner observes that giving up his plantation is for Ike a "culturally privileged gesture"; "Lucas [Beauchamp] would never do such a thing," *Faulkner on the Color Line: The Later Novels* (Jackson: University Press of Mississippi, 2000), 15.

26. *A Fable* (New York: Random House, 1954), 313.

27. *Light in August*. The Corrected Text (New York: Vintage International, 1990), 350. For previous discussions of this novel see my *The Fragile Thread: The Meaning of Form in Faulkner's Novels* (Amherst: University of Massachusetts Press, 1979), 37–68, and "'What I Chose to Be': Freud, Faulkner, Joe Christmas, and the Abandonment of Design," *Faulkner and Psychology*, ed. Donald M, Kartiganer and Ann J. Abadie (Jackson: University Press of Mississippi, 1994), 288–314.

28. Among the aspects of "gesture" I must postpone for another occasion is that of gender. Immediately obvious, even in this cursory survey of Hemingway and Faulkner, is the fact that gesture is apparently for men only, while action in the real world is for women. To adapt Addie Bundren's famous statement on words and deeds, gesture goes "straight up in a thin line, quick and harmless," whereas action "goes along the earth, clinging to it" (*As I Lay Dying*. The Corrected Text [New York: Vintage International, 1990], 173). The women characters in Hemingway and Faulkner tend to be committed to practical action rather than to the ethereal realms of style. While Harry Walden is regretting his worthless life, blaming

himself and everyone else, and ultimately meditating on the prose he has failed to write, Helen is arranging for smudge pots to be lit for the expected plane, shoots game for food, and encourages Harry not to lose hope. Margot Macomber, while her husband presumably achieves manhood through his readiness to hold his ground against a charging buffalo, at least makes the attempt to believe there is no "importance" in "whether Francis is any good at killing," relegating that particular talent to Wilson, who "is really very impressive killing anything" (8).

Faulkner creates a comparable duality, perhaps more even-handedly, cogently summarized by the character Ephraim in *Intruder in the Dust*: "In fact, you mought bear this in yo mind; someday you mought need it. If you ever needs to get anything done outside the common run, don't waste yo time on the menfolks; get the womens and children to working at it" (*Intruder in the Dust* [New York: Vintage International, 1991], 70). Throughout Faulkner's fiction we find women characters more grounded, more resourceful, far less idealistic, less "gestural" than men: Caddy Compson, as opposed to any of her brothers, Temple as opposed to Horace, Addie as opposed to all her family except possibly Jewel, Lena Grove as opposed to Joe Christmas etc.

Nevertheless, in both Hemingway and Faulkner the gestural mode is central, constituting a vision, a form of perception and courage that is somehow more valuable than practical action. It is certainly arguable that the restriction of that mode to males constitutes an inescapable sexism.

The Faulkner–Hemingway Rivalry

George Monteiro

One of the bravest and best, the strictest in principles, the severest of craftsmen, undeviating in his dedication to his craft; which is to arrest for a believable moment the antics of human beings involved in the comedy and tragedy of being alive. To the few who knew him well he was almost as good a man as the books he wrote. He is not dead. Generations not yet born of young men and women who want to write will refute that word as applied to him.

—Faulkner on Hemingway (1961)[1]

Carlos Baker, Hemingway's first biographer and editor of his letters, reports that Wyndham Lewis's essay on Hemingway in *Men without Art* (1934) so infuriated Hemingway that "he broke a vase of flowers in Sylvia Beach's bookshop."[2] Yet Lewis's "Dumb Ox" essay starts out promisingly enough in Hemingway's favor, one might think, with a comparison of Hemingway and Faulkner as artists: "Ernest Hemingway is a very considerable artist in prose-fiction. Besides this, or with this, his work possesses a penetrating quality, like an animal speaking. Compared often with Hemingway, Faulkner is an excellent, big-strong, novelist: but a conscious artist he cannot be said to be."[3] If much of what came later in Lewis's essay was, in Hemingway's view, offensive, he could not have been entirely unhappy with Lewis's opening formulation. What is relevant to our purposes, however, is that implicit throughout Lewis's essay in his pairing of Hemingway and Faulkner, beyond his recognition that the two Americans were the great forces in contemporary American fiction, is that they were already engaged in what a more recent critic has called an "ongoing subterranean rivalry."[4] Ongoing it undeniably was, with Hemingway "forever shadow-boxing the champion he never met," according to one reader, and Faulkner, for his part, carrying on a "one-sided 'dialogue'" with his most successful contemporary, according to another.[5]

What I propose to do is to look at some of the incidents and episodes—flash points, if you will—of that ongoing rivalry. It offers seldom, if ever, a pretty picture. Those flash points, considered in roughly chronological order, are grouped under headings: "Reading Tips for an Old Lady,"

"Referencing Hemingway," "Faulkner's List," "Just Another Dog," "The Dope on God," "Hawks Don't Share Prizes," "Dr. Hemingstein Teaches," "Death and Suicide," "Courage and the Hemingway Biographer," and, finally, "A Last Word."

Reading Tips for an Old Lady

Unable to get on with his writing in the months following the publication of *A Farewell to Arms* in 1929, Hemingway confessed to his editor, Maxwell Perkins, that he was fearful of losing ground to his contemporaries, especially Faulkner—even if Faulkner did tell the *New York Herald-Tribune* that Hemingway was "the best we've got."[6] For his part, Hemingway could tell Perkins that while Faulkner was "damned good when good," he was "often unnecessary."[7] Fortunately, Hemingway did not know that Perkins, who considered Faulkner to be "a writer of great talent," had already thought of trying to lure Faulkner to Scribners.[8] He had abandoned the idea, explained his fellow editor John Hall Wheelock, only "because he was afraid of arousing Hemingway's jealousy." In Hemingway's mind, "there was no more room in Max's life for another power so threatening as William Faulkner."[9] Hemingway's was "a mighty ego, and Max knew it."[10]

The public face of Hemingway's jealousy began in 1932: in *Death in the Afternoon*, specifically in material Hemingway inserted into his manuscript at a late stage of composition. Hemingway writes: "My operatives tell me that through the fine work of Mr. William Faulkner publishers now will publish anything rather than to try to get you to delete the better portions of your works." Therefore—Hemingway was writing shortly after the successful publication of *Sanctuary* in 1931—"I look forward to writing of those days of my youth which were spent in the finest whorehouses in the land amid the most brilliant society there found." His dialogue with the "Old lady" continues:

> *Old lady*: Has this Mr. Faulkner written well of these places?
> Splendidly, Madame. Mr. Faulkner writes admirably of them. He writes the best of them of any writer I have read for many years.
> *Old lady*: I must buy his works.
> Madame, you can't go wrong on Faulkner. He's prolific too. By the time you get them ordered there'll be new ones out.
> *Old lady*: If they are as you say there cannot be too many.
> Madame, you voice my own opinion.[11]

One Faulkner critic at the time found it strange that Hemingway would adopt such a "sneering" attitude toward Faulkner, that he would exhibit such pettiness, in the form of a "patronising reference to Faulkner in

Death in the Afternoon as a glorifier of bawdy houses."[12] And the novelist-critic Robert Coates complained in the *New Yorker* that the author's exchange with the *Old lady* constituted a jibe at Faulkner ("who has done him no harm save to come under his influence")—an example of malice in which Hemingway's "bitterness descends in petulance."[13] Hemingway fired off a letter to Coates, in which he denied that there were "any cracks against Faulkner."[14] To attack Faulkner was in no way his intention, he insisted disingenuously, for the implications of his words are unmistakably clear: Faulkner writes too quickly, too hurriedly, to write well—after all, his next book always comes out before you have time to finish reading his last one—indicating, perhaps, that as an artist he is undiscriminating and undisciplined. It is of course Hemingway who has a stone in his shoe. Since Hemingway's last book, in 1929, Faulkner had published *The Sound and the Fury, As I Lay Dying, Sanctuary, These Thirteen,* and *Light in August*. Conveniently, Hemingway forgot, repressed, or just did not bother to remember, what he had once said to the artist Henry Strater: he did not understand how writers like Faulkner could express themselves so freely. "It just comes out of them," he marveled, "as though they were evacuating their bowels."[15] Excrement in its various forms and many names turned out, in the long run, to be Hemingway's metaphor of choice when talking about Faulkner's work. To one correspondent, for instance, he likened *A Fable*, the war novel that earned Faulkner a Pulitzer Prize, to "the night soil from Chungking."[16]

Referencing Hemingway

One way of approaching Faulkner's 1939 novel, published as *The Wild Palms*, is to see it as a comprehensive parody of Hemingway. Faulkner himself made it certain that the knowing reader would discern the connection with Hemingway by referring to his rival's fabled style (and subject matter, I think). His tough-minded Chicago newspaperman, McCord, makes it explicit when he says, mock-heroically, "Set, ye amourous sons, in a sea of hemingwaves"—"hemingwaves" suggesting "short waves," perhaps, or the staccato sounds of Morse code.[17]

Faulkner insisted that his novel tells a single story on a familiar romantic theme. As he described it in the *Paris Review* interview attributed to Jean Stein, *The Wild Palms* is "one story—the story of Charlotte Rittenmeyer and Harry Wilbourne, who sacrificed everything for love, and then lost that."[18] But that one story, told experimentally in two separate yet thematically complementary narratives, breaks into two—a straightforwardly naturalistic tragedy and a wildly comic send-up of the theme of "all for love." Moreover, as others have noticed, the book parodies

Hemingway's very popular novel of 1929, *A Farewell to Arms*. Hemingway's childbirth scene becomes a botched abortion, his noble, grieving Henry becomes a confused, grieving Harry, an idealized, submissive Catherine hardens into the determined, domineering Charlotte, and a well-planned journey by rowboat across a lake to safety in another country becomes a helter-skelter odyssey over a raging river flood.

To the best of my knowledge, nowhere—in interviews or correspondence—does Hemingway refer to Faulkner's "sea of hemingwaves." But that he knew the book is suggested by the fact that there is a copy of *The Wild Palms*, along with thirteen other Faulkner titles, in Hemingway's personal library at the Finca Vigía farm in Cuba.[19] My suspicion is that Hemingway was emboldened by the novel's ingeniously realized final scene, in which the imprisoned hero masturbates, to introduce a masturbation scene into *For Whom the Bell Tells*, the novel Hemingway started to write two months after *The Wild Palms* was published. There is no point in looking for that scene in Hemingway's novel, however, for Hemingway—to meet the objections of his editors—carefully rewrote the "passage of onanism to make one of the love scenes less offensive."[20] But what is more interesting is that Hemingway, in other late revisions to his manuscript, rewrote several love scenes to make them not less suggestively sexual but more so. It is tempting to think that here again it was Faulkner's writing in *The Wild Palms* that encouraged Hemingway to move toward greater experimentation, to create a language that conveyed the sensuality of sexual behavior more precisely without resorting to literal descriptions of the mechanics of intercourse or other sexual acts. What I have in mind, in particular, is the writing in the more rhythmical of the "earth-moved" passages.

Faulkner's List

Faulkner, biding his time, had offered no immediate response, at least publicly, to Hemingway's sniping in *Death in the Afternoon*. Some years later he emulated Scott Fitzgerald, perhaps unwittingly, in compiling a list of the best writers of his time. Asked to comment on the literary situation in America in 1936, Fitzgerald had answered: "Ernest Hemingway, I think, is the greatest living writer of English.... Next comes Thomas Wolfe and then Faulkner and Dos Passos."[21] Meeting with students at the University of Mississippi in 1947, Faulkner was coaxed into offering his own version of Fitzgerald's list. Asked to name the five most important writers among his contemporaries, he ventured:

> 1. Thomas Wolfe; 2. Dos Passos; 3. Hemingway; 4. Cather; 5. Steinbeck. (To the above questioner, a teacher auditing the class turned and added after the above

listing: "I am afraid you are taxing Mr. Faulkner's modesty." Mr. Faulkner then listed them this way:)
1. Thomas Wolfe—he had much courage, wrote as if he didn't have long to live. 2. William Faulkner. 3. Dos Passos. 4. Hemingway—he has no courage, has never climbed out on a limb. He has never used a word where the reader might check his usage by a dictionary. 5. Steinbeck—I had great hopes for him at one time. Now I don't know.[22]

The mischief in all this is that on this second try Faulkner did not limit himself to emending his list so as to include his own name, but chose to annotate his choices as he went along, developing reasons for his rankings. Remarkably, on numerous other occasions in later years Faulkner would repeat his list, sometimes varying the rankings, but never once placing Hemingway first, as Fitzgerald had done, or even elevating him to second place.[23]

Faulkner's reason for listing Hemingway consistently at or below the median was of course even more galling to Hemingway than the ranking itself. For Hemingway, who had coined the still celebrated phrase "grace under pressure," the charge that he lacked courage went right to the heart of what most mattered to him. Faulkner had cautiously indicated that it was lack of courage in his writing that fixed him in the rankings, but Hemingway chose to construe Faulkner's remarks (accurately, I think) as impugning his manhood all round. So vehemently did Hemingway react to Faulkner's characterization of his writing—the list had been sent out to the world in a press release—that he enlisted the aid of his friend Brigadier General Charles "Buck" Lanham in an ill-advised effort to refute it.[24] Immediately Lanham wrote to Faulkner, complaining that he found it very difficult to understand "how anyone in writing of Ernest could say, 'He has no courage; he has never climbed out on a limb.'" Hemingway's whole life, Lanham points out, belies that statement—"his early days in the professional prizering; his combat experience in World War I; his fighting record with the Loyalists in Spain; his anti-submarine work in the Caribbean in the early part of World War II; his large number of hours in the air in an RAF Mosquito working over the Rocket Coast; and his subsequent work with our Army starting with the assault on the Normandy Coast on D-Day." Lanham could tell, in "a person-to-person conversation," of Hemingway's "many deeds of derring-do" performed while with his regiment, but these things, for some mysterious reason, cannot be put in writing. Nevertheless, he concludes, "Ernest Hemingway is without exception the most courageous man I have ever known, both in war and in peace. He has physical courage, and he has that far rarer commodity, moral courage. Finally, I might add this: I have never known a more truthful man or a more generous one."[25]

Except for what Lanham had actually witnessed, the good General had taken Hemingway's word about his life experiences at face value. Hemingway *was* wounded in World War I but he had not fought in battle. He was never a very good boxer, let alone a professional prizefighter. But Hemingway had pretty much done everything else. Lanham's most significant claim, however, was that Hemingway possessed not merely great physical courage but moral courage as well.

In the context of Lanham's letter, Hemingway's unquestioning acceptance as factual what is now known to be Faulkner's largely spurious military record during World War I looms large. Had Hemingway known the truth, it can be surmised, he would not have been so utterly vulnerable to what he deemed to be Faulkner's unfair criticism, nor would he have forgone the opportunity to impugn Faulkner's own claims to overseas experience during World War I. As it was, Hemingway had to resort to questioning Faulkner's bravery as a hunter. When he was sent a copy of *Big Woods*, he pretended to send its author a message through the critic Harvey Breit: "please tell him that I found them [the stories] very well written and delicately perceived but that I would be a little more moved if he hunted animals that ran both ways."[26]

General Lanham's letter to Faulkner did not go unanswered. Faulkner knew all about Hemingway's wartime exploits, "of his record in two wars and in Spain, too," he explained, but what he had meant when he referred to his contemporary's lack of courage was something else. "The statement ... was incomplete as you saw it, and in its original shape it had no reference whatever to Hemingway as a man," he claimed: "only to his craftsmanship as a writer."[27] Faulkner copied this letter to Hemingway, accompanied by a note of apology: "I'm sorry of this damn stupid thing. I was just making $250.00, I thought informally, not for publication, or I would have insisted on looking at the stuff before it was released. I have believed for years that the human voice has caused all human ills and I thought I had broken myself of talking. Maybe this will be my valedictory lesson."[28] Oddly, the language of this apology would reemerge, as will be seen, in Faulkner's Nobel Prize acceptance speech.

Hemingway's reply to Faulkner, by return mail, starts out in a conciliatory way, but it soon becomes clear that Faulkner's apology has not mollified him. Moreover, not entirely content with Lanham's argument on his behalf, Hemingway decides to argue his own case. He took risks in *For Whom the Bell Tolls*, he insists, notably in those scenes centering on the woman Pilar. "Probably bore the shit out of you to re-read," he jokes, "but as brother would like to know what you think." Even more importantly, he wants to set Faulkner straight about the two writers at or near the top of Faulkner's list: "I know what you mean about T. Wolfe and Dos [Passos] and still can't agree." Wolfe he brushes off in one short sentence: "I never felt the link-up in Wolfe except with the N.C. stuff." But the author of *U.S.A.* requires more detail, including stuff only an insider will know. "Dos I always liked and respected and thought was a 2nd rate writer on acct. no ear," he begins. "2nd rate boxer has no left hand, same as ear to writer, and so gets his brains knocked out and this happened to Dos with every book. Also terrible snob (on acct. of being a bastard) (which I would welcome) and very worried about his negro blood when could have been our best negro writer if would have just been negro as hope *we* would have."[29]

Just Another Dog

In the 1950s Hemingway's distrust of Faulkner surfaced once again. When the *New York Times* asked Faulkner to comment on *The Old Man and the Sea*, Hemingway's rival came up with a very strange statement:

> A few years ago, I forget what the occasion was, Hemingway said that writers should stick together just as doctors and lawyers and wolves do. I think there is more wit in that than truth or necessity either, at least in Hemingway's case, since the sort of writers who need to band together willy nilly or perish, resemble the wolves who are wolves only in pack, and, singly, are just another dog.
>
> Because the man who wrote the MEN WITHOUT WOMEN pieces and THE SUN ALSO RISES and A FAREWELL TO ARMS and FOR WHOM THE BELL TOLLS and most of the African stuff and most of all the rest of it, is not one of these, and needs no pack protection.
>
> So he gets this for free from one who, regardless of how he rated what remained, has never doubted the integrity of it, and who has always affirmed that no man will be quicker and harsher to judge what remained than the man who wrote MEN WITHOUT WOMEN and THE SUN ALSO RISES and A FAREWELL TO ARMS and FOR WHOM THE BELL TOLLS and the best of the African stuff and most of the rest of it; and that if even what remained had not been as honest and true as he could make it, then he himself would have burned the manuscript before the publisher ever saw it.[30]

Detecting in this piece still another instance of Faulkner's treachery, Hemingway immediately fired off a protest to the well-intentioned Harvey Breit, the critic who had sent him Faulkner's piece in the first place, hoping thereby to effect some modicum of rapprochement between the competing writers. Faulkner "did not forget what the occasion was that I wrote him that," Hemingway corrected. "He remembers it very well. In one of his rummy moments (I hope) he had said, flatly, that I was a coward. The Trib picked it up (the lecture was reprinted) and I sent it to Brig. Gen. C. T. Lanham, former commander of the 22nd Infantry Regt. We had been together a long time in 1944–5 and I let him write Faulkner. We both received apologies from Faulkner." On that occasion, Hemingway points out, he had written Faulkner "a friendly letter." It is from that letter that Faulkner quotes, Hemingway clarifies, but now he talks of writers who "'resemble the wolves who are wolves only in pack, and singly, are just another Dog.' Figure that one out."

Then Hemingway turns to what he calls "the record." Faulkner spoke well of him once, he concedes. "But that was before he was given the Nobel Prize. When I read he had won that, I sent him as good a cable of congratulations as I know how to write. He never acknowledged it. For years I had built him up in Europe. Any time anyone asked me who was the best American writer I told them Faulkner." Moreover, Hemingway had never told anyone, he reveals, that Faulkner "couldn't go nine innings, nor why, nor what I knew was wrong with him since always.... He is a good writer when he is good and could be better than anyone if he knew how to finish a book." But he wishes him the luck that he needs "because he has the one great and un-curable defect; you can't re-read him. When you re-read him you are conscious all the time of how he fooled you the first time."[31]

Still restive—even after two days—Hemingway writes, again to Harvey Breit, that he is "fed on that County." "Anything that needs genealogical tables to explain it is a little bit like James Branch Cabell. Then if you need the longest sentence in the world to give a book distinction you might as well hire Bill Veek [Veeck] and have midgets. As a technician I would say that sentence was not a sentence. It was made of many, many sentences. But when he came to the end of a sentence he simply did not put in the period." In fact, when he reads Faulkner, he claims, he can "tell exactly" when he got tired and did it—the writing—"on corn." "But that is one of the things I thought writers should not tell out-siders. But he did not understand about writers sticking together against out-siders. It is not a question of log-rolling or speaking well of each other. It is a question of knowing what is wrong with a guy and still sticking with what is good in him and not letting the out-siders in on *secrets proffesionel*."[32]

The Dope on God

When the editor of the literary journal *Shenandoah* asked Faulkner to review *The Old Man and the Sea*, he at first hesitated but then complied. This was Hemingway's "best," Faulkner pronounces. "Time may show it to be the best single piece of any of us, I mean his and my contemporaries," for "this time, he discovered God, a Creator." "Until now," he explains, "his men and women had made themselves, shaped themselves out of their own clay; their victories and defeats were at the hands of each other, just to prove to themselves or one another how tough they could be. But this time, he wrote about pity: about something somewhere that made them all: the old man who had to catch the fish and then lose it, the fish that had to be caught and then lost, the sharks which had to rob the old man of his fish; made them all and loved them all and pitied them all."[33]

Hemingway was having none of this "curt, mock-humble puff," as one Hemingway biographer calls Faulkner's review, especially his allusions to the Divinity.[34] "When Bill Faulkner talks about God as though he knew him intimately and had the word," Hemingway later explained to Charles Poore, "I would have to answer that I do not know. . . . Sometimes I have a few ideas but I do not know and sometimes I think it is like one time when an old Indian asked me, 'You Indian boy?' I said, 'Sure.' He said, 'Long time ago good. Now no good.'"[35] Incidentally, included in Blotner's edition of Faulkner's letters is the draft for a telegram congratulating Hemingway on receiving the Pulitzer Prize for *The Old Man and the Sea*. There is no evidence to indicate that it was ever sent.[36]

Faulkner continued to be Hemingway's principal target. In a letter to Lillian Ross, who had profiled Hemingway in the *New Yorker*, he drags in Faulkner to shore up his own disclaimer regarding all matters pertaining to God: "I cannot help out very much with the true dope on God as I have never played footy-footy with him; nor been a cane brake God hopper; nor won the Nobel prize." His best advice is "get the true word on God from Mr. Faulkner." "It is quite possible that Mr. Faulkner sits at table with him each night and that the deity comforts him if he has a bad dream and wipes his mouth and helps him eat his corn pone or hominy grits or wheaties in the morning. I hope Mr. Faulkner never forgets himself and gives it to the deity with his corn cob. . . . Faulkner has always been fairly fraudulent but it is only recently that he has introduced God when he is conning people."[37]

After these unseemly jibes at Faulkner as Benjy at his breakfast and Popeye in the crib, Hemingway turns to Faulkner's failure to understand Santiago. "The Old Man in the story was born a Catholic," he writes, "but he certainly believed in something more than the church and I do not think Mr. Faulkner understands it very well. He talks like a convert or a man afraid to die." Hemingway's only wishes for Faulkner are that he "not continue to write after he has lost his talent" and that he be given "the grace of a happy death."[38] But these words are for Miss Ross's ears alone, he advises, not to be conveyed to Faulkner. He signs his letter "H. von H.," an abbreviated form of "Huck von Hemingstein."

Hawks Don't Share Prizes

The Faulkner–Hemingway competition pervaded their utterly different and opposing Nobel Prize acceptance speeches. Faulkner, the first to receive the Prize, laments that young writers have "forgotten the problems of the human heart in conflict with itself which alone can make good writing because only that is worth writing about, worth the agony and the sweat." Such a writer, who "labors under a curse," must return to "the old verities and truths of the heart," he insisted, "the old universal truths lacking which any story is ephemeral and doomed—love and honor and pity and pride and compassion and sacrifice." For the writer's "privilege" is "to help man endure by lifting his heart, by reminding him of the courage and honor and hope and pride and compassion and pity and sacrifice which have been the glory of his past."[39] There was nothing new in this, for Faulkner always wrote about the old verities and absolutes of the heart—glory, sacrifice, honor, and courage. But on this occasion, if I read him correctly, he was also echoing Frederic Henry, whose rejection of wartime talk about those absolutes occurs in one of the most celebrated passages in Hemingway's fiction. "I was always embarrassed by the words sacred, glorious, and sacrifice and the expression in vain. . . . Abstract words such as glory, honor, courage, or hallow were obscene beside the concrete names of villages, the numbers of roads, the names of rivers, the numbers of regiments and the dates."[40]

But there was also something else in Faulkner's speech that must have struck Hemingway as rather odd. Toward the end of his peroration Faulkner says, famously: "when the last ding-dong of doom has clanged and faded from the last worthless rock hanging tideless in the last red and dying evening . . . even then there will still be *one more sound: that of his puny inexhaustible voice, still talking*. . . . I believe that man will not merely endure; he will prevail. He is immortal, not because he alone among creatures has *an inexhaustible voice*, but because he has a soul, a spirit capable of compassion and sacrifice and endurance."[41] There are echoes here, especially striking to the student interested in the Faulkner-Hemingway rivalry, of the terms in which Faulkner apologized to Hemingway only three years earlier. Could Hemingway have missed in Faulkner's speech the echo of his apology: "I have believed for years that the human voice has caused all human ills and I thought I had broken myself of talking"?

Hemingway's own Nobel Prize acceptance speech, four years later, does not, of course, mention Faulkner. Too ill to travel to Stockholm to receive his prize in person, Hemingway turned his absence to personal and professional advantage. "A writer should write what he has to say and not speak it," he warns, for the true writer, who perforce works alone, must defeat the temptation to turn himself into a public spokesman. (That summer Faulkner had traveled to South America at the behest of the United States State Department.) Shedding his loneliness by joining groups may help a writer grow "in public stature," he acknowledges, but his work will deteriorate. "For he does his work alone and if he is a good enough writer he must face eternity, or the lack of it, each day. For a true writer each book should be a new beginning where he tries again for something that is beyond attainment. He should always try for something that has never been done or that others have tried and failed. Then sometimes, with great luck, he will succeed."[42] It goes without saying that such writers do their work alone, not as members of a pack.

Dr. Hemingstein Teaches

Sad to say, even receiving the Nobel Prize in 1954 did not put to an end Hemingway's animosity toward Faulkner or his contentious skepticism toward anything Faulkner said on virtually any subject. Asked in 1956 to write an introduction to a collective edition of his short stories, Hemingway produced a piece that his editors, when they saw it, deemed so unequivocally inappropriate that rather than publishing it they decided to scrap the whole project. In "The Art of the Short Story," which remained unpublished until it appeared in the *Paris Review* in 1981, Hemingway assumes the situation of a classroom or lecture hall. As lecturer he takes questions from his listeners, all of them eager, presumably, to learn the tricks of the writing trade. As it happens, *Faulkner in the University*—subtitled *Class Conferences at the University of Virginia*—had just come out.

Hemingway admits that he has not always been above touting Faulkner. "When they didn't know him in Europe, I told them all how he was the best we had and so forth and I over-humbled with him plenty and built him up about as high as he could go because he never had a break then and he was good then." Now, however, whenever Faulkner "has a few shots, he'll tell students what's wrong with me or tell Japanese or anybody they send him to, to build up our local product. I get tired of this but I figure what the hell he's had a few shots and maybe he even believes it." Then his imagined students ask him an imagined question: What *does* he think of Faulkner? The professor answers, reluctantly, he implies: Faulkner "cons himself sometimes pretty bad. . . . For quite a while when he hits the sauce toward the end of a book, it shows bad. He gets tired and he goes on and on, and the sauce writing is really hard on who has to read it. I mean if they care about writing. I thought maybe it would help if I read it using the sauce myself, but it wasn't any help. Maybe it would have helped if I was fourteen. But I was only fourteen one year and then I would have been too busy. So that's what I think about Faulkner." He will admit, though, that "The Bear" is "a really fine story," one that he would be pleased to put in his book if he had written it—"but you can't write them all, Jack." Then he takes one last swipe, recalling, perhaps, Faulkner's unsatisfactory apology for his remarks at the University of Mississippi in 1947: "He's easy to handle because he talks so much for a supposed silent man. Never talk, Jack, if you are a writer, unless you have the guy write it down and have you go over it. Otherwise, they get it wrong. That's what you think until they play a tape back at you. Then you know how silly it sounds. You're a writer aren't you? Okay, shut up and write."[43]

Of this and other gratuitous, even egregious, attacks on Faulkner, Michael Reynolds writes: "Whenever he dug up his old grievance with Faulkner, he was usually on the dark side of his emotional curve. Faulkner, he claimed, was always making disparaging remarks about him but maybe that was just the 'sauce' talking. That was Faulkner's problem: he drank too much and wrote when he was drunk. That and he talked too much. A writer, said Ernest while doing the same, should never talk too much."[44]

In the year after Hemingway was awarded the Nobel Prize, Faulkner's list resurfaced several times, mainly as the result of an interview Faulkner accorded the *New York Times*. Audiences in Tokyo, Nagano, and Paris, and students in Charlottesville kept bringing up the matter of what Faulkner had meant by his list, and Faulkner never failed to accommodate them with his by now boilerplate answer.

Death and Suicide

Since Faulkner survived Hemingway, he had a last word, if not the final one. At West Point, in his own last year, Faulkner was asked if he thought that Hemingway's death was accidental. He answered thoughtfully. No, he did not think so, for in death Hemingway had followed "a deliberate pattern," just "as all his work was a deliberate pattern." "I think that every man wants to be at least as good as what he writes," he continued. "And I'm inclined to think that Ernest felt that at this time, this was the right thing, in grace and dignity, to do. I don't agree with him. I think that no man can say until the end of his life whether he's written out or not."[45] Notably, Faulkner fetched in the word "grace," a word quintessential to Hemingway's ethos. But note as well that the writer who had failed to take chances had also failed himself, decided his old rival, when he refused to face his unknown future by ending his life.[46]

Courage and the Hemingway Biographer

With Faulkner's own death a year after Hemingway's, their competition could have, and should have, come to an end. More than three decades after the deaths of its principals, however, it continues to figure, though not exclusively so, in books by Hemingway's critics and biographers. It is apparent that what Faulkner did and said—especially his questioning of Hemingway's courage—cut more deeply into Hemingway's sense of himself than anything Hemingway ever said or did affected Faulkner. Or so it seems, given the record as we now have it, and granting, of course, that much of what Hemingway said about Faulkner never reached his rival's ears. As a result, the Hemingway-Faulkner rivalry features a great deal less in Faulkner's biography than it does in Hemingway's.

It will be recalled that General Lanham in his 1947 letter to Faulkner distinguished between physical courage and moral courage, attesting to Hemingway's possession of both kinds. While Hemingway chose, at first, to believe that Faulkner had questioned his physical courage, Faulkner, for his part, insisted that it was the writer in Hemingway who had not been courageous enough to move beyond what he had already done well and could do again. When Hemingway did not venture into unknown territory, sail out into strange and dangerous seas, it was clear that Hemingway's fault was that he lacked a writer's moral courage. Having struck a nerve, Faulkner never took anything back. Even his public praise for some of Hemingway's work—the novels and stories of the 1920s, the African writing, *Across the River and into the Trees*, and *The Old Man and the Sea*—did not address, let alone erase, the charge first leveled in 1947 and voiced numerous times thereafter.

Faulkner's charge has figured, not only in the assessments of Hemingway's writing and character by literary critics and historians, but, preeminently, in the work of Hemingway's biographers. One instance will suffice, that of Michael Reynolds, whose biography of Hemingway runs to five volumes. Reynolds, in my opinion, is as objective and fair-minded as a biographer deeply sympathetic to his subject can possibly be. Not surprisingly, there is much in the last two volumes of his biography, *The 1930s* and *The Final Years,* that has as its primary intent the validation of Hemingway's popular reputation for physical courage. Each one of the instances in which Hemingway has been credited with having acted courageously in the face of great danger to himself and others—on-the-spot reporting during the Spanish Civil War, patrolling the seas looking for German U-boats, fighting with ground troops in the Hüertgenwald attack—is thoroughly investigated and, by and large, confirmed.

But Reynolds's investigations and confirmations are not limited to the question of Hemingway's physical courage. Reynolds argues as well against Faulkner's charge that Hemingway the writer lacked the courage to "try for the impossible"—Faulkner's words in 1955.[47] With every book, Reynolds argues, Hemingway as artist and craftsman had tried to do something he had never done before—that, in effect, he had had the moral courage to keep trying to do work that surpassed anything he had already accomplished. In *The Final Years* Reynolds sums up his defense of Hemingway the risk-taker. He looks back at what Hemingway had already accomplished by mid-April 1945, when the war in Europe was finally over and, after a lapse of almost five years, he could now look forward to resuming his work as a writer of fiction:

> In the previous twenty years he had published three collections of short stories, a satire (*The Torrents of Spring*), a roman à clef (*The Sun Also Rises*), a semihistorical novel (*A Farewell to Arms*), a book of natural history (*Death in the Afternoon*), a safari book (*Green Hills of Africa*), a semiproletariat novel (*To Have and Have Not*), and a play (*The Fifth Column*). *For Whom the Bell Tolls* was his epic novel just as "The Snows of Kilimanjaro" was his epic short story: in both, he gave the reader a story within which was embedded an entire collection of short stories. The critics who said he repeated himself were missing the obvious.

The truth of the matter, according to Reynolds, was that Hemingway had always pushed the limits of his craft and would continue to do so. "Always experimenting, always reaching beyond his last effort, Hemingway had never repeated the form," concludes Reynolds, "and he was not about to start."[48]

It occurs to me that no student of Faulkner's work has found it necessary to construct such an apology for its author—for the moral courage Faulkner displayed in devising his various styles and composing his innovative and highly original books. One could say that, in a sense, Faulkner himself had discovered the exact terms by which his rivalry with Hemingway might serve him in the shaping of his own lasting reputation.

And how did Faulkner's list serve Hemingway, if it did serve him in any useful way? The question can be best answered indirectly. In the years after 1945, it has been emphasized, Hemingway "referred repeatedly" to Marcel Proust.[49] *Remembrance of Things Past* is surely, in its own uncommon and brilliant way, one of those few works that comes close to fulfilling Faulkner's impossible desideratum for the writers of his or any generation: "to say it all before he dies . . . to try to put all the experience of the human heart on the head of a pin."[50]

Reynolds's *Final Years* volume rests on an important conviction about its subject. Hemingway had started out knowing that his writing began with "one true sentence," and he once wrote about a dying writer who thought "you might put it all into one paragraph if you could get it right," but in the years remaining to him after the end of World War II he set out to "say it all" in one massive, complexly structured, thematically interrelated work to be published at some future date in a series of volumes.[51] Reynolds writes critically of the hostile reaction of many readers and critics to the individual titles culled from the thousands of pages of manuscript that Hemingway left "in the vault" and published posthumously. Aimed at a market bullish for Hemingway, these works were cut, rearranged, and edited according to editorial principles that were problematic at best. Not even *A Moveable Feast*, it was argued, can be said to honor Hemingway's final intentions.

To all those who, afterwards, decided that Hemingway left these books unfinished because he was no longer able to make the final revisions they required, Reynolds has this to say: "To make that judgment one must ignore the talent and diversity at work in *The Old Man and the Sea*, *Across the River*, and the posthumous *A Moveable Feast*. One must also ignore the massive revisions he made to the Bimini novel, and completely disregard the possibility that these 'unfinished' novels were linked in ways that made their endings interdependent. Under no financial pressure to bring any of these books to completion, he always imagined there would be time to finish them." These novels "were to be his legacy, his most complex undertaking. It was like working a crossword puzzle in three dimensions. All he needed was time, which, unfortunately, was no longer on his side."[52]

A Last Word

While in Japan in 1955 Faulkner claimed to have seen an old woman beneath the gate outside the Temple selling peanuts to tourists who would feed them to the pigeons. In this woman—his stand-in for Hemingway's "Old Lady" in *Death in the Afternoon*, if you will—Faulkner saw "a face worn with living and remembering... a face durable and now even a comfort to her, as if it had by now blotted up whatever had ever ached or sorrowed behind it, leaving it free now of the anguishes and the griefs and the enduring." "Here is one anyway," he concluded, "who never read Faulkner and neither knows nor cares why he came to Japan nor gives one single damn what he thinks of Ernest Hemingway."[53]

NOTES

1. "Authors and Critics Appraise Works," *New York Times* (July 3, 1961), 6.
2. *Ernest Hemingway, Selected Letters, 1917–1961*, ed. Carlos Baker (New York: Scribners, 1981), 264 note.

3. Wyndham Lewis, "The Dumb Ox: A Study of Ernest Hemingway," *Life and Letters* 10 (April 1934): 33–45, in *Hemingway: The Critical Heritage*, ed. Jeffrey Meyers (London: Routledge and Kegan Paul, 1982), 186–209. The quotation comes from the Critical Heritage volume, 186.

4. Daniel J. Singal, *William Faulkner: The Making of a Modernist* (Chapel Hill: University of North Carolina Press, 1997), 235.

5. Thomas L. McHaney, "Watching for the Dixie Limited: Faulkner's Impact upon the Creative Writer," in *Fifty Years of Yoknapatawpha: Faulkner and Yoknapatawpha 1979*, ed. Doreen Fowler and Ann J. Abadie (Jackson: University Press of Mississippi, 1980), 242–43; and William Van O'Connor, "Faulkner's One-sided 'Dialogue' with Hemingway," *College English* 24 (December 1962): 208–15. See also M. Thomas Inge, "The Dixie Limited: Writers on Faulkner and His Influence," *Faulkner Journal of Japan* 1 (May 1999)—www.senshu-u.ac.jp/~thbo559/IngeRevd.htm.

6. *Lion in the Garden: Interviews with William Faulkner, 1926–1962*, ed. James B. Meriwether and Michael Millgate (Lincoln: University of Nebraska Press, 1980), 21.

7. Joseph Blotner, *Faulkner: A Biography*, 1-vol. ed. (New York: Random House, 1984), 275–76.

8. A. Scott Berg, *Max Perkins: Editor of Genius* (New York: Dutton, 1978), 180.

9. Ibid., 181.

10. Blotner, *Faulkner*, 1-vol. ed., 276.

11. Ernest Hemingway, *Death in the Afternoon* (New York: Scribners, 1932), 173.

12. Laurence Bell, "Faulkner in Moronia," *Literary America* (May 1934): 15–18; reprinted in *William Faulkner: The Critical Heritage*, ed. John Bassett (London: Routledge and Kegan Paul, 1975), 165–69. The quotation comes from the Critical Heritage volume, 166.

13. R[obert] M. C[oates], "Bullfighters," *New Yorker* 8 (October 1, 1932): 61–63; reprinted in Meyers, *Hemingway: Critical Heritage*, 160–62. The quotation comes from the Critical Heritage volume, 161.

14. Hemingway, *Selected Letters*, 368. Hemingway's letter appeared in Coates's "Style versus Stodginess," *New Yorker* 8 (November 5, 1932): 85–87.

15. Henry Strater, "Hemingway," *Art in America* 49, No. 4 (1961): 84–85; quoted in Scott Donaldson, *By Force of Will: The Life and Art of Ernest Hemingway* (New York: Viking, 1977), 252.

16. Hemingway, *Selected Letters*, 864 note.

17. William Faulkner, *The Wild Palms* (New York: Random House, 1939), 97. Links between Faulkner's novel and Hemingway's fiction are identified in Carlos Baker, *Hemingway: The Writer as Artist* (Princeton: Princeton University Press, 1952), 205–6; H. Edward Richardson, "The 'Hemingwaves' in Faulkner's 'Wild Palms,'" *Modern Fiction Studies* 4 (Winter 1958–59): 357–60; W. R. Moses, "Water, Water Everywhere: 'Old Man' and 'A Farewell to Arms,'" *Modern Fiction Studies* 5 (Summer 1959): 172–74; Hyatt H. Waggoner, *William Faulkner: From Jefferson to the World* (Lexington: University of Kentucky Press, 1959), 134–36; Edmond L. Volpe, *A Reader's Guide to William Faulkner* (New York: Farrar, Straus, 1964), 214–15, 227–30; Thomas L. McHaney, "Anderson, Hemingway, and Faulkner's *The Wild Palms*," *PMLA* 87 (May 1972): 465–74 (reprinted as "Anderson, Hemingway, and the Origins of *The Wild Palms*," the first chapter of *William Faulkner's "The Wild Palms": A Study* [Jackson: University Press of Mississippi, 1975], 3–24); and Singal, *Making of a Modernist*, 235–44.

18. Jean Stein vanden Heuvel, "William Faulkner," in *Writers at Work: The Paris Review Interviews*, ed. Malcolm Cowley (New York: Viking, 1959), 133.

19. The fourteen Faulkner titles found in the library at Hemingway's farm in Cuba are *Absalom, Absalom!*, *As I Lay Dying*, *Big Woods*, *Collected Stories of William Faulkner*, *A Fable*, *Go Down, Moses*, *Light in August*, *The Mansion*, *The Portable Faulkner*, *Pylon*, *Sanctuary*, *Soldiers' Pay*, *The Unvanquished*, and *The Wild Palms* (*Hemingway's Library: A Composite Record*, compiled by James D. Brasch and Joseph Sigman [New York: Garland, 1981], 119–20).

20. Carlos Baker, *Ernest Hemingway: A Life Story* (New York: Scribners, 1969), 351. See also George Monteiro, "'Between Grief and Nothing': Hemingway and Faulkner,"

Hemingway Notes 1 (Spring 1971): 13–15; and Thomas E. Gould, "'A Tiny Operation with Great Effect': Authorial Revision and Editorial Emasculation in the Manuscript of Hemingway's *For Whom the Bell Tolls*," in *Blowing the Bridge: Essays on Hemingway and "For Whom the Bell Tolls*," ed. Rena Sanderson (New York: Greenwood, 1992), 78–81.

21. Michel Mok, "The Other Side of Paradise," *New York Post* (September 25, 1936); reprinted as "'A Writer Like Me Must Have an Utter Confidence, an Utter Faith in His Star,'" in *F. Scott Fitzgerald in His Own Time: A Miscellany*, ed. Matthew J. Bruccoli and Jackson R. Bryer (New York: Popular Library, 1971), 299.

22. Meriwether and Millgate, *Lion in the Garden*, 58.

23. Faulkner's "list" appears in various forms in Meriwether and Millgate, *Lion in the Garden*, 81, 88–91, 121–22, 179–80, and 225; *Faulkner in the University: Class Conferences at the University of Virginia, 1957–1958*, ed. Frederick L. Gwynn and Joseph L. Blotner (Charlottesville: University of Virginia Press, 1959), 143–44, 206–7; and *Conversations with William Faulkner*, ed. M. Thomas Inge (Jackson: University Press of Mississippi, 1999), 46, 64, 71, 79–80, 138, and 148.

24. Marvin M. Black's press release is reproduced in Louis Daniel Brodsky, *William Faulkner, Life Glimpses* (Austin: University of Texas Press, 1990), 91.

25. Brodsky, *Life Glimpses*, 94–95.

26. Hemingway, *Selected Letters*, 850. It was not until well after Hemingway's death that a disinterested critic of major prominence came forth to defend Hemingway against Faulkner's charges. In 1970 Irving Howe, the author of an early book on Faulkner, wrote: "Despite Faulkner's notorious and unjustified slur, Hemingway did take risks. He took the risk of moving beyond the relative safety of his stylization and of trying not merely for the large novel as a form but also for what the large novel implies: a commanding idea or vision about man's place in society" ("Great Man Going Down," *Harper's* 241 [October 1970]: 120–25; reprinted in Meyers, *Hemingway: Critical Heritage*, 566–72. The quotation comes from the Critical Heritage volume, 571).

27. Brodsky, *Life Glimpses*, 95.

28. Ibid., 96.

29. Hemingway, *Selected Letters*, 623–24. Hemingway offered his opinion of Wolfe, "a great child," in letters to Maxwell Perkins, beginning in 1932 when he reminded Perkins that "Geniuses" of Wolfe's sort are always "a hell of a responsibility." A year later he wrote: "Glad you've got Tom Wolfe to the printers but I swear to God that last story in the magazine opened in the phoniest way and had the most Christ-awful grandiloquent title of anything I ever read ["Dark in the Forest, Strange as Time," *Scribner's Magazine*, August 1934]. You know why your geniuses stall so long and are afraid to publish may very well be because they have a big fear inside of them that it's phoney instead of being a World Masterpiece and are afraid somebody will find it out." When Wolfe left Scribners for Harpers in 1938, Hemingway no longer had to worry about Wolfe's competition for the attention of the editor they had been sharing. He then acknowledged Wolfe's defection simply: "Am sorry about the Tom Wolfe business. All I know is what I read in Time. I guess he is like Franco [of Spain]. He got to believeing [sic] his own communiques" (*The Only Thing That Counts: The Ernest Hemingway/Maxwell Perkins Correspondence, 1925–1947*, ed. Matthew J. Bruccoli [New York: Scribner, 1996], 180, 214, 253).

Remarkably, Faulkner, too, had "no particular great admiration for Wolfe." "To tell the truth," he confessed, "I haven't read much of Wolfe. I've read one or two of his stories. I've opened his books and read pages or paragraphs" (Gwynn and Blotner, *Faulkner in the University*, 143, 206). Faulkner's fullest explanation of why he always placed Wolfe at the top of his notorious list appears in Richard Walser's *The Enigma of Thomas Wolfe: Biographical and Critical Selections* (Cambridge: Harvard University Press, 1953), vii.

30. *Selected Letters of William Faulkner*, ed. Joseph Blotner (New York: Random House, 1977), 333–34. Faulkner's statement incorporates notions expressed in his letter to *Time* magazine on November 13, 1950, dismissing the reviewers who had savaged *Across the River and into the Trees*.

31. Hemingway, *Selected Letters*, 768–70.

32. Ibid., 772.

33. William Faulkner, "A Review," *Shenandoah* (Autumn 1952): 55; reprinted in *Shenandoah: An Anthology*, ed. James Boatwright (Wainscott, N.Y.: Pushcart, 1985), 123.
34. Meyers, "Introduction," *Hemingway: Critical Heritage*, 47.
35. *Kenneth W. Rendell Inc. Catalogue 185* (Newton, Mass.: n.p., 1988), 24.
36. Faulkner, *Selected Letters*, 348.
37. Hemingway, *Selected Letters*, 807.
38. Ibid. Hemingway's widow later claimed that she could not recall his ever "having deplored the award to William Faulkner" (Mary Welsh Hemingway, *How It Was* [New York: Knopf, 1976], 472).
39. William Faulkner, "Address upon Receiving the Nobel Prize for Literature," in *Essays, Speeches, and Public Letters*, ed. James B. Meriwether (New York: Random House, 1965), 119–20.
40. Ernest Hemingway, *A Farewell to Arms* (New York: Scribners, 1929), 196. It is unlikely that Faulkner would have missed Archibald MacLeish's essay, in *Life* magazine in 1940, criticizing postwar writers, like Hemingway, for devaluing the "old verities." According to Michael Reynolds, "MacLeish said publicly that the postwar writers, like Hemingway, in their disillusionment with the 'war to end all wars' had 'educated a generation to believe that all declarations, all beliefs are fraudulent, that all statements of conviction are sales-talk, that nothing men can put into words is worth fighting for.'" In fact, argues MacLeish, "those writers must face the fact that the books they wrote in the years just after the war have done more to disarm democracy in the face of fascism than any other single influence." Hemingway in turn, writes Reynolds, accused "MacLeish of having a bad conscience while Ernest had fought fascism every way he knew how and had no remorse, 'neither literary nor political.... If the Germans have learned how to fight a war and the Allies have not learned, MacLeish can hardly put the blame on our books'" (Michael Reynolds, *Hemingway: The Final Years* [New York: Norton, 1999], 24–25).
41. Faulkner, "Address.... Nobel Prize," *Essays, Speeches*, 120. Italics added.
42. Ernest Hemingway, "Nobel Prize Acceptance Speech," in *Ernest Hemingway: A Literary Reference*, ed. Robert W. Trogdon (New York: Carroll & Graf, 1999), 295–97.
43. Ernest Hemingway, "The Art of the Short Story," *Paris Review*, 25th Anniversary Double Issue 79 (1981): 96–97. In the same year, Hemingway cautions Harvey Breit: "Faulkner gives me the creeps. Harvey[,] remember that Papa's last words were Never trust a man with a Southern Accent. They could talk reasonable English as we talk it if they were not phony." Yet, he admits, "I wish I could write well enough to write about air-craft. Faulkner did it very well in Pylon but you cannot do something some one else has done though you might have done it if they hadn't. He must have felt pretty strongly about them at one time" (*Selected Letters*, 862, 863).
44. Reynolds, *Final Years*, 324–25.
45. *Faulkner at West Point*, ed. Joseph L. Fant, III and Robert Ashley (New York: Random House, 1964), 49–50. Upon hearing the still sketchy news of Hemingway's death, Faulkner immediately remarked to his daughter: "It wasn't an accident. He killed himself" (Blotner, *Faulkner*, 1-vol. ed., 690).
46. Faulkner's view of Hemingway's suicide is turned back on Faulkner by Albert I. Bezzerides, who knew him in Hollywood in the 1940s and later stated in the PBS program *William Faulkner: A Life on Paper for PBS*: "As a conclusion to the PBS script, I wrote that at the end of his life Hemingway discovered the loss of his faculties and that the grief over this made him put a shotgun in his mouth and pull the trigger. Likewise, Faulkner surely committed suicide by getting drunk so incessantly and riding the least manageable horse, the one that had thrown him several times before and he knew would throw him again. I think the last few months of Faulkner's life were dedicated to committing suicide in a way because he had sensed a loss of faculty" ("Bill and Buzz: Fellow Scenarists," in Brodsky, *Life Glimpses*, 78).
47. Meriwether and Millgate, *Lion in the Garden*, 81.
48. Reynolds, *Final Years*, 129.
49. Ibid., 257.
50. Walser, *Enigma*, vii.

51. Ernest Hemingway, *A Moveable Feast* (New York: Scribners, 1964), 12; and "The Snows of Kilimanjaro," in *The Complete Short Stories of Ernest Hemingway*, Finca Vigía Edition (New York: Scribners, 1987), 50.

52. Reynolds, *Final Years*, 319.

53. Faulkner, "Impressions of Japan," in *Essays, Speeches*, 77.

William Faulkner and Henry Ford: Cars, Men, Bodies, and History as Bunk

Deborah Clarke

> *The chicken, weighed down by the burden of a thousand chickens before her who in the swirling dust of the lightbespeckled dusk of far fields in the long gone time of Gettysburg and Cold Harbor and Vicksburg, picked her way through the brown and muddy road as she sought to relive the faded glory and dying dreams of Grandmother—Grandmother whose eggs were sacrificed in one swirling raid upon the General's tent one crisp October morning because Jeb Stuart was lacking coffee.*
> —William Faulkner

> *Chickens are bunk.*
> —Henry Ford[1]

Listening to these alleged responses to why the chicken crossed the road, no one could confuse one individual for the other. Faulkner, after all, has made his name as one of the most complex of the high modernists, with an incredible sensitivity for language and an obsession with the sense of place and the role of history in determining human identity and fate. Ford, on the other hand, was the great simplifier. He made his fortune by making cars easy—easy to drive, easy to repair, and easy to assemble. He had a simple formula for success—keep the prices down. He was a health nut and a tee-totaler (unlike Faulkner) with an innate suspicion of experts and higher learning and a distrust of the history taught in books. He was only partially literate; he could read but his writing is full of misspellings and errors, and his published work was ghostwritten. He was, apparently, an engineer who couldn't read a blueprint but worked from models. And yet there are points of comparison. Both, most obviously, are giants within their own milieus, and while Ford was clearly much better known, Faulkner's stock has consistently risen while Ford's has gone down. Both have a strong populist streak with a genuine interest in rural life, farming, and the common man. While Ford was quoted as claiming that history is "more or less bunk,"[2] he was obsessed with his personal history and created, in Greenfield Village, a kind of living history that was entirely fabricated to fit his own personal vision. Both examine the significance of the human body—as working entity and as an innate part of human identity. Finally, both are fascinated with the role of machinery and technology in American culture and what it means for the future and for human identity, particularly male identity.

At first glance, it seems relatively easy to pigeonhole Ford as the straw man against which Faulkner's tormented humanity can be measured. But Ford is more complicated than one might realize initially. While deploring his virulent anti-Semitism and tyrannical control—over his company, his workers, and his son—you cannot help feeling a reluctant admiration for a man who, at nearly 70 years old, managed to make the V-8 engine viable on moderately priced cars. He was a hell of an engineer. And reading his insistence that profits should be banked for reinvestment in the industry to maintain its innovative potential and competitive edge is a refreshing change from the daily newscasts of CEOs pillaging the assets of their companies to feed their own greed. Indeed, whatever the sins of the Ford Motor Company under Henry I—and they were considerable—no one raided the coffers or cooked the books to any significant degree. Ford hated accountants, at one point firing the entire accounting staff; his son Edsel had to squeeze them into other jobs in the firm. One of the most interesting details of Ford's career is his commitment to hiring the disabled to work on his assembly lines; as he pointed out, there were plenty of jobs that could be competently performed by the blind, deaf, and lame. "It is a waste," he wrote, "to put an able-bodied man in a job that might be just as well cared for by a cripple. It is a frightful waste to put the blind at weaving baskets."[3] Waste was anathema to Henry Ford. Let it also be noted that he hired African Americans in greater numbers and to better positions than his competitors; Josephine Gomon, a member of Detroit's first interracial committee in 1926, noted, "Mr. Ford took this problem very seriously and gave it his personal attention. He tried to increase and upgrade jobs for Negroes in the plant."[4]

Ford's influence, of course, is far greater and more interesting than his life—though that does have its moments as well. In some ways, he has an undeserved reputation as the father of the automobile. He invented neither the car nor the internal combustion engine nor even the idea behind the assembly line. What he brought to the assembly line was movement: bringing the task to the worker and at a height and location best suited for the worker to perform his job as quickly and efficiently as possible. More importantly, though, is his own ideal for what the car could accomplish along with the symbolic significance of the dominance of assembly-line labor. Ford was dedicated to bringing the car to the common people, to the wage earners. One of the motivations behind his widely hailed five-dollar a day wages was to provide his workers with the means to purchase a Model T, thus ensuring its continued sales. Another was to stem the extremely high turnover rate of his employees, who suffered under the relentless pressure of assembly-line labor. The price of the Model T dropped nearly every year it was in production, reflecting Ford's belief that customers simply wanted bargains. In fact, his stubborn refusal to look beyond that philosophy and the car that made him a household name nearly brought the company down. By 1927 General Motors, with its emphasis on style over engineering, overtook Ford as the top-selling auto company; Ford sales dropped to only 15 percent of the market.[5] Alfred P. Sloan, at GM, understood what Ford did not: that people bought cars not just as tools but as symbols, as expressions of self. And yet Ford did have some inkling of this; as he remarked in 1926, "we have not yet found out what the automobile means."[6] One thing he did know was that "what the motor car does among other things, quite apart from its own usefulness, is to familiarize people generally with the use of developed power—to teach what power is and to get them about and out of the shells in which they have been living."[7] Cars, then, transform people's lives and make them aware of the shifting paradigms of power—in ways, I would postulate, that Henry Ford never anticipated. The power of automobility is not limited to the internal combustion engine.

Faulkner too was interested in examining what the automobile means. Like Ford, he saw the car as an emblem of the future, that "toy and symbol of modernity," as W. J. Cash puts it in *The Mind of the South*.[8] To a far greater degree than Ford, however, Faulkner perceived the nuances of automobility, its potential as well as its liability. The fact that Herbert Head's prenuptial gift to Caddy Compson is an automobile is enough to give us pause, even without realizing that Jason's car was illicitly bought with the thousand dollars his mother gave him to invest in Earl's business. Faulkner certainly did not view the car in Ford's messianic light. He did recognize, however, its role in shaping men. For Faulkner, the automobile is often explicitly linked to masculine identity. In this, he echoes some of Ford's obsession over the identity of the men who built his cars, but Faulkner's interest veered sharply from Ford's almost pathological insistence that his workers, like his cars, needed to be standardized. Ford's infamous policing of the homelife of his workers stands as one of his most disturbing legacies—alongside his anti-Semitism and the ferocity with which he resisted union organization.

Ford's vaunted five-dollar a day wages, established in 1914 as a significant jump from the previous average of roughly two dollars a day, provided him with the opportunity to enforce his vision of what a man should be. The salary came with strings attached. First, it was restricted to men. They had to have been working for the company at least six months, be over the age of twenty-two unless they were married or supporting a widowed mother, and as Ford put it, "The man and his home had to come up to certain standards of cleanliness and citizenship."[9] In order to judge cleanliness and citizenship, Ford sent inspectors from his Sociology Department out into Detroit to gather information on his employees. They asked, among other things, about marital status, religion, citizenship, savings (including passbook number), value of house, hobbies, number and ages of children, health, and name of the family doctor.[10] In monitoring the conditions of his men we see Ford, the great automotive engineer, experiment with human engineering. All foreign-born employees were required to take English-language courses after working hours, taught by American-born workers for no pay. The graduation ceremony featured a large cauldron bearing the sign *"Ford English School Melting Pot"*—a literal melting pot, which employees entered wearing the garb of their native countries and emerged "dressed in American clothes," carrying American flags.[11] The whole procedure is eerily reminiscent of Hank Morgan's man factory in Twain's *A Connecticut Yankee in King Arthur's Court*. In fact, Ford claimed that, given "the most shiftless and worthless fellow in the crowd," by means of giving him a job with a decent wage and hope for the future, he could "guarantee that I'll make a man out of him."[12] As Antonio Gramsci later wrote in his *Prison Notebooks*, Americanism and Fordism constituted "the biggest collective effort to date to create, with unprecedented speed, and with a consciousness of purpose unmatched in history, a new type of worker and a new type of man."[13] In other words, Ford created the mass-produced man, efficient and interchangeable.

In fact, Ford was also in the business of making women. A 1912 pamphlet issued by the company entitled "The Woman and the Ford," gushed, "It's a woman's day. Her own is coming home to her—her 'ownest own.' She shares the responsibilities—and demands the opportunities and pleasure of the new order. No longer a 'shut in,' she reaches for an ever wider sphere of action—that she may be more the woman. And in this happy change the automobile is playing no small part." The pamphlet goes on to cite a letter from a woman driver who writes, "There must be women . . . who love the outdoor life, who crave exercise and excitement, who long for relief from the monotony of social and household duties, who have said, 'I wish I were a man.' Why don't you tell them that your motor car is a solution to all their troubles?"[14] If you can drive, you may not need a sex-change operation. But making women "more the woman" seems largely symbolic; Ford is not looking to remake women, merely to remind them that womanliness and automobility are not mutually exclusive. Making men, however, demands overt and material intervention along with constant policing.

The process of making men goes hand in hand with making cars. "A business," Ford says, "is men and machines united in the production of a commodity, and both the man and the machines need repairs and replacements."[15] "There is every reason to believe," he adds elsewhere, "that we should be able to renew our human bodies in the same manner as we renew a defect in a boiler."[16] Some of his closest associates regretted that Ford himself was not put together as well as he might have been. Samuel Marquis, former director of Ford's Sociology Department, lamented in 1923 that while Ford was "a genius in the use of methods for the assembly of the parts of a machine, he has failed to appreciate the supreme importance of the proper assembly, adjustment, and balance of the mental and moral machine within him. He has in him the makings of a great man, the parts lying about in more or less disorder. If only Henry Ford were properly assembled! If only he would do in himself that which he has done in the factory!"[17] While challenging Ford's own assemblage, Marquis fully accedes to the Fordist philosophy on the making of men— it is an assembly-line procedure. The implied interchangeability between the human and the machine, one of the strongest components of Fordism, incurred considerable resistance from "his" men. One former Ford worker, attracted by the five dollar wages, discovered that the salary was not worth the experience, describing the Ford Motor Company as "a form of hell on earth that turned human beings into driven robots. I resented the thought that Ford publicists had made the company seem beneficent and imaginative when in fact the firm exploited its employees more ruthlessly than any of the other automobile firms, dominating their lives in ways that deprived them of privacy and individuality."[18]

These concerns over human identity in the machine age strike a chord in any reader of Faulkner. While certainly not known primarily as an industrial novelist, his fiction reveals the encroaching industrialization of the South, from the remark that Doane's Mill, Lena Grove's hometown in *Light in August*, will soon be abandoned once the lumber industry has denuded the timber (the same fate that overtakes Major de Spain's hunting camp), to the growing realization in his postwar novels that, as Gavin Stevens puts it in *Intruder in the Dust*, "The American really loves nothing but his automobile: not his wife his child nor country nor even his bank-account... but his motorcar."[19] Faulkner was well aware of twentieth-century automobile culture—and everything it stood for.

The automobile age did not initiate the machine age, but modernist technology was producing machinery with a much greater impact on personal lives than the great factory industrialization of the nineteenth century. The telephone, the telegraph, and radio all brought the world of the machine into the home. And the automobile brought the individual out into the world. While Henry Ford was facilitating this automotive victory, writers were questioning the role of men in an increasingly technological age. One thinks of Eugene O'Neill's Yank of *The Hairy Ape*, for example, as a man reduced to a pre-evolutionary state through running the engine room on an ocean liner. As Martha Banta puts it, the forces of Fordism and Taylorism were "producing a nation whose notion of wholeness was inspired not by Emerson's man redeemed from the ruins but by the Model T."[20] Men were to become standardized and interchangeable, valued less for their individuality than their efficiency and conformity. The perception of the human body could not help but be shaped by this growing dependence on machinery. Tim Armstrong notes, "Modernity, then, brings both a fragmentation and augmentation of the body in relation to technology; it offers the body as lack, at the same time as it offers technological compensation."[21] This sounds remarkably similar to Ford's attempts to engineer better men through the use of technology; men find their identities through working on the assembly line, engaged in mass production to earn the means for mass consumption. Whatever the body lacks can be provided by purchasing the very technological products that have revealed the body's inadequacy, such as cars. As David Harvey points out, one of the basic tenets of Fordism is "his explicit recognition that mass production meant mass consumption."[22] Bringing the assembly line into prominence meant committing oneself to standardization and consumer culture.

The commitment was particularly problematic in the South, where, as one might expect, the forces of automobility met with considerable resistance. First of all, the roads were deplorable, reinforcing Southern isolationism. In 1902 Charles A. Bland, mayor of Charlotte, North Carolina, announced, "I do not believe that there would have been a Civil War if we had had good roads, because the [North and South] would have been so mingled together." North Carolina was spared Sherman's invasion, he suggested, "because the roads were so bad he could not get through."[23] The implication is that good roads would erase a distinct Southern identity. In 1911, the mayor of Atlanta heralded the arrival of the automobile which, he said, "will weld together . . . the most distant parts of our beloved country."[24] The statement is fully in accord with the vision of Henry Ford, who claimed that the car would broaden "geographical horizons" and "will ultimately bring about a redistribution in which each person will naturally gravitate to that part of the country in which he is best satisfied to live."[25] "Life, as I see it," he wrote, "is not a location, but a journey."[26]

Ford's migratory philosophy would not go down well in much of the South, especially in Faulkner's work where location is everything. Indeed, Andrew Nelson Lytle, in his contribution to the Southern Agrarian manifesto *I'll Take My Stand*, expressed his deep concern over the good roads movement of the early twentieth century and the impact it would have on Southern rural life. Once the roads were in place, he worried, "Automobile salesmen, radio salesmen, and every other kind of salesman descends to take away the farmer's money. The railroad had no such universal sweep into a family's privacy."[27] Ford, of course, didn't see it this way, given his own violation of his workers' homes and privacy. Lytle also shared modernists' concerns over issues of human identity in a machine age. "This conflict," he wrote, "is between the unnatural progeny of inventive genius and men. It is a war to the death between technology and the ordinary human functions of living."[28] Yet the Agrarians also realized that "ordinary human functions of living" changed with technological progress. In an essay in *Who Owns America*, the 1936 sequel to *I'll Take My Stand*, John Crowe Ransom wryly noted, "The Agrarians have been rather belabored both in the South and out of it by persons who have understood them as denying bathtubs to the Southern rural population. But I believe that they are fully prepared to concede the bathtubs."[29] It turns out that much of rural populace valued cars even more than bathtubs. When a USDA inspector questioned a woman about why her family had purchased a car when they didn't own a bathtub, she immediately responded, "Why, you can't go to town in a bathtub."[30] The people apparently preferred cars to cleanliness, validating Agrarian uneasiness over the ways technology shaped human lives and bodies, particularly since cars not only triumphed over bathtubs, they also impinged upon the glory of the past. In 1926, the city of Birmingham issued an appeal to motorists not to run down "any of the old soldiers in town for the annual reunion of Confederate veterans."[31] There could hardly be a greater desecration of Southern tradition.

Faulkner shared these Agrarian concerns about the preservation of Southern tradition. But his work reveals a much more complex awareness of the meaning of modernity. In "Was," the opening story of *Go Down, Moses*, Uncle Buck remarks that in their territory, "ladies were so damn seldom thank God that a man could ride for days in a straight line without having to dodge a single one."[32] He's referring, of course, to riding on horseback, for cars were as yet unheard of and even after they made their appearance, they remained scarcer than ladies for many years to come. Cars feature prominently in Faulkner's work, from the death car that kills old Bayard Sartoris, to the car for which Jason Compson robs his mother, to the red roadster which is the site of Manfred de Spain's macho posturing. As even this brief survey indicates, the automobile hardly comes off as a positive influence. Faulkner expressed some of his reservations about automobility by linking the car with criminality, troubled male identity, and the passing of history.

It's no accident that I just now forged a connection between cars and ladies. These two entities reflect Faulkner's uneasiness about modernity, progress, and male independence. Further on in *Go Down, Moses*, Lucas Beauchamp passes judgment on the McCaslin descendents based on the vehicles they own. "There was a tractor under the mule-shed which Zack Edmonds would not have allowed on the place too, and an automobile in a house built especially for it which old Cass would not even have put his foot in. But they were the old days, the old time, and better men than these" (43–44). The degeneracy of the family line and of male identity—"better men"—is revealed in its increasing dependence on machinery, not just for farming but for mere convenience and pleasure. Similarly, in the old time, as Uncle Buck pointed out, ladies were seldom seen. The Golden Age, then, comes to be defined by a scarcity of women (or, at least, white women, since it is unlikely that Buck and Buddy are counting black women as ladies) and a lack of cars. Cars and women seem to have had an emasculating impact on men, a subject that was under intense cultural scrutiny by advertisers, automobile companies, and writers. As Mark Seltzer observes, late nineteenth-century realist fiction attempts to replace "female generative power with an alternative practice, at once technological and male."[33] There appears to have been some hope that new technology could finally render the female womb obsolete. By the modernist era, that technological generative power was fully ensconced, though not as male-dominated as some could have hoped. The popularity of the Tin Lizzie—both as car and as cultural icon—certainly indicates that a significant trace of feminine power lingers in the machinery. Female generative power, whether figured through maternity or machinery, was not so easily erased. Faulkner, while he may have robbed the mother, did not replace her with a machine.

We all know that, as a young man, Faulkner was fascinated by flying. He joined the RAF during World War I though he did not, of course, get into the war itself or even into the air, despite his claims to the contrary. Later in life, he complained that flying had become too mechanized, that it used to be that anyone with a plane and a tank of gas could go up, but all that had changed.[34] With mechanization and technology comes a loss of individual control, reducing both the sense of accomplishment and the numbers of men who could hope to assert what control was left them. As Ford observed, technology is about power, though, as Faulkner illustrates, that doesn't necessarily mean an increase of it. But if flying was becoming more complicated, driving was getting easier. The addition of self-starters and paved roads, just to name the most obvious, brought the car to many—far and wide, even in the South. By 1930, there were just under one million cars on farms and in towns with populations under 2,500, a number which constituted 47 percent of the total registered passenger cars.[35] The automobile had ceased being a toy of the rich city dweller to become a rural and small town necessity. Herein lie some of Faulkner's reservations about the car as a measure and expression of self. Once one becomes dependent on it, it controls and shapes not only one's life but also one's identity. Faulkner remarked in a speech in Manila in 1955, "[man] has created machinery to be his slave, but his danger is that he will become the slave of that machine he has created. He will have to conquer that slavery, he will have to conquer and control his machinery because he has a soul."[36] And what becomes of man's soul, once he enslaves himself to automobility?

Many attempted to answer that question, though the automobile was, in general, welcomed with enthusiasm. A 1919 article in *Harper's Weekly* noted that cars bring the "feeling of independence—the freedom from timetables, from fixed and inflexible routes, from the proximity of other human beings than one's chosen companions; the ability to go where and when one wills, to linger and stop where the country is beautiful and the way pleasant, or to rush through unattractive surroundings to select the best places to eat and sleep; and the satisfaction that comes from a knowledge that one need ask favors or accommodation from no one nor trespass on anybody's property or privacy."[37] This description sounds remarkably Edenic, allowing one to linger in pleasant country surroundings and evoking a kind of nostalgia for a Golden Age lost to the age of automobility which, paradoxically, the automobile restores. It further offers a sense of control—to reclaim the past and reorder the present. Yet these implications are also troubling for Faulkner; those who attempt to reclaim the past often render themselves unfit for the present. Faulkner was much wiser than the Henry Ford who constructed, in Greenfield Village, a recreation of his idyllic vision of the past and then retreated into it in his final days, seemingly blind to its fantasy and to his own contribution to the passing of the era he came to worship.[38] Only a man who really did believe that history is bunk could fool himself so thoroughly. Faulkner, however, for whom history was emphatically *not* bunk, was well aware of the dangers of such willful fabrication. One must ultimately learn to live within history, within real historical communities, rather than fantasies.

Faulkner is a writer of communities; for him, identity and, particularly, masculinity are constructed within social relations. By and large, his most tortured male characters are the loners: Quentin Compson, Darl Bundren, Thomas Sutpen, and Joe Christmas. None of them bear the slightest resemblance to factory-made standards. Not a Model T in the lot. For Faulkner, community did not mean interchangeability, as it did for Ford who discouraged any type of fellowship or individuality on the job. Even Faulkner's twin characters are unique individuals. Buck and Buddy will "fight anyone who claimed he could not tell them apart," and, it is said, "any man who ever played poker once with Uncle Buddy would never mistake him again for Uncle Buck or anybody else" (*GDM* 7). The two men may look alike, but they are far from interchangeable, either in poker skills or in awareness of human tragedy, as evidenced by Buddy's superior understanding of Eunice's suicide recorded in the family ledgers. Young Bayard and Johnny Sartoris appear to come closer replicating each other; when Aunt Sally mistakenly identifies Bayard rather than Johnny as having gone up in a hot air balloon, she retorts, "Well, it dont matter which one it was. One's bad as the other."[39] The text, however, does not entirely bear this out. Clearly, the wrong twin has died in the war; young Bayard lacks his brother's lightheartedness, though he spends the course of the novel attempting to use his car to match Johnny's feats in the air, to become like Johnny. For Faulkner, and thus for young Bayard, to become interchangeable is not a viable option; the only way Bayard can replicate Johnny is to die like him. Flaming deaths may be interchangeable; human beings are not. Standardization of men has no place in Yoknapatawpha County.[40]

Also implicit in the 1919 *Harper's* piece is the ability the car offers to evade what one doesn't like, whether schedules or bad scenery or, by implication, evidence of modernity and progress. The American conviction that we can control our surroundings and reconstruct our history resonates strongly in the South, where one hasn't always had such control and where the memories of defeat and occupation lead to a nostalgia for a lost time, a preautomotive age in which communities flourished and men had souls. That those communities engaged in slavery makes this nostalgia all the more complicated, as any reader of Faulkner can attest. Isaac McCaslin's misguided but understandable desire to erase the past of incest and rape by abjuring his inheritance is rendered even more problematic by his outraged rejection of the African American woman who bears Roth's child at the end of "Delta Autumn." "*Maybe in a thousand or two thousand years in America*, he thought. *But not now! Not now!* He cried, in a voice of amazement, pity, and outrage: 'You're a nigger!'" (*GDM* 344). Neither the automobile that brings Ike to the rapidly vanishing wilderness nor the motor boat that brings the young woman to the hunting camp has altered the existence of miscegenation; past and present alike share troubled and abusive racial relations, which nostalgia for a vanishing wilderness cannot eradicate. The car offers no panacea for the legacy of slavery or the exploitation of the land. At times, the presence of technology only illustrates how little we control because some things never change; only the mode of transportation is different. Yet that technological presence also hints at some of the broader implications of industrialization and mass production. Once standardization is the rule of the day and all is interchangeable, segregation becomes much harder to justify and uphold. Certainly the episode leaves us unable to read Ike as any kind of savior, despite his attempts—as he sees it—to emulate Christ.

Nostalgia is linked even more explicitly to the car in *Flags in the Dust*, where Simon laments the neglected horses and carriage, the emblems of gentility, which have given way to the automobile. Interestingly, it is the fact of the Sartoris men driving the car that disturbs him most. "It didn't make much difference what women rode in, their menfolks permitting of course. They only showed off a gentleman's equipage anyhow; they were but the barometers of a gentleman's establishment, the glass of his gentility; horses themselves knew that" (*FD* 121). Women and vehicles, then, reflect the status of their male owner, and replacing the horse and carriage with the automobile seems to diminish his position and manhood, even more than replacing the women might. To quote the Clint Eastwood movie *Pink Cadillac*, "never mess with a man's vehicles." But Simon, of course, is lamenting the passing of a bygone era, refusing to see that while manhood may still depend on a man's vehicles, it is now defined not by equipage but by speed. Regardless of what one drives, one's vehicle asserts one's manhood, as young Bayard Sartoris is determined to replicate the airplane by driving his car at suicidal—and murderous—speeds. He seems to be desperately trying to catch up to his past, thinking if he moves quickly enough he can somehow get back to that past and prevent his brother's death. Speed, rather than propelling him into the future, takes him back to his past, evoking memories of flying in the war. In each case the automobile is linked to the past, either by contrast or as a means of returning to it. To control one's past is to be a real man, and to control one's past one needs a car. Somehow, the technology of the future becomes the preservation of the past—or it does if you're as desperate and clueless as young Bayard Sartoris, an automotive outlaw who pursues the past in order to erase the present.

The past, of course, is always suspect in Faulkner, and may be constructed not just by those with active and selective imaginations, like Quentin Compson, but also by technology itself. Stephen Kern has argued that "the impact of the automobile and of all the accelerating technology was at least twofold—it speeded up the tempo of current existence and transformed the memory of years past, the stuff of everyone's identity, into something slow."[41] If the notion of an easy-going golden age is constructed by the very technology which seems to destroy it, then we have a typically Faulknerian dilemma; the past cannot be dead because it is constructed only by the present. Thus, it never really existed in the first place. Those who build their lives around it, such as Quentin Compson or Ike McCaslin, are doomed to failure, trapped by their faith in a time that never was. I'd like to say that they'd be better off learning to drive, but driving doesn't seem to do much for either young Bayard or Jason Compson, possibly because the car functions in many ways, and its connection to the past constitutes only a portion of its symbolic import.

Faulkner's one rather regrettable trip down memory lane with the automobile is detailed in his final novel, *The Reivers*. In this novel, what starts off as an illicit joyride with a "borrowed" car ends up as a horse race, as if Faulkner was hoping to erase the age of automobility and return to a simpler time of horses and prostitutes redeemed by eleven-year-old boys. Indeed, the book bears witness to the issues surrounding the good roads movement. The episode in Hell Creek bottom, where Boon has to pay six dollars to get towed out of a massive mud hole, illustrates the concerns that the condition of the roads were stagnating the region. However, once on the road to Memphis, at the sight of cars passing, Lucius (in retrospect) waxes poetic about "the antlike to and fro, the incurable down-payment itch-foot; the mechanised, the mobilised, the inescapable destiny of America."[42] The novel, narrated retrospectively by Lucius, eleven at the time of the trip and now a grandfather, certainly recognizes the car as the future, noting the absurd machinations through which the city fathers of Jefferson ineffectively attempted to stave off the automobile age. But it is nonetheless the story of a horse race. In this text Faulkner comes dangerously close to Ford's naïve assumptions about how the automobile would preserve rather than transform rural America. While one can read the book as resisting the oversimplification of the past—certainly it reflects violence and corruption—Faulkner seems to suggest, in this instance, that nothing will replace the horse, that there are some things that the car will never change.

It is not just the car's curious association with nostalgia that makes it a useful perspective through which to examine Faulkner; it is also its connection to gender. Almost from its outset, the car was coded, somewhat uneasily, as female but its mastery was assumed to be the province of men. Early names for car parts often came from women's clothing: the bonnet or hood which enclosed the engine and the skirt or modesty panels which covered the inner workings, and everyone knows of the designation of Tin Lizzie for the Model T. Vehicles are often gendered female—like ships. But machinery is supposed to be masculine, and we all know of the car advertisements that flaunt the car as a phallic symbol. To associate masculinity with automobile mastery, then, suggests a tinge of homoeroticism that is, of course, entirely appropriate when thinking about Faulknerian masculinity. And even if one goes with the stronger coding of the car as female, mastering her is still not easy. Paul Frankl, American auto designer, remarked in 1932, "Twentieth-century Man is in the toils of a new mistress . . . the Machine. . . . Roughshod she trampled over all traditional values; she crushed out the lives of men, women, and children; she destroyed the old beauty and replaced it with a 'new ugliness.' "[43] While Frankl seems to accept a concept of existence from a previous golden age, now obliterated by the automobile, he also sees this conquering force as that of aberrant female sexuality. Quentin Compson, I suspect, might agree with him. Many have written about the fragility of masculine identity in Faulkner's work, and the perceived threat that women pose towards masculinity.[44] Speed may be one of the few remaining avenues of escape from female entrapment; one remembers all the young men who fled to Texas throughout the Yoknapatawpha chronicles.

But speed doesn't always work as an escape route; rather, it gives the illusion of independence, of control, that is so necessary to so many of Faulkner's men. And the car, which one might assume would offer the fastest way out of town and away from women, doesn't function that way. Women, after all, are associated with cars; it is telling that as young Bayard careens through town on a stallion, he passes Narcissa in her car. His glimpse of her reflects all the complications of the connection between women and the automobile. Her image "seemed to have some relation to the instant itself as it culminated in crashing blackness; at the same time it seemed, for all its aloofness, to be a part of the whirling ensuing chaos which now enveloped him; a part of it, yet bringing into the vortex a sort of constant coolness like a faint, shady breeze" (*FD* 143). Both aloof from and an integral element of the "whirling chaos," even the serene Narcissa becomes inextricably imbricated with the technology of speed and automobility. The car, then, offers no escape from women. Thus, using the car to assert one's masculinity guarantees failure, if one defines masculinity as separation from femininity.

The significance of the link between cars and criminality in Faulkner's work lies precisely in this connection to masculinity, or rather, failed masculinity, in most cases. Young Bayard, who could probably have been charged with reckless endangerment and vehicular homicide in his grandfather's death, runs off rather than face the consequences. It is only through deliberately flouting law and safety that he can find any purpose or meaning, as if being a criminal is the only way he can be a man in the post–World War I era. With the war over and his brother dead, he has no other notion of appropriate male behavior. Asserting control over machinery is his only option and, as Faulkner noted in his 1955 speech, such control only constitutes further slavery. By associating masculine identity with speed and mechanization, Bayard becomes an outlaw and an exile, unable to function within a community or a relationship, finding solace only in the dangerous freedom of automobility and later, airplanes. It's worth noting that Ford cars had a particular association with the criminal element. To his horror, Ford received testimonials from some of the most infamous crooks of the day who appreciated the power of his V-8 engine to outrun the law. John Dillinger wrote to him in 1934, "Hello Old Pal. You have a wonderful car. It's a treat to drive one." Similarly Clyde Barrow sent a letter saying, "I have drove Fords exclusively when I could get away with one."[45] Bonnie and Clyde were to die in a Ford; the car took 107 bullets, and the engine still started the next day.[46] While Faulkner was detailing less spectacular examples of criminality, the car was widely perceived as damaging morality not just through its use by criminals but also by weakening family ties, encouraging joyrides, even on Sundays, and allowing young people a site for fornication.[47]

Jason Compson, while he is hardly the speedster that young Bayard is, has similar problems with masculinity, criminality, and cars. He spends his mother's thousand dollars on a car rather than investing it in Earl's store as she intended. Jason perceives himself to be a shrewd businessman, constantly chaffing at being cheated out of his chance at a job in the bank; even Earl admits, "You'd be a good business man if you'd let yourself" (246). But Jason, who must be one of the few men in America to lose money in the stock market in 1928, cannot "let himself." The fact that he buys a car rather than a partnership casts further doubt on his business acumen and reveals the flaws in his self-image. Clearly, there is something about the car that means more to him than pursuing a career as a part owner of a business, rather than an employee. If being deprived the job at the bank costs him his manhood, the car, he seems to feel, may restore it, may give him the power and control he so desperately wants. Like young Bayard, he seeks to replenish something that is lost by means of automobility. Like young Bayard's, his pursuit of automobility takes on a vaguely criminal aura. It gives him the chance to reduce his dependence on his mother, to be his own man rather than a mama's boy.

And, like young Bayard, he fails. He fails in his pursuit of Miss Quentin and the young man in the Ford during the afternoon chase, ending up with a flat tire, and fails in his attempt to track them down after they have robbed him, ending up, even more ignominiously, forced to hire an African American driver to get him home. Even the smell of gasoline makes him sick. The car, rather than restoring his masculinity, reinscribes its loss, his inability to drive linked to his failures as a man. "'Maybe I can drive slow,' he said. 'Maybe I can drive slow, thinking of something else . . .' and so he thought about Lorraine. He imagined himself in bed with her, only he was just lying beside her, pleading with her to help him."[48] The car, fraudulently if not criminally obtained, literally drives home to him his failed masculinity.

The most significant moment of women being associated with automotive criminality comes in *The Mansion*, when Linda Snopes Kohl rewards herself with a Jaguar, her vehicle out of town after she has helped to orchestrate the murder of her stepfather, Flem Snopes. And yet while Linda is legally guilty, in the terms of the Yoknapatawpha chronicles, her act has a kind of ethical justice; Flem, the source of so much corruption, has finally been brought down. Linda's "criminal" behavior has a justification that both young Bayard and Jason lack, thereby reducing the intersection between femininity and the automobile. For her, the car is a prize for a job well done; she has none of Gavin Stevens's tortured moral qualms, and can celebrate her triumph with a Jaguar without becoming emotionally invested in either the car or in what it symbolizes.

Jason, however, needs not just a car, but a particular kind of car. Though we never learn its make (it's highly unlikely that it's a Jaguar or anything close to that bracket), we do know that it's not a Ford. "I think too much of my car; I'm not going to hammer it to pieces like it was a ford" (*SF* 238). Ford, of course, would have been delighted at the comment; Model Ts were meant to be hammered—they could take it. But Jason's thousand-dollar car is roughly double the price of most 1920s era Fords, necessary for him in his attempt to maintain his class status. "I says my people owned slaves here when you all were running little shirt tail country stores and farming land no nigger would look at on shares" (*SF* 239). While cars were initially the toys of the rich, Ford promoted cars as a means of class unity—anyone and everyone could own one. Indeed, this appears to be one of Simon's grudges in *Flags in the Dust*, that "Sartorises come and go in a machine a gentleman of his day would have scorned and which any pauper could own and only a fool would ride in" (*FD* 119). But, says automobile historian David Gartman, cars "united classes not in reality, by narrowing the gap of economic and political power, but merely in appearance, by obscuring class differences behind a façade of mass consumption."[49] He's largely correct, but cars do level, if not as objects of consumption then as vehicles that can get you off the farm, on the road, and into a wider public sphere. For Jason, however, the car is simply a status symbol and thus totally inadequate to maintain either his masculinity or his family's social rank, reflecting just how far the Compsons have fallen: trying to shore up their position through consumer goods rather than community leadership.

The phenomenon of consumerism recurs in the second novel of the Snopes trilogy. And what's particularly scary about *The Town* is that, by 1957, Faulkner had come to realize that it worked: consumer goods triumphed over family history, behavior, and ethics. Manfred de Spain celebrates his sexual triumphs by racing his car through the streets of

Jefferson, going out of his way to pass the house of Gavin Stevens, his erstwhile rival. The Mayor of Jefferson, de Spain, unlike earlier Faulknerian men, finds in the red roadster the perfect expression of his masculinity—loud, insolent, and triumphant. De Spain, of course, fulfills Faulkner's 1955 concern: he has no soul and has become enslaved to his machine, defining his manhood through commodity culture like the rest of America. The roads have let in the cars and now North and South are indeed mingling together. The North may have won the war but it is the car that conquers the South. To paraphrase Wash Jones, the Yankees mought have kilt us, but car has finally whupped us. And yet, Southern culture has put its distinctive stamp on automobile culture; NASCAR has Southern roots and retains a distinct Southern flavor.[50] Not even the automobile can entirely erase Southern identity or escape its influence. One might see, then, in de Spain the origins of new Southern masculinity, inextricably tied to automobility. But in linking his identity to racing his car, de Spain not only loses soul; he also loses class. Southern racing culture is a distinctively working class phenomenon. As Pete Daniel observes, "Southerners manifested an inordinate interest in automobiles. With aggressive drivers, fast cars, and wild fans, automobile racing became the ultimate working class sport."[51] Thus we see in de Spain the final defeat of the Southern gentleman and a new era of masculine expression.

I'd like to conclude by returning to the issue of the body and the car, and those disabled workers that Ford employed. I remain struck by that detail because it evokes Faulkner's emphasis on the often mutilated or damaged body. For Ford, hiring the disabled was greatly superior to charity and demanded not accommodation but simply an analysis of the kinds of work that needed to be done. He launched an inquiry and determined that of the 7,882 different jobs in the factory, "670 could be filled by legless men, 2,637 by one-legged men, 2 by armless men, 715 by one-armed men and 10 by blind men."[52] Ford was extremely progressive for his time in this consideration. Yet despite Ford's admirable determination to employ the disabled, it is troubling to see how he reduces the body to its functioning parts. In this continuation of the assembly line metaphor, the human body is judged by its ability to perform specific physical functions. One gets the sense that it is waste, especially recalling his statement about waste and disability, that Ford wants to avoid more than anything else. Indeed, when his workers were convalescing in the hospital, he set them to work screwing nuts and bolts together while in bed.[53] He claimed it was a matter of choice on their part but it was also a matter of economics; he wasn't advanced enough to fund sick leave, and if they worked they got paid. Nonetheless, his policies regarding the sick and disabled reveal his focus on the body as the integral component of production. In this he reflects the Faulknerian grounding of human identity; it lies in the body. But for him, the body is shaped by machine-age technology.

Faulkner's emphasis on the disabled body is less on physical than mental disability. There are a few minor references to physical disability such as Grandfather Compson's lost arm or Cash Bundren's probable lameness after having his broken leg set in concrete. But it is the idiots who stand out: Benjy Compson, Ike Snopes, and Darl Bundren, pushed into insanity by his crazy family. Interestingly, even Ford admitted that idiots were probably best supported by charity.[54] But for Faulkner, such affliction was a test of ethics, not an economic problem. Furthermore, mental disability in his work also seems to be embodied, in very literal ways. We always remember Ike Snopes's "female thighs," the physical description being as necessary to understanding his character as his mental disability. Similarly, Benjy Compson, unlike his brothers and sister, is physically described. He is "a big man who appeared to have been shaped of some substance whose particles would not or did not cohere to one another or to the frame which supported it. His skin was dead looking and hairless; dropsical too, he moved with a shambling gait like a trained bear" (SF 274).

The shock of this visual image reminds the reader of Benjy's idiocy, though it is telling that Faulkner first grounds Benjy as both disabled and intensely human in the first section, long before this damning physical description which seems to dehumanize him. Thus Faulkner challenges common stereotyping of the mentally disabled; having read Benjy's immensely moving narrative, we can never see him as the world does—physically incoherent and like a trained bear. Benjy's disabilities, both mental and physical, demand an ethical response rather than figuring out what work he might be able to perform. We are judged based on how we judge him. As Michael Berubé, who looks at the novel in the context of disability studies, asserts, Caddy's refusal to pity Benjy—"You're not a poor baby" (SF 9)—stands as the "key to the novel's moral index."[55] Benjy, mute and castrated, comes across as the most human character of the book and, indeed, as one of Faulkner's most powerful characters overall. For Faulkner, the disabled body stands as a monument to the human spirit rather than a cog in an automotive assembly line. Ford sees human imperfection as something to be erased or equalized; Faulkner sees it as something to be reverenced.

And herein lies the true significance of bringing together Faulkner and Ford: to examine the role of art versus industry in determining human identity. Ford reports, rather smugly, the plaint of a highly educated Persian visitor who toured the River Rouge plant. After seeing the immensity of the plant, he remarked, "My education began in words and ended in words and when I go back to my country I have nothing to offer my people." Ford agreed that the man "could do very little that a phonograph could not do."[56] This recalls Mr. Compson's bafflement at trying to understand the Sutpen story when one is left with "just the words."[57] With Faulkner, however, the words are more than enough. Despite his reservations about the culture of automobility, he was savvier than the Agrarians. He may have associated the car with criminality, but it was generally petty criminality, particularly when compared to the apocalyptic crime of slavery. He may have been a bit nostalgic, but he wasn't stupid. Faulkner was fully engaged with the social issues of his day, and he recognized that the automotive condition was part of the human condition. As powerful as it is to speak of him as a mythmaker, we must also remember that he and Henry Ford shared living space on earth for fifty years, and he knew exactly what Fordism meant. If Henry Ford really wanted to know what the car meant, he should have read Faulkner because part of understanding the significance of automobility lies in understanding that bodies exist independent of the factory line, that cars are full of contradictory symbolism, and that history is not bunk.

NOTES

I am greatly indebted to Kristin Jacobson, my research assistant, who provided invaluable assistance in tracking down a wealth of material for this article. I am also grateful to the many people at the Faulkner and Yoknapatawpha Conference who made various suggestions and reminded me of many significant car scenes in Faulkner's work.

1. Both quotations come from the following website: http://chickenology.virtualave.netlf.htm: 7/18/2002.
2. See Robert Lacey, *Ford: The Men and the Machine* (Boston: Little, Brown and Company, 1986), 238.
3. Henry Ford, in collaboration with Samuel Crowther, *My Life and Work* (New York: Doubleday, Page & Company, 1922), 209.
4. Quoted in Lacey, 222.
5. David Gartman, *Auto Opium: A Social History of American Automobile Design* (New York: Routledge, 1994), 77.
6. Henry Ford, in collaboration with Samuel Crowther, *Today and Tomorrow* (New York: Doubleday, Page & Company, 1926), 209.
7. Ford, *Today*, 7.
8. W. J. Cash, *The Mind of the South* (New York: Random House, 1941), 260.
9. Ford, *My Life*, 128.
10. See Lacey, 125, and Martha Banta, *Taylored Lives: Narrative Productions in the Age of Taylor, Veblen, and Ford* (Chicago: University of Chicago Press, 1993), 213.
11. Lacey, 126.
12. Quoted in Lacey, 127.
13. Quoted in David Harvey, *The Condition of Postmodernity* (Cambridge: Blackwell Press, 1990), 126.
14. Ford Motor Company, "The Woman and the Ford" (Dearborn: Ford Motor Company, 1912), 3, 11.
15. *My Life*, 159.
16. Henry Ford, *My Philosophy of Industry*. Authorized interview by Fay Leone Faurote (New York: Coward-McCann, Inc., 1929), 12.

17. Quoted in Banta, 273–74.
18. Quoted in Lacey, 128.
19. William Faulkner, *Intruder in the Dust* (1948; New York: Vintage International, 1991), 233.
20. Banta, 277.
21. Tim Armstrong, *Modernism, Technology, and the Body: A Cultural Study* (Cambridge: Cambridge University Press, 1998), 3.
22. Harvey, 125–26.
23. Quoted in Howard Lawrence Preston, *Dirt Roads to Dixie: Accessibility and Modernism in the South, 1885–1935* (Knoxville: University of Tennessee Press, 1991), 11.
24. Quoted in Preston, 41.
25. *My Philosophy*, 46–47.
26. *My Life*, 43.
27. Andrew Nelson Lytle, "The Hind Tit," in *I'll Take My Stand: The South and the Agrarian Tradition. By Twelve Southerners* (New York: Harper & Brothers Publishers, 1930), 255–56.
28. Lytle, 202.
29. John Crowe Ransom, "What Does the South Want?" *Who Owns America? A New Declaration of Independence*, ed. Herbert Agar and Allen Tate (Boston: Houghton Mifflin Company, 1936), 190. I thank Grace Hale, whose talk included a reference to this point and who generously provided me with the citation information.
30. Quoted in Michael L. Berger, *The Devil Wagon in God's Country: The Automobile and Social Change in Rural America, 1893–1929* (Hamden: Archon Books, 1979), 65.
31. Blaine A. Brownell, "A Symbol of Modernity: Attitudes Toward the Automobile in Southern Cites in the 1920s," *American Quarterly* 24.1 (March, 1972): 31–32.
32. William Faulkner, *Go Down, Moses* (1942; New York: Vintage International, 1990), 7. Subsequent references will be to this edition and will be cited parenthetically within the text, indicated by the abbreviation *GDM*.
33. Mark Seltzer, *Bodies and Machines* (New York: Routledge, 1992), 28.
34. See *Lion in the Garden: Interviews with William Faulkner, 1926–1962*, ed. James B. Meriwether and Michael Millgate (Lincoln: University of Nebraska Press, 1968), 139.
35. Quoted in Berger, 51.
36. *Lion in the Garden*, 200.
37. Quoted in Gartman, 35.
38. Greenfield Village represents Ford's attempt to reconstruct a nineteenth-century American village. He collected eighteenth- and nineteenth-century artifacts from all over the United States and even England, often with little concern over the authenticity of his overall creation. The "village" contains the Wright brothers' bicycle shop, the courthouse where Abraham Lincoln practiced law, and Thomas Edison's workshop, among other shops and businesses. It is, as Robert Lacey remarks, "a never-never land." See Lacey, 237–49.
39. William Faulkner, *Flags in the Dust* (New York: Random House, 1973), 75. Subsequent references will be to this edition and will be cited parenthetically within the text, indicated by the abbreviation *FD*.
40. I am indebted to Jay Watson for pointing out to me the significance of twins and interchangeability in Faulkner's work.
41. Stephen Kern, *The Culture of Time and Space, 1880–1918* (Cambridge: Harvard University Press, 1983), 129.
42. William Faulkner, *The Reivers* (New York: New American Library, 1962), 71.
43. Quoted in Gartman, 56.
44. See, for example, Susan V. Donaldson, "Introduction: Faulkner and Masculinity," *Faulkner Journal* 15.1–2 (1999/2000): 3–13; John N. Duvall, "Faulkner's Crying Game: Male Homosexual Panic," *Faulkner and Gender: Faulkner and Yoknapatawpha, 1994*, ed. Donald M. Kartiganer and Ann J. Abadie (Jackson: University Press of Mississippi, 1996), 48–72; Doreen Fowler, *Faulkner: The Return of the Repressed* (Charlottesville: University Press of Virginia, 1997); Robert Dale Parker, "Sex and Gender, Feminine and Masculine: Faulkner and the Polymorphous Exchange of Cultural Binaries," *Faulkner and Gender*,

73–96; Noel Polk, *Children of the Dark House: Text and Context in Faulkner* (Jackson: University Press of Mississippi, 1996); Jay Watson, "Overdoing Masculinity in *Light in August*; or Joe Christmas and the Gender Guard," *Faulkner Journal* 9.1–2 (1993/1994): 149–77.

45. Quoted in Lacey, 311.
46. See Lacey, 312.
47. See Robert S. and Helen Merrell Lynd, *Middletown in Transition: A Study of Cultural Conflicts* (1937; New York: Harcourt Brace Jovanovich, 1957). A judge in "Middletown" identified the car as "a house of prostitution on wheels" (163–64n).
48. William Faulkner, *The Sound and the Fury*. The Corrected Text (1929; New York: Vintage International, 1990), 238. Subsequent references will be to this edition and will be cited parenthetically within the text, indicated by the abbreviation *SF*.
49. Gartman, 15.
50. For more on NASCAR as a Southern enterprise, see Pete Daniel, *Lost Revolutions: The South in the 1950s* (Chapel Hill: University of North Carolina Press, 2000), 91–120.
51. Daniel, 93.
52. Ford, *My Life*, 108.
53. Ibid., 110.
54. See Ford, *My Life*, 109.
55. Michael Berubé, *Life As We Know It: A Father, A Family, and an Exceptional Child* (New York: Random House, 1996), xv.
56. Ford, *Today*, 177.
57. William Faulkner, *Absalom, Absalom!* The Corrected Text (1936; New York: Vintage International, 1990), 80.

Surveying the Postage-Stamp Territory: Eudora Welty, Elizabeth Spencer, and Ellen Douglas

PEGGY WHITMAN PRENSHAW

In the spring of 1936, perhaps just at the time that William Faulkner was drawing a map to accompany the publication of his new novel, *Absalom, Absalom!*, Eudora Welty was awaiting the publication of her short story "Death of a Traveling Salesman" in the little magazine *Manuscript*. For Welty, it was the launching of what would be a long writing career. For Faulkner, it was a culminating moment of his vast ambition to gather the Southern story between the covers of one book. He identified his sketched map as "Jefferson, Yoknapatawpha Co., Mississippi, Area 2400 sq. mi., Population, Whites, 6298, Negroes, 9313," and then he added, "William Faulkner, Sole Owner and Proprietor." Laying claim to the imaginative landscape of Yoknapatawpha County was as bold an exercise of power as any of the maneuvers of his great-grandfather, the Old Colonel, William Clark Falkner, the slave-owning planter, railroad builder, lawyer, novelist, duelist. Whatever anxiety of belatedness the great-grandson might have suffered, following as he did upon the wake of such an illustrious forebear and denied witness to the South's great war, he countered by means of a sweeping appropriation of that earlier William Faulkner's story, along with the multitudinous stories, past and present, located in Mississippi history and fleshed out in the imagining of a county that Malcolm Cowley once described as the habitation of the "legend" of the South.

If one were a young Mississippi writer launching a career in the mid-1930s, or afterwards, where might one look for unclaimed space after surveying the imaginative territory already colonized by the territorial giant? Critics often recall Flannery O'Connor's remark that one best not have a mule and wagon on the same track the Dixie Limited was roaring down, but O'Connor was a Georgian and a Catholic. By birth and faith she already had more breathing room than Welty, or her younger contemporaries, Elizabeth Spencer and Ellen Douglas, all natives of Mississippi who shared a common state identity and history with Faulkner. Potentially, he posed for them not just an anxiety-producing influence but an exhaustion of the raw-material resources necessary to narrative. The extent to which he laid claim to this material as a representative semblance of the nineteenth- and early twentieth-century American South is suggested by historian Don Doyle in his recent book on the historical roots of Yoknapatawpha. Doyle describes Lafayette County, Mississippi, as a place recoverable in part through documents and oral accounts, but even more expansively in Faulkner's transformations of Lafayette into Yoknapatawpha. He identifies the features of the historical county, like that of Faulkner's fictional postage-stamp, as "rather typical, even ordinary," not a site of any special historical significance, not "in any way exceptional."[1] The historical authority of Yoknapatawpha lies, in fact, largely in its representativeness of the state and the Deep South, a "case study" in Doyle's words, a richly elaborated metonymy that has incited successive critiques showing how Faulkner's county encapsulates Southern history.

In his essay "Mississippi," published in April 1954 in *Holiday* magazine, Faulkner does indeed seamlessly conflate the characters and events that are his own invention with Mississippi historical figures and sites, just as he had done throughout his fiction.[2] And into his portrait of the state's history and geography, he inserts an autobiographical surrogate, a character who is at first simply "the boy" and later "Mr. Bill," a character whose life span gives focus and measure to the story of a place. His gaze defines and encompasses the whole of Mississippi, though it is clearly the Oxford area and nearby counties that he regards as most personally "his." In fact, biographer Joseph Blotner quotes a letter from him to his agent Harold Ober regarding a request from *Holiday* shortly after the publication of the "Mississippi" essay. The magazine wanted another essay devoted solely to Vicksburg. Faulkner wrote Ober: "I get nothing from VICKSBURG yet. I dont believe I shall get anything by going there, though I will try that as soon as I can. . . . Vicksburg is not my town for me to have the right to do an imaginative piece about it; the Vicksburgians who really own the town might feel the same way about intrusion and violation that I did about the violation of my privacy by Life magazine."[3]

Noel Polk has observed that although Faulkner was much aware of his differences from other Mississippians, in this essay he does negotiate a reconciliation between the autobiographical narrator and his home state, taking on the voice of an "everymississippian" in the process.[4] He may not own Vicksburg in the way that he does Oxford, but he clearly feels comfortable in representing his experience of Lafayette County as a legitimate general knowledge of the history of the state and even of a wider South. In his one-page introduction to the *Holiday* essay, billed as "The Magazine Story of the Year," Malcolm Cowley's opening paragraph indicates the sweep of Faulkner's territory, both in the autobiographical essay and in the fictional Yoknapatawpha: "Here is William Faulkner's tour of his native state, through space and history and his own life story. In the time dimension he takes us from the days of Mound Builders to those of the mechanical cotton picker. In space he takes us from a hotel lobby in Memphis to the barrier islands fringing the Gulf Coast, where he used to be captain of a rum-running launch, then north again through the piney woods and the prairies along the Alabama line to the little town of Jefferson, which he knows best of all" (33).

Born in 1897, Faulkner acknowledges in the essay that he entered the historical scene after the era of the wild beasts, the great Indian warriors, the frontier heroes, and even the Civil War drama, but there was still virgin land to be hunted when he first set out in the early 1900s and, further offering a direct link to the heroic days, "the people the boy crept with were the descendants of the Sartorises and DeSpains and Compsons who had commanded the Manassas and Sharpsburg and Shiloh and Chickamauga regiments." In this passage the narrator goes on to name the other main players in the cast of his youth, the fictional McCaslins and Ewells and Hogganbecks, and adding "now and then a Snopes too because by the beginning of the twentieth century the Snopeses were everywhere: not only behind the counters of grubby little side streets . . . but behind the presidents' desks of banks and the directors' tables of wholesale grocery corporations and in the deaconries of Baptist churches" (12). We recognize here, with help from Faulkner's biographers, the references to persons who are unmistakably drawn from Faulkner's personal—and Oxford's public—history. For the Bill Faulkner writing in 1953, and certainly for the narrator of the essay "Mississippi," the political and the personal, the statewide and the local were almost interchangeable. Mystery and alienation might attach to the inward human heart, but the outer world of Yoknapatawpha County, every foot of it, he had traversed.

Of course, as several scholars have recently pointed out, this presentation of himself as a deeply rooted regionalist, tied to his land and his people, is just one of many masks that Faulkner employs, although Lothar Hönnighausen argues that it was his most continuous self-presentation, iterated and reiterated in his writing from the mid-1920s until his death.[5] This regional or pastoral self-portrait would change over the years, Hönnighausen shows, in response to shifts in politics and, especially, in race relations, but the self-displays that one finds in photographs of Faulkner, as well as in his words, characteristically link him to farm, to horses, to Yoknapatawpha. James G. Watson also reminds us in his recent book on Faulkner's self-presentations that the author deftly and deliberately constructs a range of narratives, both in autobiographical documents and in the fiction, in which he recasts personal and regional history to fit textual purposes and, doubtless, his own psychic needs. Watson writes that Faulkner's "distrust of fact; his daring, multifaceted constructions; his insistence on imaginative license to create characters from diverse sources and move them around in his role as Player, stage manager, God—all these speak to the willed artistic reality of the work he fathered, the outcome, again, of very personal performances of *his* knowing and imagining, of *his* mind and experience."[6]

We can well argue that there was much about Mississippi and the South generally that Faulkner omitted in his portraits of self and region, much that his mind and experience did not allow him to see, given the trajectory of his gaze. Certainly his vantage was not that of Richard Wright, and, as critics have discussed over the past quarter century, his depiction of women was necessarily shaped by his perspective from outside woman's experience. But his engagement of public history, especially as demarcated by race and class, was entirely familiar to an Elizabeth Spencer of Carrollton, Mississippi, or a Josephine Ayres Haxton of Natchez and Greenville, and, significantly, his was predecessor to theirs. Like Welty, they were inheritors not only of the society and history that he wrote about; they were also heirs of his shaping vision of Mississippi.

What I propose to consider in this paper is the response that Welty, Spencer, and Douglas individually and collectively made to the writer Faulkner, both directly in interviews and essays, and indirectly in fiction and memoir, in which they imagined an alternate mapping of the region, one originating in their different experience of it. They have demonstrably taken into account their celebrated literary forebear, but principally they reflect another Mississippi, another South, and so show us a different region.

Haxton, or Ellen Douglas, as we know her by her pseudonym, has given a telling example of the complication posed by a master storyteller's power to imprint his version of the past so definitively upon the general memory as to make one's own life narrative seem derivative or inconsequentially anemic. In the second story of *Truth: Four Stories I Am Finally Old Enough to Tell*, a book in which the first-person narrator identifies herself as an autobiographer, Douglas recounts an episode that occurred in 1948 on a chance drive from Greenville, Mississippi, with a Miss Adah, "an elderly friend of my mother-in-law's who had caught a ride with me as far as Vicksburg.... I was going to Natchez to see my grandmothers, both in their late eighties."[7]

> "Natchez isn't a real town, is it?" she said. "Faulkner might have invented it."
> Miss Adah was one of those gracious, self-confident women who used to be the product of regular army families. She sorted people out: officers, nomcoms,

privates, and foreigners.... And she'd married a wealthy Delta planter and no doubt could cope with him, too.

"Well," I said, "the landscape.... The woods. The Spanish moss. All those movie-set pre-Civil War houses. But—I don't know—I see it differently. Longwood, for example. My father's family (he and his parents and his three brothers) lived at Longwood for a year or two when the boys were in high school.... [W]hen they needed to learn geometry and trig and Latin to prepare for college, they rented the Longwood house. Near enough to town to ride their horses to school. Later, my grandfather inherited a little money and they bought a house in town." (33–34)

The narrator's rebuttal in defense of the reality of Natchez is loaded with details, family particulars to ground the story in authentic event and testify to the lived experience. But Adah is more disappointed than impressed with the mundane story of the Ayres family's residence at Longwood, a large spooky mansion noted for its Moorish castle design and its uncompleted upper stories, the carpenters having laid down their tools in 1861 when they left to join the fighting.

"Lived there?" Miss Adah said. "At Longwood?"
"So in a way, for me," I went on, "there's nothing Faulknerian about it. I see that finished ground floor as a home, with my grandmother's furniture in it—the music box, the square piano, my grandmother's little desk, littered with bills and letters to answer, her brown wicker rocker drawn up to the coal grate, the Bible on her sewing table, just as I remember it in the house in town."

The story Miss Adah is driving toward is one she recollects having once heard, a Gothic tale about adultery and Catholics and the removal of a body from one grave to another—Faulknerian! Contesting the narrator's family story, she insists that "Miss Julia Nutt—Dr. Haller Nutt's daughter—she always lived at Longwood." But the narrator persists, at least for one more round: "No, I think—let's see—I think she lived there sometimes. But I know my father and his brother.... She must have been living somewhere else when she rented Longwood to my grandfather. I seem to recall that sometimes she lived at The Forest. Maybe that's where she was when...." We notice the power of Miss Adah's tale slowly overtaking the personal recollection of the narrator, whose attenuating confidence in her own memory is signaled by the qualifying phrases, "I think" and "I know," which give way to "I seem to recall that sometimes...." In 1948, the reader infers, the narrator-companion of Miss Adah was not yet "old enough" to know, not yet ready to imagine the fragments of memory into a story of Julia Nutt and her close friend, Nellie Henderson Ayres, Josephine Haxton's paternal grandmother. Josephine was not then ready to give her story competitive standing. The storyteller on that car ride was Miss Adah, insisting, in a voice that sounds like Rosa Coldfield.

"There was a madwoman living at The Forest. A madwoman named Davis."
"Oh?" I said. "But . . ."
"Yes. I suppose she's dead now," she said. "A countrywoman, I think—*plain*—but I'm not sure. Maybe from an old family."
I'd been about to say, "But that was probably later." Now, though, I felt myself closing down. I wouldn't volunteer any more of my own vaguely remembered family gossip. I'd listen instead, noncommittally, to what Miss Adah had to say about a madwoman named Davis, who was in fact my great-aunt, whom I knew well, and who in my view was not mad at all. (34–35)

The problem that the narrator encounters in this scene is not so mundane or circumventable as Faulkner's (or even Miss Adah's) having stamped "Kilroy was here first" on a story about a decaying mansion, thwarted love, obsession and scandal. It is rather a problem of the narrator's identity, her claim upon her own subjectivity. Human beings *are* what they remember. The sense of self is available to us in the present only as we have access to memory. The narrator of this text *Truth* gives us in this scene a portrait of a youthful self who is not yet engaged, or perhaps not even yet fully aware, that truth about one's past has to be imagined, created from memory, built upon recollection and interpretation. In a deep sense, the past changes every time it is recalled, as William Faulkner, the master ruminator upon the nature of the past, well knew. And for writers, especially those like Ellen Douglas who shared a culture and place with Faulkner, reading his fiction and therefore reading their culture and place through his eyes meant inevitably that his vision encroached upon *and informed* their memory—this is the shaping force of "influence." In making this rather obvious point, I am reminded of T. S. Eliot's retort in his essay "Tradition and the Individual Talent" to the "someone" who remarked that we know so much more than the writers who preceded us. "Precisely," writes Eliot, "they are that which we know."

Welty, Spencer, and Douglas all well knew the work of Faulkner, and time and time again they are asked in interviews about his influence upon their own writing of fiction. In two volumes of Welty interviews, for example, there are almost twice as many entries in the index on Faulkner as on *The Golden Apples*, arguably Welty's masterpiece.[8] Welty reviewed *Intruder in the Dust* and Joseph Blotner's edition of the *Selected Letters*, and in one of her most quoted essays, "Must the Novelist Crusade?" she defended Faulkner's literary reputation against a charge in 1965 that, since "he was 'after all, only a white Mississippian,'" his fiction "would have to be reassessed."[9] Welty's sensitivity was sharpened in this essay not only by the smugness of the Faulkner critic but by accusations directed at her during this time of increasing racial tensions in the state and across the South. "All right, Eudora Welty, what are you going to do about it? Sit down there with your mouth shut?" Such calls by strangers at midnight, she remarks, linked together "most writers in the South from time to time" (147). In this essay she claims an alliance with Faulkner and other writers of fiction that is based not on raw material or themes, and certainly not on crusading messages, but on their shared effort to take life "as it already exists, not to report it but to make an object, toward the end that the finished work might contain this life inside it, and offer it to the reader" (147).

Over the years Welty employed two main strategies in answering queries put to her about Faulkner. First, she repeatedly rejected the interviewer's impulse to establish some kind of comparison, emphasizing instead Faulkner's achievement as monumental and unique. In 1980, when asked by Bill Ferris whether she ever thought of her work as a sort of map of Mississippi, she answered, "An internal map . . . of minds and imagination." Then she added, "No, I know what you mean . . . Faulkner's marvelous work, which is really just a triumph of the first order. . . . But I have no such abilities or ambition. I locate a story, but that's all."[10] As she earlier wrote in "Must the Novelist Crusade?" what she regarded as essential to the creative process was not a focusing of her gaze upon an object; rather, she insisted that the artist works toward a vision that the material gives rise to; the story is born of the conjunction of the passionate observer and the manifold world.

Welty also reminds her interviewers of the general invisibility of Faulkner's novels in the Mississippi she knew in the 1930s and early '40s. During her early and most formative years as a reader and apprentice writer, as she tells John Griffin Jones, "I hadn't read Faulkner . . . for the reason that you almost couldn't find any books of his. I tried to. They weren't in the library. You know, he was almost out of print until Malcolm Cowley brought out the *Portable*. I used to buy his books second hand in New Orleans and places, and I read them as I could find them. But I didn't connect myself to any kind of tradition or to any other writer."[11] On several occasions she does recount the pleasure she took when in one instance Faulkner expressed notice of her work. As she relates to Patricia Wheatley during the filming of the BBC Welty documentary, Faulkner wrote her a note while in Hollywood, some years after the 1942 publication of her short novel *The Robber Bridegroom*, to ask who she was and to say he liked the book.[12] She was so pleased that in a moment of "showing off," as she says, she sent the letter to a friend in Oxford. Many years later it would end up in the collection at the University of Virginia. On balance, though, I think we have to accept Welty's judgment that Faulkner was a distant presence in her imagination and her craft. By the time of Faulkner's Nobel Prize award in 1950, Welty had published *A Curtain of Green*

(1941) and *The Wide Net* (1943) collections of stories, *The Robber Bridegroom* (1942), the full-length novel *Delta Wedding* (1946), and the collection of cycle stories, *The Golden Apples* (1949). By that time the proximity to Faulkner had doubtless come to seem like living near a "big mountain," as she recalls to Linda Kuehl in 1972, "but it wasn't a helping or a hindering presence," she said.[13]

In her study of *The Golden Apples*, Rebecca Mark has convincingly argued that, though the Faulkner presence may not have been a help or hindrance in any direct way, it provided a stimulus for Welty's imagination. Mark maintains, for example, that several of the stories, particularly "The Whole World Knows," constitute a direct response to *The Sound and the Fury*, a dialogic move whereby Welty reimagines a Faulknerian narrative from a quite different perspective. Mark writes, "Welty's vision is completely different from, perhaps diametrically opposed to Faulkner's. She shares the same textual universe with Faulkner, but her engagement with him is more active, and transformative than the word 'influence' allows."[14] "Transformative" is a well chosen word here. It names the process, I should say, by which all literary influence is, in practice, actually enacted. But whether the work that is produced is freshly engaging, is emotionally and intellectually vital, or whether it is a weak and lifeless imitation of some predecessor, does not hang upon the argument of influence. There is almost nothing prior to the literary object but what we can call "influence." "We start from scratch," Welty once wrote, "and words don't."[15] The point I am driving toward is simply that Faulkner's Yoknapatawpha territory and the denizens of it came to be not only part of the general textual universe, but part and parcel of the imaginative universe of writers like Welty and Spencer and Douglas as they read Faulkner. The literary mountain in Oxford that was rising to greater and greater eminence throughout the 1940s and '50s did in fact change the landscape for anyone who cast an eye in its direction. In 1971, in a special session at the annual MLA conference, James B. Meriwether aptly observed that Faulkner's fiction is "a historical fact; his novels have as real an existence as those battles he lists in his essay."[16] The urgency to maintain one's distance was, if anything, more pressing for Welty a decade after Faulkner's death, as we see in 1972 when she applied her trademark modesty to resist her interviewer's questions about Faulkner. His achievement, "its magnitude," she said in the Linda Kuehl interview, "all by itself, made it something remote in my own working life" (80).

Like Welty, Elizabeth Spencer and Ellen Douglas have been asked repeatedly throughout their long careers, "What about Faulkner? How is your work, your Mississippi, related to his?" Younger than Welty by eleven years and coming to Faulkner's fiction at an earlier age, they both speak of the explosive power of the encounter. Born within a week of one another in 1921, Spencer and Douglas read Faulkner as young women who loved books and who aspired to be writers, though early on it was Spencer who determinedly sought a full-time literary career. Daughter of a devout Presbyterian family from north central Mississippi, she was sent to Belhaven College in Jackson for a baccalaureate education that emphasized traditional studies. Not until she arrived at Vanderbilt as a graduate student did she begin to read seriously many of the contemporary writers. Queried by interviewers who often posed a series of questions to her about Faulkner's influence, typically asking her to compare the characters and themes of her fiction to his—especially those of her first three novels that were set in Mississippi, *Fire in the Morning* (1948), *This Crooked Way* (1952) and *The Voice at the Back Door* (1956)—she said:

> I only began to read Faulkner after I got to graduate school. It was a great discovery. It really was. Writing about my terrain and things I'd seen and heard. Very few people can ever make that kind of discovery because very few people have a novelist of genius living right up the road. Oh, I'll never forget the experience. Here was life as I knew it rendered in the highest literary form. Everything I've heard all my life, people I've seen, types I've seen all my life, speech I've heard all my life.[17]

Although Ellen Douglas would not publish her first novel, *A Family's Affairs*, until 1962, fourteen years after Spencer's *Fire in the Morning*, she came to her reading of Faulkner at an earlier age, as she describes in a 1996 interview: "I remember reading *Light in August* when I was sixteen. What in the world did I think of *Light in August* when I was sixteen, you know? I couldn't have understood what was going on. I was sheltered and naive—a Southern girl-child. But somehow, I think that all penetrated."[18] As Douglas recalls, the effect was almost a neural shock, one that gave her a new way of seeing her Southern girl-child world, gave a differently imagined Mississippi that would be permanently lodged in her memory.

Years earlier, when Douglas was invited to address the 1980 Faulkner and Yoknapatawpha Conference, she spoke at length of Faulkner's role in her and her Southern contemporaries' literary development. In the essay "Faulkner in Time," she writes that he had "loomed at one time or another as a huge part of the process of learning to write," contributing to "how we became what we are and do what we do."[19] She goes on to discuss, however, a sort of punctuated evolution in her reading of Faulkner, a transition prompted by her critical assessment of his later work but, more importantly, as she writes, by her own "needs and capacity to put his work to use." I think we can infer from her fiction—and from her remarks in a companion essay presented at the 1980 conference—that a sharp questioning of Faulkner's portrayal of women lay at the core of her revised connection to his fiction. Although in interviews she has generally been reticent about the subject, she takes it up explicitly in the essay "Faulkner's Women." Direct and unequivocal, she charges Faulkner with tunnel vision in his abstracting and symbolizing of women, his incomplete understanding of their situatedness in society. She writes that he seemed to accept "without examination or question his own society's evaluation of women," adding that "it never once crossed his mind that women *must* define their lives in sexual terms in order to survive at all in a world which is wholly controlled by men. He believed that what is sometimes a societal problem is always an unalterable genetic predicament."[20] Douglas continues with some suggestive remarks about Faulkner's linking of the female, the wilderness, and the South as symbols of lost innocence, with woman, ultimately, the image of "failed and sinful humanity" (166), her point being that, however much his fiction "loomed," it did not apprehend or show what she had to say about the female, the wilderness, or the South.

In thinking about these writers' accounts of their relationship to Faulkner, I find theories about the anxiety of literary influence to be less helpful than a wider consideration of the subtle ways in which influence is felt and expressed as a general human condition. Here I am drawn to thinking about Faulkner's or anyone else's impact upon another's memory of one's own lived experience, that is, upon the shaping of one's subjectivity, or identity. Certainly in this postmodern era of theorizing about consciousness, we are mindful of the malleability and instability of memory—and by the mapping of imagination upon memory, indeed, the near indistinguishability of imagination and memory. We can look to a Jacques Lacan or Samuel Beckett or to our own experience to verify the relational, intersubjective nature of the imagining self, its origins in its vast social surround. We of course have a millennium and more of philosophical thought to draw upon in taking up these ideas, but the European intellectual Tzvetan Todorov in his recent monograph, *Life in Common*, has ably summarized the social nature of one's imagining faculty, what he refers to as the "internal plurality of each being."[21]

The relevance of Todorov's passage to this paper is simply this: the effect of Faulkner's use of the useable past, which he located in Lafayette County, Mississippi, and transformed into Yoknapatawpha, upon such writers as Spencer and Douglas, and even Welty, was not only inevitable, but was more galvanizing and empowering than it was inhibiting. As Keats reminds us, looking upon Homer can fire the imagination and invigorate passion. Lackluster imitation is rather the weakened and failed response to an apprehension of the greatly gifted. I suspect that the way we blithely ask questions and make assertions about "influence" does not move us very far along in understanding the workings of memory or imagination. Todorov writes that "the membrane that separates the self from others, the inside from the outside, is not airtight. Others are not only around us from the beginning, but also from the youngest age we internalize them and their images begin to be part of us. In this sense, the poet is absolutely right: *I* is another. The internal plurality of each being is the correlative of the plurality of people who surround him, the multiplicity of roles that each one of them assumes. . . . The self is the product of others that it, in its turn, produces" (122).

Intertextuality is the essential condition of life and art, as Bakhtin also shows us, so let us agree that the Dixie Limited bears down upon all of us, the community of readers who read Faulkner, whether we get off the track or not. As Welty herself wrote three years after Faulkner's death, "Once Faulkner had written, we could never unknow what he told us and showed us. And his work will do the same thing tomorrow. We inherit from him, while we can get fresh and first hand news of ourselves from his work at any time."[22] But of course acknowledging the literary vitality of such a predecessor is not to say that the best or only way to approach the domains of other Mississippi writers is to walk across Yoknapatawpha to get to them. In her recent book on Southern women's writing, Patricia Yaeger complains of the "Faulkner industry" that "enshrines William Faulkner as *the* literary icon of Southern studies" and thereby forces a comparative if not derivative status upon other writers. "The mythifying energy of Faulkner studies takes my breath away,"[23] she claims, though I think her objection is not so much that Faulkner studies suck the oxygen from other literary study as undervalue the principle of textual relationality and reciprocity as a general principle of criticism. Beyond any consideration of what writers read of other writers' work, we do know that as readers we bring to our readings of Faulkner or Welty or anyone else the whole accumulation of our literary experience and perceptive faculties. Influence is manifold and endless, an interesting topic to entertain as one thinks about human development or about literary traditions, but the more arresting insights arise not from surveying or, worse, policing of the boundaries between texts, assigning ownership, but from our curious questioning of how various texts complement and contradict and inform one another.

On this note, I would like to make a concluding turn to consider briefly a few of the intertextual links between the fiction and autobiographical writings of Faulkner and the three writers who are my subjects here. It will probably not surprise anyone that the narrator's experience of Mississippi as reflected in the 1954 essay is not only coeval and coextensive of the history of the state, as I noted at the outset, but is drawn from a traditionally masculine sphere—hunting, business enterprise and money-making, lumbering, railroading, banking, warfare, politics, poker playing, and whiskey drinking. The boy—and the older Mr. Bill—speak of rivers and floods, of men's drive to own and dominate the land, and of white men's determination to invest their whiteness with dominating power. The autobiographical narrator writes of lynching, public greed, and finally, at the end of the essay, of family and intimate relationships. He remembers Ned, "born in a cabin in the backyard in 1865, in the time of the middleaged's great-grandfather and [who] had outlived three generations of them." At age eighty-four Ned had begun calling him "not only 'Master' but sometimes 'Master Murry', who was the middleaged's father, and 'Colonel' too, coming once a week through the kitchen and in to the parlor . . . saying: 'Here's where I wants to lay. . . . And I wants you to preach the sermon. I wants you to take a dram of whiskey for me, and lay yourself back and preach the best sermon you ever preached" (39).

Faulkner follows the Ned section with an even longer account of Caroline Barr's last years, of her "matriarchal and imperial" dignity and his loyal obedience. Bed-ridden by a stroke, she would send some messenger in the middle of the night with words that carried such a claim upon him that he arose and drove thirty miles and further because "She want the ice cream" (41). But in these vignettes of Ned and Caroline Barr, even as Faulkner expresses a deep affiliation with these beloved figures, an attachment that presumably symbolizes his intense emotional connection to the place of his birth, his stance seems solitary and strangely distant. He portrays himself as a man whose responsibilities for—and power over—others ultimately betray him to alienation. He is meant to pronounce the epitaph of a dignified old woman who represents a whole past era, but whereas she and his mother, Maud Butler Falkner, actually shared that past, he is largely relegated to mourning its passage. He imagines them together, "talking, he liked to think, of the old days of his father and himself and the three younger brothers, the two of them two women who together had never weighed two hundred pounds in a house roaring with five men: though they probably didn't since women, unlike men, have learned how to live uncomplicated by that sort of sentimentality" (41–42).

A profound nostalgia that seems to issue more from his sense of dispossession than from mutability—or mortality—pervades this passage, which continues through an account of Caroline Barr's death. Doubtless the tone owes in part to the general bad health and depression that afflicted Faulkner during the time he was writing the piece in early 1953 in a hotel in New York.[24] In this quasi-memoir, he bestows upon himself what he calls a manly disposition for "sentimentality," a characterization of masculinity that is both self mocking and self aggrandizing, reminiscent of Quentin and Horace Benbow, of Ratliff and Gavin Stevens, and other Yoknapatawphans one can think of. But he stands outside the circle of Mammy Barr and his mother, who even in their last days constitute the active guardians of the hearth, if not its reflecting memorializers.

Welty's *One Writer's Beginnings*, like Faulkner's essay in *Holiday* magazine, was initiated by outside offer and contract, in her case, an invitation to give a series of lectures at Harvard University in 1983. Although at first reluctant, she was persuaded that a subject she could pursue that might interest her audience was, as she said, what aspects of her life she thought accounted for her becoming a writer.[25] Reading the published version of the lectures, one finds a narrator who, beginning with the title, makes few claims to speak for any experience beyond her own personal one and whose early years were mostly defined by the family circle.[26] Although born in Mississippi, she had no long family history of the state, her father from Ohio and her mother a West Virginian for whom "back home" was a distant place. She describes her life as "sheltered," and the account she gives of her development as a writer accentuates her move outward, away from the security of family and toward a riskier and wider territory. This territory was not the extravagant sweep of history and space that Faulkner assumed as his birthright but a more circumscribed realm of human relationships. Her desire, as she has written, was to "part a curtain, that invisible shadow that falls between people, the veil of indifference to each other's presence, each other's wonder, each other's human plight."[27] Having a reserve to the point of shyness, as well as the sensibility of an outsider, Welty, a white girl growing up in a deeply gendered and racialized society, was segregated from Faulkner's Mississippi, as from Richard Wright's Mississippi, in profound ways. She knew differently from they—and from the inside—the experiences of such characters as her Laura in *Delta Wedding*, Cassie Morrison in *The Golden Apples*, and Laurel Hand in *The Optimist's Daughter*.

In addition to Welty's intimate familiarity with characters like these, who grew directly from her own firsthand knowledge, she brought curiosity and empathy to the places and people of Mississippi that lay beyond her sheltered life in Jackson. Her work as a photographer and writer in the 1930s with the WPA gave her a first real introduction to the expanse of Mississippi, and these travels proved crucial to her career as a writer. In the published fiction of the 1940s—*A Curtain of Green* through *The Golden Apples*—Welty's approach to home state material, interestingly, is often that of an attentive, but detached observer. She fully comprehends, for example, the egregious ambition of a Thomas Sutpen, as well as the decimation of the wilderness that came as the cost of settlers' frenzied rush toward wealth and dominion. She even imagines the quite literal rape of an Indian girl, but she composes her tale of early ambition and greed not as an epic or tragedy but as a comic fairy tale, albeit one like those of Grimm, with dark, subterranean implications. In *The Robber Bridegroom* the patriarch-adventurer Clement Musgrove comes down the Natchez Trace to seek his fortune, but ends up forfeiting his daughter to an outlaw, who is a man more than savvy about how to make one's fortune in a new world. Thus Jamie Lockhart transforms fair Rosamond into a grand lady, his father-in-law Clement into a proud gentleman, and his own former bandit ways into entrepreneurial capitalism. There are other Southern patriarchs in the Welty canon but unlike a Colonel Sartoris or DeSpain, Welty's Battle Fairchild in *Delta Wedding* and King MacLain in *The Golden Apples* are continually slipping away from the central drama unfolding. MacLain can be depended upon to drop in occasionally, to bring some mystery and rumored adventures, plant new seed, generate new life in Morgana, Mississippi, and then properly to disappear and let the ladies get back to organizing daily life. On Welty's map of the northeast Mississippi hill country that is the setting of her later novel, *Losing Battles* (1970), she designates a few place names of towns and waterways, but she marks only one site that "belongs" to a character—the house where the 436-page daylong family reunion takes place, the home of matriarch Granny Vaughn and the Renfros. Though Welty's interest and empathetic characterizations extend across race and gender and nationality and location, her deepest knowledge comes from her own sphere of experience. In surveying Welty territory, I would hold to an argument that I first made years ago (and here at the University of Mississippi) that what stands most revealed in her fiction is woman's world and man's place in it.[28]

Elizabeth Spencer's relation to her native state and to Faulkner differs markedly from that of Welty. In her recent memoir, *Landscapes of the Heart*, she traces through her mother's McCain family the deep roots that lead eastward of Carrollton in the direction of the Delta, the plantation Mississippi, and toward the family home with its Choctaw name, Teoc Tillila. She places the beginning of this book at a site of journeying outward, much as Welty had done, but for Spencer it is a journey toward her origins as much as toward independence. At age twelve she rides alone on her horse to Teoc, but she is ready to claim safety, if necessary, by telling anyone who would stop her, "I am Mr. Spencer's daughter from Carrollton, and my uncle is Joe McCain."[29] She grew up relishing the book-loving, music-loving, company-loving McCains, and it is in their direction that she first rides out. But the McCains, no less than her father's family, the Spencers—a much less cosmopolitan clan from the hill country to the east—is a family clearly dominated by fathers and grandfathers and uncles and brothers. Perhaps daughter Elizabeth's ambition to write candidly, and with impunity, about such a land of fathers, hoping for and expecting her own father's support, was never realistic. Certainly her early career was so fraught with family controversy that by the time *The Voice at the Back Door* was published in 1956, she faced a stark life choice between her writing and her family. Although the racial themes were the most contentious matter, her traditional family wanted a traditional life for their only daughter—marriage and children—not a stirring-up-trouble career.

By 1956 she had written three novels, all set in a Mississippi recognizably adjacent to, if not lying within, Yoknapatawpha country. With central protagonists who were male, she portrayed feuds, betrayals, lost inheritances, secret thievery, cover-ups, obsessive land acquisition, county political campaigns, and bootlegging, to name a few of the topics of these densely plotted stories. They are inventive, engaging novels, but they clearly have to contend with the Faulkner canon. For example, Amos Dudley in *This Crooked Way* is as obsessive as Thomas Sutpen, except that the inciting motive for his ambition is a religious vision rather than a humiliating rejection at the front door. Like Sutpen, Dudley is determined to marry a respectable woman and establish a great estate, but Spencer turns her novel from the Faulkner model dramatically in the conclusion, where, like Welty, she subjects her patriarch to comic deflation and thereby humanizes and saves him from Sutpen's fate. She would return to the Mississippi material that was most familiar to her once more—in *The Voice at the Back Door*, a novel that confronts white supremacy and social injustice. In the memoir, as in numerous interviews, she speaks of the tensions of the mid 1950s, both personal and political, that caused her to turn away from Mississippi. These were the days of *Brown* vs. *Board of Education* and the Emmett Till murder, which took place just a few miles from Carrollton. There was an angry confrontation with her father, as well as her developing sense that the homeland she knew was disappearing and, along with it, a closing off of the possibilities of writing about the culture that she had shared with William Faulkner. In 1956 she would turn in a different direction, marrying John Rusher, an Englishman, moving to Montreal for many years, eventually residing in Chapel Hill, as she presently does, and writing fiction with characters— mostly female protagonists—who live in Europe and Canada, New Orleans and the Gulf Coast, Carolina and elsewhere, but not in the Mississippi hill country that stands at the edge of the Delta, not anywhere near Yoknapatawpha.

In 1962, the year of Faulkner's death, Ellen Douglas published her first novel, *A Family's Affairs*. Like Welty and Spencer, she locates her home base in a domestic and familial setting, and it is this experience that informs much of her fiction. The adoption of the pseudonym was a strategy for protecting family members from an unwelcome exposure of personal stories and secrets that Douglas drew upon for the novel. Although she writes from an admittedly personal engagement of her own contemporary Mississippi scene, she brings to this material a high degree of uncertain witness and ambivalence about the possibility of remembering past events or interpreting them without truth-crippling biases. Postmodernist, she searches in vain for boundaries between remembering and forgetting, between history and fiction, and meditates, as she writes at the end of the final section of the memoir *Truth*, upon "the lies we live by" (200). Neither her autobiographical narrator in *Truth* nor her fictional narrators smoothly incorporate the wider experience of "everymississippian," or that of Southerners—or women—or Caucasians—in their construction of selfhood. They instead work hard just to connect the dots in a spotty apprehension of their own present moment or in an even more uncertain memory of moments past. The narrator of *Truth*, unlike the narrator of "Mississippi," demonstrates no assured sense of entitlement to appropriate the larger world of country or state or region to complete and complement the self. I will state the obvious here: the female world, as well as the postmodernist world, is a territory more modestly scaled than the postage stamp Yoknapatawpha, more ephemeral in memory, more contingent upon a daily shifting reality.

Whereas Quentin Compson in *Absalom, Absalom!* is obsessed with Thomas Sutpen's story for what it radiates upon his own condition, his history and his life choices, Cornelia O'Kelly in Ellen Douglas's *Can't Quit You, Baby* is largely deaf to the world, a sheltered woman who barely engages the stories of her family or of the other central character in the novel, Tweet, her black maid. Faulkner employs four narrators to demonstrate the intricate puzzle that history and memory pose for human interpretation, but the self-reflexive, fictionalized—and yet authorial—narrator of *Can't Quit You, Baby* imposes herself between reader and characters to demonstrate not only the limits of truth-seeking but the solipsism of the truth-seeker. "I encourage myself that, although it is difficult, it's perhaps not impossible for the tale-teller to rise above her limitations, escape the straitjacket of her own life," writes the narrator.[30] But this narrator grapples with the truth that she cannot shed her whiteness, that she in fact sees Tweet through Cornelia's eyes, and that the only novel she can write is one impeded by her limits. "Can't someone else search for the end of this story?" she asks. "Discover where it is leading us?" (250).

In a special 1995 issue of the *Southern Quarterly* devoted to Ellen Douglas, Susan Donaldson, Deborah Wilson, Jan Shoemaker, and others helpfully elucidate the many ways in which the author foregrounds in her fiction the limits and failures of her authority as storymaker. What she ponders—and presses upon the reader—is the recognition that the fundamental process of fiction writing is exactly the agency that undercuts a novel's ability to "tell the truth." The work issues from a single consciousness, however capacious its breadth of experience and imagination (or legacy of literary tradition), and so is ultimately monologic, she suggests, not dialogic. Fister argues that Douglas devises an ending for *Can't Quit You, Baby* that poses a different process for telling truth: an African American call-and-response pattern embodied by the exchange between Cornelia and Tweet. The composition of the scene rests upon the alternating two voices, with the reader left to "imagine how each woman might decipher and respond to the other's call/message."[31] Nonetheless, as the authorial narrator signals throughout the book, the dialogue between the two characters issues from Ellen Douglas's peephole upon the world, a vantage that she never confuses with a global satellite.

As a young woman in 1948, traveling from Greenville to Natchez with an elderly companion who insisted upon telling her a Faulkneresque story about her own family of a generation past, she was amused and somewhat dismissive, as she recalls fifty years later. But, of course, she cannot recover that earlier self, for there's no way to mute the intervening years, and so her detailed account of their conversation is mostly fabricated—the dialogue, the facial expressions, the feelings of the moment, all fabricated. "Maybe she said that and maybe she didn't," says the narrator. "I suppose it just may be *that I have the memory now* of wanting to sympathize with Dunny" (italics mine).[32] The distance offered by years of experience and reflection has produced a different memory, one that may be as faithful to the meaning of that moment as her interpretation had been then, a half century earlier. Perhaps the revised memory of Ellen Douglas is even "truer" to that conversation than Josephine Haxton's momentary perception of it had been, Douglas's the more knowing of the complicated triangle of love and power involving her great-aunt Julia Davis, Dunbar Marshall, and his wife Fanny. At the conclusion of "Julia and Nellie" the narrator gives up fretting over the vagaries of memory—"Does it matter at all whether I recall or imagine this scene?" she writes at one point. Inevitably, the past speaks obliquely and in coded voice. One doubtless gets the stories wrong, but a determined empathy can cross the boundaries, can part the curtain. Recalling the death of her paternal grandmother, she remembers being in the hospital room with her great-aunt Corinne, sitting in the familiar brown wicker rocker, along with the black sitter Jintzy. "Juh . . . juh . . . juh," her grandmother whispered, and the narrator rushed to decode the half-spoken name. Was it Julia, who had been her dear friend, or perhaps Jack, her husband, the narrator's grandfather? These are the characters, after all, that Ellen Douglas is constructing in her narrative—her memory—of these lives. Either name would have worked to make a fit story, but when the grandmother finally spoke, "Jintzy" was the word she uttered. And so, as a gesture of respect for the truth one can never parse or finally know, Douglas ends the narrative with a blunt recording of the word spoken, its meaning untranslated, uninterpreted.

In many ways Douglas's work formulates perhaps the most direct response to Faulkner's representation of Mississippi and the South. In the 1998 *Truth*, she too takes possession of regional history by way of personal narrative, in this instance, that of a later moment in history than Faulkner's and that of a woman whose sense of mystery and relativism destabilizes the possibility of a knowable region or even a knowable self. Her perspective upon the inevitable failure of the writer to capture either the past or the self is not so tragic as Faulkner's; it is rather more reconciled with and acquiescent to mortal limits. I find similar views in Welty's and Spencer's perspective upon the elusiveness of originality and the constraints upon truth. Each has of course come to occupy her own postage-stamp territory, but as a wayfaring observer rather than possessor. "We start from scratch and words don't," says Welty, and thus we are reminded that even the sole owner of Yoknapatawpha began as a literary heir. His legacy takes its place in the long list of literary "begats" that now in turn comprises Welty and Spencer and Douglas as well, all expanding that universe of words through which future writers will construct whatever truth they have wit and will enough to imagine.

NOTES

1. Don H. Doyle, *Faulkner's Country: The Historical Roots of Yoknapatawpha* (Chapel Hill: North Carolina, 2001), 3.
2. "Mississippi" is reprinted in *Essays, Speeches, and Public Letters by William Faulkner*, ed. James B. Meriwether (New York: Random House, 1965), 11–43.
3. Joseph Blotner, *Faulkner: A Biography*, 2 vols. (New York: Random House, 1974), 2:1519–20.
4. Noel Polk, *Children of the Dark House* (Jackson: University Press of Mississippi, 1996), 257. Polk refers to two other works of this period, "Mr. Acarius" and "A Note on Sherwood Anderson," as "veiled autobiographical explorations of Faulkner's sense of his differences from other people," whereas he notes that the writer appears as a "fully contextualized citizen" in the essay "Mississippi."
5. Lothar Hönnighausen, *Faulkner: Masks and Metaphors* (Jackson: University Press of Mississippi, 1997), 183–222. See especially 204.
6. James G. Watson, *William Faulkner: Self Presentation and Performance* (Austin: University of Texas Press, 2000), 191–92.
7. Ellen Douglas, *Truth: Four Stories I Am Finally Old Enough to Tell* (Chapel Hill: Algonquin Books of Chapel Hill, 1998), 33.
8. *Conversations with Eudora Welty*, ed. Peggy Whitman Prenshaw (Jackson: University Press of Mississippi, 1982) and *More Conversations with Eudora Welty*, ed. Prenshaw (Jackson: University Press of Mississippi, 1996).

9. The essay is collected in *The Eye of the Story* (New York: Random House, 1978), 146–58.
10. "A Visit with Eudora Welty" (1975, 1976) in *Conversations with Eudora Welty*, 160.
11. "Eudora Welty" (1981) in *Conversations with Eudora Welty*, 321.
12. "Eudora Welty: A Writer's Beginnings" (1986) in *More Conversations with Eudora Welty*, 135.
13. "The Art of Fiction: XLVII: Eudora Welty" (1972) in *Conversations with Eudora Welty*, 80.
14. Rebecca Mark, *The Dragon's Blood: Feminist Intertextuality in Eudora Welty's "The Golden Apples"* (Jackson: University Press of Mississippi: 1994), 147.
15. Eudora Welty, "Words into Fiction" (1965) in *The Eye of the Story*, 134.
16. James B. Meriwether, "Faulkner's 'Mississippi,'" *Mississippi Quarterly*, 25, Supplement (1972): 23.
17. "'In That Time and at That Place': The Literary World of Elizabeth Spencer" (1972) in *Conversations with Elizabeth Spencer* (Jackson: University Press of Mississippi, 1991), 21.
18. "An Interview with Ellen Douglas" (1996) in *Conversations with Ellen Douglas*, ed. Panthea Reid (Jackson: University Press of Mississippi, 2000), 144.
19. Ellen Douglas, "Faulkner in Time," in *"A Cosmos of My Own,"* ed. Doreen Fowler and Ann J. Abadie (Jackson: University Press of Mississippi, 1981), 284–85.
20. Ellen Douglas, "Faulkner's Women," in *"A Cosmos of My Own,"* 164.
21. Tzvetan Todorov, *Life in Common: An Essay in General Anthropology*, trans. Katherine Golsan and Lucy Golsan (Lincoln: University of Nebraska Press, 2001), 122.
22. Eudora Welty, "Must the Novelist Crusade?" (1965) in *The Eye of the Story*, 158.
23. Patricia Yaeger, *Dirt and Desire: Reconstructing Southern Women's Writing, 1930–1990* (Chicago: University of Chicago Press, 2000), 96.
24. See Blotner, 2:1456.
25. See "A Conversation with Eudora Welty" (1986) in *More Conversations with Eudora Welty*, 117.
26. Eudora Welty, *One Writer's Beginnings* (Cambridge: Harvard University Press, 1984).
27. Eudora Welty, "One Time, One Place" (1971) in *The Eye of the Story*, 355.
28. Peggy W. Prenshaw, "Woman's World, Man's Place: The Fiction of Eudora Welty," in *Eudora Welty: A Form of Thanks*, ed. Louis Dollarhide and Ann J. Abadie (Jackson: University Press of Mississippi, 1979), 46–77.
29. Elizabeth Spencer, *Landscapes of the Heart: A Memoir* (New York: Random House, 1998), 4.
30. Ellen Douglas, *Can't Quit You, Baby* (New York: Atheneum, 1988), 4.
31. Charles Fister, "Not Just Whistlin' Dixie: Music, Functional Silence, and the Arbitrary Semiotics of Oppression in Ellen Douglas's *Can't Quit You, Baby*," *Southern Quarterly* 33 (Summer 1995): 118. See also Susan V. Donaldson on the fragmentation of narrative in Douglas's *Black Cloud, White Cloud* stories; Deborah Wilson on Douglas's *A Lifetime Burning* as a study of "otherness"; Jan Shoemaker on the struggles to reconstruct voice in "Hold On" and *Can't Quit You, Baby*; and Leslie Petty on the complexities of "autobiographical acts" in *Can't Quit You, Baby*.
32. Ellen Douglas, *Truth*, 49.

"Blacks and Other Very Dark Colors": William Faulkner and Eudora Welty

Danièle Pitavy-Souques

Although an even north light is preferable in the greater number of cases, direct bright sunlight is sometimes useful in examining blacks and other very dark colours.

—Ralph Mayer
The Artist's Handbook of Materials and Techniques

The late 1940s and early 1950s were times of national hysteria and war on social and political heretics, times which deeply affected the South with the rise of the civil rights movement and serious commitment for or against a reconsideration of racial issues, and which affected the nation at large with the fear of communism inside the country. Such times could not leave American writers indifferent. Each, following his or her own aesthetic sensibilities, felt the urge to produce works that translated the social and political turmoil as well as reflected a deeper vision of literature and its role.

William Faulkner's *Intruder in the Dust* (1948) and Eudora Welty's *The Ponder Heart* (1953) belong to that same troubled period and share the same moral, political, and aesthetic concerns.[1] A comparison will help identify the subtle or blatant differences between two literary sensibilities as they fictionalized what they each considered as pure evil. Everything differs, it seems, except the artist's commitment to the higher function of art. Each book encapsulates its author's manner, tone, and privileged theme. The South is there, as landscape and atmosphere, as language and violence. Yet, the *mise en oeuvre* and angle of vision are radically different. Faulkner focuses on guilt and racial issues and produces his own comic, yet prophetic, version of the civil rights movement. Welty's novella focuses on the exorbitant power of language that wields life and death, raises the question of feminism (another strong political issue of the period), and parodies the political trials of McCarthysm. More intriguing is the choice of stance: Faulkner's book can be read as *utopia*, whereas Welty's novel is definitely a *dystopia*. Circumstances may explain the more pessimistic mood of Welty's book: Faulkner wrote a *prescriptive* work at the beginning of the civil rights movement, Welty wrote a *cautionary tale*, an admonitory piece of fiction whose final redaction coincided with Ethel Rosenberg's execution.[2]

Yet, rather than emphasize the horrors of the lynching of innocent blacks or the infamous trials of American citizens during the witch-hunt, they chose the comic mode. The two novels privilege dramatization, and their gradual momentum builds towards a trial, virtual or actual: an open debate with proofs of guilt presented or denied, and a verdict. An insistence on visibility in the numerous comic turns of event, feeding on a comic vein, assuages anger. Whereas Faulkner parodies the detective stories whose scripts he had written in Hollywood, Welty gives full rein to humor, "a process of revealing," she says. The unusual mood of the two novels may be ascribed to their having been produced in "direct bright sunlight" in order to examine "blacks and other very dark colors."

The two plots revolve around a complex event and its effects upon the community and its individuals. A brief examination of the titles will help define those events. The word *intruder* suggests encroachment, forcing one's presence, and its etymology is related to threat. The military use of the word ("an aircraft assigned to penetrate alone into enemy territory usually at night") further implies spying upon the enemy and possibly doing harm. Used in the singular, "intruder" refers, it seems, to Lucas Beauchamp, the black man intruding upon the illicit activities of Crawford Gowrie, a white man who is systematically stealing lumber from the mill which he operates in partnership with his brother Vinson. However, "intruder" could equally apply to Crawford Gowrie the fratricide, or to Chick, the boy deciding to save Lucas by opening a grave at night. An intruder is someone who creates an *event*, who upsets the expected course of things, and forces a reconsideration of values, private or public: all three characters qualify. Lucas Beauchamp is this *event* because he is "the nigger who refuses to act like a nigger." After falling into the trap laid for him by a white murderer—Crawford Gowrie who deliberately kills his brother Vinson—Lucas is accused and arrested, and neither protests nor explains. And this momentarily upsets the order of the racist community, whose immediate response is to reestablish "order" by taking for granted that the Gowrie kin and other inhabitants of Beat Four will come and avenge Gowrie's murder by burning Lucas. Order is further upset by the transgression of two taboos—digging up corpses and fratricide—until the resolution of the plot establishes primordial similarities. We may choose instead to read the event in this novel as the ghost of an unaccomplished event—the absence of the expected, dreaded, and wished for lynching by the people in Jefferson.

In Welty's title, we hear two words: "ponder" and "heart." In this ferocious anatomy of love and marriage, irony rests on the discrepancy between the narrator's constantly protesting of the presence of love and the dire facts that deny this presence, while the plot functions on the confusion between the literal and the figurative, between heart as a vital organ and heart as the seat of emotions, character, and love. Both meanings can lead to failure, since to ponder suggests "a careful weighing and balancing of considerations," and also "inconclusive thinking about something" (Webster). We note then how both words "heart" and "ponder" ring with failing and failure: people die of heart failure, just as they fail other people through "neglect of an assigned, expected, or appropriate action." Inconclusive thinking leads to that very lack or absence of performance or achievement which failure implies. The novel is Edna Earle's narrative of the recent dramatic events that have upset the small town of Clay. Everything is seen, evaluated, and reported by the talkative spinster, who keeps the Beulah Hotel on the Square in front of the court house. She tells the unexpected and unexplained death of young Bonny Dee Peacock on the day she returned to her husband's home, then Uncle Daniel's trial for the murder of his wife and its outcome. Everything, including the absence of love and care, separates the spouses: she is twenty-two, and he is over fifty; she comes from a poor white family, and he is a member of a once prominent and still rich Southern family; and she proves more independent than expected in front of this simple-minded man perhaps suffering from down syndrome or hydrocephalus ("see what a large head size he wears?" [3]). The text is built upon a double mirror effect: with the choice of the main characters uncannily close yet different (Edna Earle a not too bright spinster of fifty and her uncle Daniel Ponder about the same age), Welty plays with distortion and blurred reflections. Then, with the organization of the narrative in two almost equal parts, she offers two different stagings of the same indictment of language. The first part is wonderfully funny as it makes fun of commonplaces and easy empty discourse, the second part is more polemical and stages the trial of a trial, denouncing the absurdity or real danger of literalness and the traps laid by the fascism of language, thus dismantling the tricks that had made us laugh in the first part.

To stop Uncle Daniel from giving away everything he owns, his father and niece marry him to a respectable widow, Miss Maggie Teacake, who dismisses her husband after two months. When Uncle Daniel starts giving built property away, the father has his forty-year-old son committed to the county asylum until Uncle Daniel seizes upon the attendant's mistake, lets his father be locked up in his place, and picks himself a wife at the Woolworth's cashier's desk, a pretty girl of seventeen, from a poor white family. Wasting no time, he marries her in Silver Spring with the help of his parents' black cook, Narciss, and causes his father's fatal heart attack on his return. Bonnie Dee Peacock has married Daniel "on trial," and after five years and six months of solitude and boredom without a cent to herself in the large isolated Ponder House, "she decided No." The promise of a retroactive allowance brings her back, well decided to have her way, and after establishing some form of separation at home, she "runs [her husband] off." Money is used again as a ploy to bring husband and wife together. When they stop paying Bonnie Dee's monthly allowance, she summons Edna Earle to the Ponder House "before it storms" only to die a few hours later during a terrific thunderstorm. "Well, to make a long story short, Bonnie Dee sent him word Monday after dinner, and was dead as a doornail Monday before supper. Tuesday she was in her grave" (55).

Right after the funeral, advised by a county attorney Doris Gladney presented as a muck racker and "no friend of the Ponders," the Peacocks charge Uncle Daniel with murder. Narratively, the trial and what pertains to it occupy more than half the novel. All kinds of witnesses, black and white, embroider on the circumstances of Bonnie's death, and when Daniel Ponder realizes that Edna Earle will prevent him from telling the truth, he resorts to another form of language—money—and distributes all his riches in bank notes. The verdict is "not guilty." Silence now prevails in the deserted Beulah Hotel.

Just as *Intruder in the Dust* revolves around the ghost of an event—a nonevent—*The Ponder Heart* revolves around the ghost of love—the failure of the heart: Bonnie Dee's heart failure, the Ponders failure to love, and the trial's failure to bring out the truth. A sinister parody of discourse replaces the discourse of truth during the trial and the ghosts of the once brilliant and humorous voices and conversation now haunt the Beulah Hotel.

I want to explore the ways comedy is both misleading and revealing. I will first examine some of the comic devices Faulkner and Welty use to fictionalize contemporary dark events. Then I will discuss the strategies of language as revelatory of darker issues, and finally I will analyze how transgression, as Bataille defined it for literature, leads Faulkner to utopia and Welty to dystopia.

Why the use of comedy as a priviliged mode? Whereas tragedy creates empathy for the victims and cleanses the audience of its guilt through the purifying process of catharsis, comedy creates distance, disorientation, and is essentially misleading because of the ambiguity of laughter, which approves and disapproves and is death's harbinger, as Bataille wrote. The texts precisely exemplify the strident or weird quality of laughter.

In both novels, comedy arises from a strategy of displacement, that is, the application of techniques used for popular genres, such as the detective novel or the western in cinema, to the higher genre of the political essay. The result is two highly entertaining novels with all the ingredients of the detective story or the western: suspense, dead end tracks, violence, old weapons and missing bullets, lurid scenes at night or in bright daylight, and many corpses. Both writers were familiar with those artistic productions and quite appreciative of the techniques. Faulkner had worked on film scripts in Hollywood, and Eudora Welty was a great amateur of cinema, Broadway productions, music hall, and other such popular entertainments.

The plots, for instance, are built on the lines of a regular detective story: there is a sudden and violent death, and the question is "who dun it and why" in *Intruder in the Dust* and "what caused death" in *The Ponder Heart*, with the enigma solved only at the end. *Intruder in the Dust* opens with this statement:

> It was just noon that Sunday morning when the sheriff reached the jail with Lucas Beauchamp though the whole town (the whole county too for that matter) had known since the night before that Lucas had killed a white man. (3)

With remarkable economy the information given in this first paragraph defines the action: time and racial issues are the key words. The plot rests on a race with time to refute the first assertion given as a fact, which becomes a truth because it is shared by the whole town and county, and leads to the disclosure of more sinister truths about the community. Since Lucas Beauchamp is threatened with lynching without trial, it is urgent to prove his innocence and convince the community of its denial of justice. Comedy springs from a series of discrepancies: the apparent helplessness of the rescuing party, and the outrageous course adopted: three people, whose age, race, and social position place them on the social fringe—Miss Habersham, over seventy and unmarried, and two adolescents of sixteen, one white, Chick, the nephew of Lawyer Gavin Stevens, and one black, Aleck Sander, Chick's companion. Only these three persons, "an old woman and two children," Gavin keeps repeating, are brave enough to transgress taboos because their perceptiveness enables them to be convinced of Lucas's innocence. "Young folks and womens, they aint cluttered. They can listen," says Old Ephraim (71). This is why Chick understands Lucas's silent message in his prison cell, "looking at him with whatever it was in his face so that he thought for a second that Lucas had spoken aloud. But he hadn't, he was making no sound: just looking at him that mute patient urgency" (66). Chick and the other two characters acknowledge a secret bond with Lucas—a pure human bond—that creates obligation if not some form of identification. The three of them agree to "go out there and look at him," as requested by Lucas, since only an examination of the corpse can prove that Vinson Gowrie was not shot by Lucas's "fawty-one colt."

The expedition itself partakes of the burlesque. Like a modern knight or some avatar of Don Quixote on Rossinante, Chick insists upon riding on his horse Highboy to the plot where the Gowries bury their dead while Alec Sander drives with Miss Habersham in her truck. The digging up of the grave sounds and looks like a parody of something already known or seen. To the first readers, the grotesque figure of Boris Karloff in a recent production of RKO, *The Body Snatcher* (1945), must have come to mind, while I think there are also unmistakable echoes of Dickens's *A Tale of Two Cities*.³ Echoes include the empty coffin open at night after the sham funeral of a spy in the humorous episode of the "resurrectionist" Jeremiah Cruncher, who digs up and sells to surgeons recently buried corpses. Or again, Madame Defarge's ominously knitting the names of suspects before turning them in during the French Revolution emerges as the benevolent Miss Habersham protecting Lucas Beauchamp in the prison corridor while mending stockings taken from a huge basket at her feet.

Faulkner's use of repetition with differences emphasizes comedy while suggesting the uncanny—a disquieting signal of evil to the reader. In the narrative treatment of the several expeditions to the Gowries burial plot, Faulkner's strategy exploits all the ambivalence of parody. The first time, for instance, an accumulation of details slows down the progress of the narrative and emphasizes the ordinariness of the occasion—a realistic treatment—yet, on the other hand, Aleck Sander's uncannily acute "sense beyond sight or hearing" detects odd things, either comic because unexpected, or ominous and threatening, such as the horse smelling quicksand, or "a darker shadow than shadow" silently going down the hill "toting something on the saddle in front of him" that could be a man, or again when he digs up the grave with something like rage to expose with the flashlight a corpse that is not Vinson Gowrie but Montgomery (100–104). Other repetitions, such as the trick of the unexpected contents of the coffin or the ludicrous play with flowers snatched away from the grave then hastily flung back, prove both burlesque and disquieting and, it seems, parody Chandler's *The Big Sleep*, whose script Faulkner had written while in Hollywood.⁴

Another burlesque strategy, subtle and complex, is the use of traffic as an objective correlative of the community, as the visible formula of Chick's and Gavin's particular emotion in reaction to the people around them. Described three times at three critical narrative stages, automobile traffic represents both the different moods of racist Jefferson and the emotional response of its viewers. The first time, the mass of cars and pickup trucks on the Square is the sign of the community awaiting the lynching of Lucas as a form of collective entertainment as well as a ceremonial reenactment of the "white man's high estate" (137). As in a western, such as *Stagecoach* or *High Noon,* people are waiting for the small party of avengers from Beat Four to appear, drag Lucas Beauchamp out of jail, and burn him alive. The second time, the sudden emptying of the Square reflects the horror inspired by the disclosure of fratricide. Finally, two long meditations, as Chick and his uncle watch the traffic from above, conclude the novel with a poetical yet moral and sociological portrait of Jefferson and the South. The adolescent resents the excessive slowness and closeness of the traffic, which blocks the view of the Square and all possible evasion. He then envisions his horse Highboy jumping from top to top towards the outer edge of the city, or a plank bridge over the car tops, "thinking of the gallant the splendid the really magnificent noise a horse would make racking in any direction on a loose plank bridge two miles long"(238). His uncle, on the other hand, tempers this idealistic and youthful vision and sees in the closed circle of cars slowly revolving around the Square a representation of an American society: "The American really loves nothing but his automobile: not his wife, his child, his country nor even his bank account first . . . but his car. Because the automobile has become our national sex symbol" (238–39). And he pursues with the image of a vicious circle in which men whose wives deny them their beds are forced to having mistresses who in their turn force them to divorce and marry them, and so the game goes on and on because of that American combination of puritanism with materialism.

With Eudora Welty, comedy arises from a brilliant combination of excess and severe control of her material and technique. She cleverly manipulates characters and readers as she plays with literalness to the verge of sheer ridicule, when, for instance, Uncle Daniel's attitude toward riches and money suggests a parody of communism, quite appropriate indeed to the general background. But the reader is subtly warned not to pursue the analogy too far through Uncle Daniel's erratic redistribution of his possessions. What matters is the tragicomic mood and the possibilities of interpreting rather than strictly decoding. The point is to destabilize readers by opening up too many paths, suggesting too many possibilities, slowly luring them into a narrative maze that oozes the weird and uncanny.

A series of comic incidents, almost slapstick comedy, generated by Uncle Daniel builds up the family background and the figure of the man who has "been a general favorite all these years" (4). All have an unpleasant edge. For instance, money given and then taken back when he is carried away by the voice of Miss Teacake Magee singing solo in the Baptist church: "And before I could stop his hand, he'd dropped three silver dollars, his whole month's allowance, in the collection plate, with a clatter that echoed all over that church. Grandpa fished the dollars out when the plate came by him and sent me a frown, but he didn't catch on"(17). Or again, Uncle Daniel's favorite story, the time when at the entrance of the asylum "he turned the tables" on his own father. This apparently very funny story has an even more grating edge when we learn that Grandpa died of heart failure on his return:

> the lady asked *him* who the old *man* was. Uncle Daniel was far away the best dressed and most cheerful of the two, of course. Uncle Daniel says, "Man alive! Don't you know that's *Mr. Ponder?*"And the lady was loading the Coca-Cola machine and says, "Oh, foot, I can't remember everybody," and called somebody and they took Grandpa. Hat, stick, and everything, they backed him right down the hall and shut the door on him boom. And Uncle Daniel waited and dallied and had a Coca-Cola with his nickel when they got cold, and then lifted his hat and politely backed out the front door and found Grandpa's car with the engine running still. (12)

The most dramatic of these double-edged incidents comes at the end of the trial when prevented from telling the truth by Edna Earle, Uncle Daniel finds another language—money. This creates bedlam within the courthouse as everyone tries to grab some bills. He "starts up the aisle, and commences handing out big green handfuls as he comes, on both sides. Eloise Clanahan climbed over her new beau and scooted out of the courtroom like the Devil was after her" (107).

For all the funny incidents crowding the narration of the trial, Welty with a light yet unmistakable touch contrives to remind her readers of the trial carried on at the time of McCathyism, when so many writers, film directors, and performers were put under pressure, confessed, and gave names, thus turning the tables on their friends, times when nobody could be trusted, and no friend still relied upon. See for instance, the awkward moment when the defense counsel, De Yancee Clanahan, is outwitted by Narciss, the black cook, finally confessing that she saw nothing since she was hiding under a bed in another room during the storm, and Edna Earle's sense of betrayal: "She just washed her hands of us. You can't count on them for a single minute. Old Gladney threw his hands in the air, but so did De Yancey" (76), or again, when the doctor's testimony proves more ambiguous than expected. When pressed by Gladney to "swear that the death [he] ascribes to heart failure might not also be ascribed to suffocation," he answers: "That distinction would be perfectly pointless, Mr. Gladney. Misadventure, Mr. Gladney, in case you'd like to remember this for future occasions . . . is for all practical purposes an act of God" (80).

In order to present their vision of contemporary events, both writers use the strategy of exposing the Southern infatuation with language—eloquence and rhetoric as the best-loved forms of the Southern art of living—in order to present their vision of contemporary events. While Faulkner exposes the bombastic rhetoric of political discourse ("it was his uncle's abnegant and rhetorical self-lacerating which was the phony one." [133]),[5] Welty exposes the drama and vacuity of humorous chitchat. Whether staged for large audiences or restricted to the intimacy of a front porch, Southern discourse can prove a terrible weapon in many ways. Words are as dangerous as they are magical, they are the fruit of love as much as of hatred or indifference. Discourse plays with emotions and feelings rather than with rational thinking and can rouse audiences and mobs to the most heroic or the most debased actions. At other times, discourse is like a drug to fevered minds and stops people from acting as they revel in the pure joy of discourse, or conversely, like a poison that festers within hearts and consciences, throws suspicion on innocents, and embraces them in a deadly clasp. Discourse is also sheer vacuity when it produces the deafening noise of pure rhetoric, or the slumber-conducive drone of clichés. Yet, there is another trick that language can play with phrases and metaphors: harmless and dream-creating when in the hands of poets, it becomes terrifying when it opens up the invisible gates of the world of uncontrollable forces. The borderline between reality and high-flown fiction is thin indeed, and this is what these two highly political novels are about. With differences in modes and moods, both writers build their argumentation on the opposition between two discourses—the consensual discourse of the community, misleading and slippery since it convinces the careless reader, and the progressive discourse of the novelist's spokesman.

Faulkner has one character, Gavin Stevens, converse with his nephew, a boy of sixteen, who paradoxically is at the same time more of an idealist than his uncle yet more down to earth and a pragmatist. *Intruder in the Dust* becomes challenging in its own context once the reader accepts its contrapuntal effect between Chick's restricted language and Gavin's flamboyant rhetoric fed by centuries of black and white eloquence, political and religious. The role of the first speaker is to bring about radical change by opening up a historical and ontological perspective, and to prove by his action that things can be done *now*. The role of the second speaker is to slow down things: to begin by reconstructing the South's self-image positively, then to confront the South in its delusion that it will take time. Thus Faulkner's language strategy rests on breaking barriers and compartments, then on dedramatizing the issues—*restoring the norm*—or what should be the norm in any civilized country. In this strategy of deconstruction and reconstruction it is important for the novelist to create empathy for his characters, black and white, and to modulate their voices so that facts and positions at the beginning of the novel are proved untrue, narrow-minded, and false at the end. This strategy reflects William Faulkner's awareness of the divided mind of the South at that time and his own commitment to such central issues at this stage of his career.

Gavin speaks the discourse of the traditional South, still jealous of its politics and history and adamantly refusing the interference of the nation in matters of desegregation. At the same time, as a continuation and broadening of Gavin's first discourse, Chick recalls another discourse, which it is his own specific role to impart to the reader: a visionary and heroic discourse which might have been pronounced by Gavin Stevens himself because of the historical background, but which reflects Chick's heroic attitude in the novel. This discourse opens up the problematics of the civil rights movement in the South and extends the debate to the continuing threat of racism all over the United States (*"their ancestral horror and scorn and fear of Indian and Chinese and Mexican and Carib and Jew"*) and further away in time and space to all totalitarian regimes that force people to adhere to one ideology unless they prefer death. The very fine point, it seems to me, is that this heroic discourse comparing the Southern situation to what prevailed in Nazi Germany and then in Communist Russia (two regimes fought by the USA) should be relayed by Chick, the boy who said no and found a way out within his own community. Only at this price, says the writer, can rights—civil rights and human rights, be respected:

> We are in the position of the German after 1933 who had no other alternative between being either a Nazi or a Jew or the present Russian (European too for that matter) who hasn't even that but must be either a Communist or dead, only we must do it and we alone without help or interference. (216)

When the novelist requires his reader's more active participation to grasp complex political and moral issues, he adopts a maieutic strategy in the dialogue between uncle and nephew. Just as Socrates' dialectic method elicited and clarified the ideas of others, the conversation helps the reader to clarify such issues as the prohibition of murder and the interdict of fratricide, racism, and totalitarianism. The key moment comes when Chick firmly rejects Gavin Stevens's statement that racist murder and fratricide are different, by saying: "You can't say that" (200). The boy is already one step ahead. Yet his uncle finds it necessary to explain that only a full realization of the interdict of fratricide can put an end to racist murder. Indirection here slowly brings the reader to equate a racist murder with fratricide.

If the discourse about racism and segregation is Faulkner's theme in *Intruder in the Dust*, women and the fascism of language is Welty's theme in *The Ponder Heart*. As Welty explained, once the writer has found his subject, he will explore it through a variety of themes (*Conversations* 11). And Welty's subject, I say, is man's relationship with language. Throughout her work, we see how this preoccupation with words—the writer's tool, just as color is the painter's tool—determines her approach to writing fiction. It is *this* specific challenge which she picks up again and again in a variety of ways. See her abrupt and illuminating answer, "No, I wrote it," to a question about the characters in *The Ponder Heart*; the writing comes first, strictly controlled:

> Mr. Greenway: "I was sort of wondering about *The Ponder Heart*. You see [the characters] through the eyes of Edna Earle, but you consider each of the people as a separate entity? Then you follow them all through Edna Earle?
> Miss Welty: "No. *I wrote it*. It was the other way around. My story really was about her, and it was her vision of these people that I was writing about. So, I knew them through her. I did everything through her, *including my own ideas*, of course, *I worked back and forth* and made—oh, well you know what I mean." (*Conversations* 10, my italics).

The Ponder Heart is about the exorbitant power of language, with the dark play of clichés moving around under masks. Social comedy turns into the indictment of a society and of the terrorism inherent in language. In this short piece of fiction whose atmosphere recalls Kafka's novels, the true theme is the exploration of the terrorist laws that govern clichés. For clichés are but the reflection of suspicion, of the fear of the other, and of the disgusting fascination of mercenary generosity. Then as the novelist warns against the danger of taking words and phrases literally, she projects a disquieting light upon the deadly power of language. The issue is no longer the necessity to institutionalize rights in order to end injustice as in Faulkner, but the denunciation of evil present in rumors, calumny, and small betrayals—to show the havoc that mere words can bring to human relationships inside a whole nation hysterical with the fear of communism.

The enveloping discourse of Edna Earle, the woman narrator, creates the circumstances of the events she relates. (Faulkner says in *Intruder in the Dust* that women like circumstances and men facts). Edna Earle ambiguously functions as both producer and publicity agent of small-town Southern culture, sketching atmosphere and background with funny details and small events such as a fair with a Ferris Wheel and "Intrepid Elsie Fleming riding a motorcycle around the Wall of Death," a Sunday choir in the Baptist Church, or a rummage sale "conducted" in the yard, together with the eccentric behavior of her Uncle Daniel melting into this general background. The artistic achievement of Edna Earle's discourse comes from Welty's masterful play with what Jean-Paul Sartre called the sphere of general discourse in the preface he wrote for

Nathalie Sarraute's novel *Portrait d'un inconnu* in 1947.[6] Exclusively composed of moral, psychological, and cultural cliches, Edna Earle's discourse weaves a brilliant fabric or backdrop representing the town of Clay, and embroiders the adventures of its inhabitants on top of it.

The difficulty for the writer is to produce two discourses at the same time: one that will ensure readers' adhesion through laughter, and one that will prick their critical sense. In other words, comedy functions at two levels. The first level is pure clichés and relies on surprise and poetic invention. It is comforting because renewed surprise delights, convinces, and reassures as it covers well-established ground. This discourse represents that safe place of polite conversation where people exchange such commonplaces that no one is hurt. All the time, Edna Earle's constant reference to the reader's experience or opinion implies a sharing *a priori* of that level of generalities and prejudice. Edna Earle is what Sarraute called an original because of the unusual way she assembles clichés. Invention lies in this assemblage. See, for instance, how the description of the Ponder place built by Grandpa belongs to the sphere of everyday life and activity:

> "[He] painted the whole thing bright as a railroad station. Anything to outdo the Beulah Hotel.
> And I think maybe he did outdo it. For one thing he sprinkled that roof with lightning rods the way Grandma would sprinkle coconut on a cake, and was just as pleased with himself as she was with herself." (31–32)

On the second level comedy rises from the difference between the language heard/read and the language understood: the readers are asked to translate. Discourse is cautionary, so to speak, it warns the reader as well as confirms the mask effect of the cliches. Welty uses repetition among other devices. Compare for instance two portraits of Uncle Daniel drawn by his niece. By a brilliant stroke the norm which will enable the reader to gauge the character suggests the abnormal. The whole first paragraph denies the first reassuring sentence: "My Uncle Daniel's just like your uncle if you've got one." We are presented odd behavior, a disfunctioning mind, and an oversized head, even the comment "sweetest disposition in the world" sounds suspicious. A second portrait denies the norm by erasing anomalies, and therefore requires a translation: Edna Earle's discourse is affected by her prejudice in favor of Uncle Daniel; worse, it is emptied of its meaning by clichés; consequently, it cannot be trusted. Moreover, Edna Earle's prejudiced discourse reveals a closed society, almost feudal in the relationship between old families like the Ponders and poor whites like the Peacocks. The decoding of humor is once again necessary.

Language so ambiguously invested with power leads to a more general debate about the larger issues fictionalized in those two novels. When finally considered, both texts are reflections on literature itself, which can be discussed with the help of Bataille. In *Literature and Evil* (1957), Georges Bataille shows how transgressing taboos is as much a necessity as respecting them. Transgression requires courage and is man's accomplishment; more specifically, it is the accomplishment of Literature—Promethean since the authentic writer dares to contravene the fundamental laws of active society. Literature brings into play the principles of essential regulations, and prudence and the writer accepts his guilt with orgiastic fever—the sign of his election.

Both works reflect Kafka's transgression, as Bataille sees it: the desire of every authentic writer to write within the sphere of the present and to refuse values subordinated to the future. From the beginning, William Faulkner's hero, Lucas Beauchamp, stands as the black man who quietly "refuses to act like a nigger." Eudora Welty endows Daniel Ponder with the graces and seductions of a child obstinately immerged in the present, heedless of consequences, playing pranks on his own father and subverting the establishment with his disregard for riches and social conventions. Lucas Beauchamp is indicted for a murder he did not commit, Uncle Daniel for a murder he did not intend to commit. Faulkner multiplies incidents and actions before showing how proving Lucas Beauchamp's innocence means expiation and initiation for young Chick, and he brings the community to a new awareness of racial issues. On the other hand, Welty's novella seems to be lighter until one realizes that the true manipulator of the plot is the standardizing and deadly power of language. Welty proves truly innovative since her translation of the political and social situation of the time is the staging of the seizing of power by language from the moment it leaves the world of metaphors and imagination to enter the world of facts and violence.

Bearing in mind this Promethean gesture/accomplishment, which is literature's chief glory because it will save men—at least bring them the knowledge of something formidable, I will say that the transgression in Faulkner's novel centers on fratricide. The announcement of the news is sufficiently elaborated in the narrative to transform the incident into something meaningful. Besides, Faulkner is clearly establishing the distinction between a crowd, a mob, and a lynching party. The crowd on the square, eagerly waiting for the public lynching by the mob (a small group of people) of a black man, has the sudden awful revelation of its symbolic, ontological guilt. People had blindly declared a man guilty just because he was black and the witness of a murder. The revelation of fratricide (as opposed to simple murder) is to establish, though this remains unsaid, a correlation between unjustly killing/lynching black people and fratricide. Whenever Southerners condone the lynching of innocent blacks, they reiterate Cain's gesture, they participate in that archetypal fratricide—the murdering of Abel by Cain. And the worse, and truly subversive revelation, is that they get into the skin of Cain the pariah, the damned. "They were running from themselves, they ran home to hide their heads under the bedclothes from their own shame," says Chick (202). If we remember that shame means firstly "a painful sense of one's indignity" and secondly "the opprobrious gaze of the others," we see that what is being narrated here is for a brief moment, a moment of Joycian epiphany, the passage from white Southern blind self-righteousness to a black Southern sense of rejection. In other words, the white people see themselves as niggers, Chick implies, with the clear-sightedness of youth. Gavin Stevens is far less explicit. In this remarkable passage, Faulkner fictionalizes the simple words inscribed in the Declaration des Droits de l'Homme et du Citoyen (Paris, 1792): "Liberté, Egalité, Fraternité/Freedom, Equality, Fraternity"—exactly what the civil rights movement was demanding at the time. We also hear an echo of Dostoïevsky's "we are all responsible for everything."

In its implications and daring, Welty's transgression is ideologically on a par with Faulkner's in *Intruder in the Dust* and hits on the very foundations of the American orthodoxy. Just as Hawthorne probed into the fallacy of the Pilgrim Fathers sternly advocating the elevated principles of religious freedom to found their New Jerusalem when in reality their repressive theocracy could be called the first totalitarian regime of the New Colonies, Welty probes into the contemporary fallacy of the United States and the Cold War. How could the champion of freedom, and recent victor with the Allies over the totalitarian regimes of Hitler and Mussolini establish at home, as strategy in its new war against its former ally, comparable forms of totalitarianism as those it was claiming to fight in the USSR (and had fought against in Germany and its allied countries less than ten years earlier)? Similarities in the methods of investigation and in the trials between the two countries were disquieting, and the general atmosphere of fear and distrust strangely reminiscent of the Salem Witch-Hunt in the 1690s during another period of deep political and religious unrest.[7] They led Welty to take a courageous, if oblique, stand as she felt it her moral responsibility as the *écrivain engagé* (whom few people had suspected she was until then) to warn the nation against the fascist power of language. Besides, the Rosenbergs' trial must have recalled Dos Passos's treatment of the Sacco-Vanzetti case in *The Big Money*. But unlike Dos Passos, Welty refused to preach and chose comedy to denounce how the general compliance of the nation with the methods, trials, and death sentences was equally appalling for her. Sharon Baris[8] suggests that the target of the novella may have been President Eisenhower himself portrayed as Uncle Daniel, with clear allusions to this "nationally beloved spokesman," and his rationale for justifying his denying clemency to Ethel Rosenberg. Welty's transgression, I will argue, is of a different order and considerably widens the political scope of her fiction. A blacker transgression incriminating the country itself was Welty's real target. The "anguish" the writer felt as she was drafting the book, her "misgivings about Uncle Daniel finishing Bonnie Dee off at the end," what Welty called the "flawed" ending,[9] must have come, I think, first from a realization of the coincidence between actual events and the philosophical and artistic necessity that made her end her "funny story" in the same way, and secondly from something comparable to what Nathaniel Hawthorne felt on the completion of *The Scarlet Letter*.

In their warnings against fascist thinking and power Faulkner and Welty use two different methods. By openly naming Nazi Germany and Communist Russia, Faulkner establishes a fascist background against which the present situation in the South and in the United States is to be evaluated. Welty, on the other hand, suggests but does not name, yet she offers a comic version of a totalitarian regime headed by a half-wit, a puppet, loved by everyone and apparently harmless, but whom everyone will reject in the end. Welty's transgression is comparable to what Kafka does in *The Trial*: the creation of a world all the more baffling and disquieting as it resembles the world of everyday life. The victim is not a character, like Mr. K in *The Trial*, but the reader. Welty's art is to create a place, apparently so close and similar to what her readers know or have experienced, that at first they are in danger of being deceived by the illusion of realism as they yield to Welty's humor. Only at the end of the book can they realize that in Clay Uncle Daniel controls language. The pleasant Southern town, so emblematic of small town life in the United States that it could be a version of what threatens the country, or is already happening as some trials demonstrated. People are framed not by what Kafka called "the Law," for all its vagueness, but by language. To the extent that he makes language come true, Uncle Daniel is a comic version of Big Brother. His first transgression is the actualization of language phrases. He literally tickles his wife to death, and at the trial he literally throws money away. These are only signs of some deeper disruption. By the same logic, we can infer that *The Ponder Heart* is also a text about the fascism of the heart. Everyone feels caught in and by the general protestations of love and benevolence. "[Uncle Daniel's] been brought up in a world of love," repeats Edna Earle, a sentence that deserves circumspection (106). All his life, the man has tried to force himself and his love on people, spending his allowance on treats for children, giving away his possessions, killing his wife out of love, and finally distributing all the Ponder money because "all he wanted was our approval" (110). Following Eloise Clanahan, the whole town will flee from him "like the Devil was after [them]." In reality, as the terrifying silence of the Beulah Hotel indicates at the end, the novella is about the end of the world, the end of the Ponder rule over the community and Edna Earle's sense of superiority. *The Ponder Heart* is another name for paternalism, the domination of money, and "aristocracy." Old money becomes strangely suspicious when its distribution frees tongues and liberates buried resentments on the origin of the money: The Ponders "did not burn their cotton when Sherman came," and after selling it to the Yankees they sold timber to "the same Yankees." This is another brilliant instance of the transgressive use of money as language in this novel. Thus, transgression in Welty's text is about perverted forms of language. Language is no longer a creative means of communication but an instrument of oppression, and this reversal is the very sign of totalitarianism—what was happening in the United States during McCarthyism.

I suggested earlier that properly placed in their political context, the two novels borrowed from those highly fashionable literary genres: utopia and dystopia, in spirit at least. Faulkner's utopia participates of what Paul Ricoeur recently defined as "a dream that wants to become true,"[10] utopia seen not as a flight from reality but as a text aiming to provide a serious realistic program for lasting social change. As the French philosopher points out, there is a current of utopian thought which veers away from fantasy and is informed by a powerful impulse to intervene and change reality. This is why the keyword about Chick is "to intervene": action as opposed to discourse with positive transgression. As Gavin says, it takes but few people to change things. And Chick meditates:"three amateurs, an old white spinster and a white child and a black one to expose Lucas's would-be murderer, Lucas himself and the county sheriff to catch him" (214–15). Hence, also, Gavin's speech about resistance to injustice: "Some things you must always be unable to bear. Some things you must never stop refusing to bear. Injustice and outrage and dishonor and shame" (206). The novel ends on this short dialogue with Lucas, who has come to the lawyer's office to pay for his "defense":

"Now what?" his uncle said. What are you waiting for now?
"My receipt," Lucas said.

The new order which Chick's romantic courage has just established is based on the enforcement of the law and the respect of rights. The receipt as a legal document becomes the sign of a transaction officialized by the law. It marks Lucas's final triumph: the old black man holds in his hand the icon of his statute as man and citizen of The United States. He no longer is "the Nigger who refuses to act like a Nigger." Yet, if we replace this ending in its historical perspective—Faulkner's providing for the possibility of rescuing an innocent black man from lynching at the very beginning of the civil rights movement, with Southerners as sole agents—we see that nothing was less certain at the time; the novel partakes of utopia for offering lasting social change by banking on the younger generation. The key is provided just before the final scene by the dual and displaced meditation on traffic (the real topic is the future of America). The boy's hopeful reverie is counterbalanced by the mature man's disillusion. Faulkner's daring young hero envisions a town and a country liberated from the evil of segregation and social injustice, since the bird imagery combining with the fantasy about his horse Highboy suggests Pegasus, the winged horse, born of the blood of the Medusa after Perseus's triumph over that figure of evil: "a hard-driving rack seven feet in the air like a bird and travelling fast as a hawk or an eagle" (238). This poetic vision is somewhat tempered by Gavin's matter of fact view of America as a consumer society, an endless circle imprisoning men within desire and repetition.

On the other hand, *The Ponder Heart* is one of the darkest books Welty ever wrote because this brilliant novella, so widely popular and acclaimed for its hilarious monologue and dialogues, should be read as a dystopia. Dystopia surfaces, says Ricoeur, when an excess of the necessary critique of the *status quo* leads to totalitarianism, presents negative features of the utopian model, and contains "the seeds of its potential distortion into the *worst* of all possible worlds." The term appears in the nineteenth century to become a major and obsessive theme of twentieth-century thinking. See Zamyatin's *We* (1924), Huxley's *Brave New World* (1932), and the more recent and most influential at the time Welty wrote her novella, Orwell's *Nineteen Eighty-Four* (1949). Rather than terror and horror, Welty chose comedy, "direct bright sunlight," and kept referring to her novella in the writing as "the funny story." Yet her dismay before the changes brought to the New York stage version proves she intended it as a serious text, and Edna Earle is essential. Her discourse betrays self-delusion, blindness, and prejudice not only about the town of Clay and the Ponders' social position, but also about Uncle Daniel, a well-loved man, Edna says, as she tries to minimize that he "may not have a whole *lot* brains, but what's there is Ponder" (24).[11]

I will briefly examine some of the characteristics of dystopia that can be found in *The Ponder Heart*: a panoptical and repressive structure of supervision, power maintained and nourished through rituals, enforcement of a distinctive speech. Obviously Eudora Welty never intended them to establish some rigid network in what was, after all, a kind of fantasy, yet because of their role in the novella such features are worth considering. Uncle Daniel, that "unmistakable," "big," and "well-known" fellow, always dressed "fit to kill," in a snow-white suit with a rose in his lapel, is a humorous and parodic counterpart of Big Brother. His excessive visibility is doubled by the way he imposes himself on everyone, including perfect strangers ("he's liable to give you a little hug" [6]), monopolizes discourse: "the stranger don't have to open his mouth. Uncle Daniel is ready to do all the talking" (11), and imposes his version of facts: "Oh, the stories! He made free with everybody's—he'd tell yours and his and the Man in the Moon's. Not mine: he wouldn't dream I had one" (51). His power over the town of Clay comes from his money (he is "rich as Croesus"), his birth, and his gift for talking. Welty transposes the terrifying blind power of Big Bother and creates a character out of cinema or comic strips, whose control of private lives can bring death. Two burlesque episodes—his turning the tables on his father and his distributing masses of banknotes—belong to comic strips; in reality they are evil: Grandpa dies of a heart attack, and Edna Earle is ruined. More sinister, his tickling his wife to death, "with the sweetest, most forbearing smile on his face, a forgetful smile" (104) reminds readers of the pitiful yet dangerous Lennie, Steinbeck's simple-minded migrant-worker in *Of Mice and Men*, who kills a young woman when he wanted to stroke her hair.[12] Another parodied feature of dystopia is the ritual established by Uncle Daniel's telling of his conjugal bliss or woes every night before a large audience. This public staging of a one actor show functions as a cement of society, since his audience's strong empathy creates communal cheers or tears, and the Beulah Hotel becomes the social center of Clay: "We had all that company to crowd in at the Beulah dinner table, had to serve it twice, but there was plenty and it was good" (89). Because it is a ritual, endlessly repeated and gradually emptied of meaning, this discourse expresses no real feeling. Daniel Ponder as narrator presents Bonnie Dee as a pure object of masculine discourse:

> And here at the Beulah, coming in singing, Uncle Daniel commenced on, "Oh, my bride has come back to me. Pretty as a picture, and I'm happy beyond compare. . . . Well, I don't have to cry any more. She's perched out there on the sofa till I get home tonight. I'll hug her and kiss her and I'll give her twenty-five dollars in her little hand. Oh, it would do you good to see her take it." (45)

Thirdly, people use a distinctive speech in Clay, at least in the Ponder Family, where violence and exageration are quite common. Gladney's strategy during the trial rests on proving murder through the threatening language used by Uncle Daniel to summon his wife two days before her death: "I'm going to kill you dead, Miss Bonnie Dee, if you don't take me back" (67). The defense counsel, De Yancee Clanahan, tries to prove that such open violence was ordinary with the Ponders, a trait, which Welty had used before as a sign of the arrogant power of the planters in *Delta Wedding*.

All these features show that *The Ponder Heart* functions like a feminine dystopia in its relation to language. Welty's particular brand of feminism, in this text at least, works less to commiserate with spinsters on their day-dreamings and aborted sexual lives, than to offer a philosophical reflection on discourse by and about women, including its absence. Women have no access to language, unless it were the language of money—seen as a transgressive substitutive for the norm, used by "minorities." Money represents the only verbal exchange between husband and wife, foretelling Daniel's dramatic use of money as language when prevented from speaking during the trial. Bonnie Dee nearly never speaks; instead, she is spoken. The pure object of her husband's discourse, Bonnie Dee, is presented as *absence*: literally and figuratively husband and wife do not live together. Yet, paradoxically, we track her presence in the profusion of miscellaneous objects and commodities she orders by mail. And this strangely substitutive presence is itself an absence as the many holes in the papers from which she has cut off the coupons attest. Furthermore, the ghost of the linguisitic presence of the ads as commercial messages strangely lingers and attests the ambiguous, or sinister, nature of Daniel Ponder's relationship with his pretty young wife: the man is not in love with the woman herself since her absence brings him no real suffering, he is in love with her as a sign, as a verbal object to advertize widely and wildly to any audience in the Beulah Hotel. He does not miss Bonnie Dee as much as he says he does, Edna Earl concludes. The young woman's departure has offered him the opportunity to modulate his discourse about her, and his reiterated professions of love amount to nothing else than his own selfish love for his own discourse. Likewise, Edna Earle feels dispossessed of a personal language, reduced to the function of a mirror reflecting the society she depicts: "'I'm the go-between, that's what I am, between my family and the world, I hardly ever get a word in for myself'" (89). Uncle Daniel's silence about Edna Earle's story corroborates this.

After the dreadful events of the trial, the major threat for Edna Earle is a loss of self, which is countered by her recourse to narration. By telling her story retrospectively, she creates a position for herself as speaking subject, or witness. Thus, for Edna Earle, the act of telling creates an imaginary circuit of communication with the unknown and unique guest of the Beulah Hotel, briefly alluded to at the beginning of the book. Identity is constructed through the use of first- and second-person pronouns. Narration becomes, in fact, the sole possible locus and safe haven for identity in a society which rejects the Ponders and their power. Her mode of survival lies in her speech. Yet, her speech act is an affirmation of identity only insofar as it postulates an addressee on whom this identity is predicated. Margaret Atwood, will use this device again in her appalling dystopia *The Handmaid's Tale*.[13]

Is it fair to compare the two writers and to use the term *influence* restrictively, when Eudora Welty so persistently eluded the question, when like Flannery O'Connor, who spoke of the necessary progression along different tracks for younger writers, she herself pursued one narrative experimentation after another? Is it fair indeed? The answer is no—unless we use the word influence to designate the more or less conscious circulation of ideas, themes, and techniques, such as we find among artists of the same generation, among painters, for instance; then we can risk some conclusions.

Firstly, we note that Faulkner himself was not unaware of what Welty was doing and his praising *The Robber Bridegroom* in a private letter to her acknowledges his appreciation of the young artist's dissident use of the fairy tale as genre in order to present a Southern version of Willa Cather's *A Lost Lady*, or Fitzgerald's *The Great Gatsby*. And just as Faulkner was influenced by American and European writers of the preceding generation (Conrad, Joyce, Proust, for instance) so was Eudora Welty, for she is heir to such great women writers as Edith Wharton, Willa Cather, Virginia Woolf, and to male writers such as the Joyce of *Dubliners* or the Kafka of *The Trial*.

Secondly, to suggest the spirit of the difference between Faulkner and Welty, I will use two detours, one pertains to literature, the other to painting.

Take two great nineteenth-century French novelists, whom both Faulkner and Welty had read: Balzac and Stendhal. In terms of scope, width, and breadth and recreation of a whole society with its historical, economic, and political background, Faulkner's work is comparable to Balzac's world, of whom Faulkner said: "he created an intact world of his own, a bloodstream running through twenty books of his own."[14] On the other hand, Welty's method and vision compare with Stendhal's achievement in a short story entitled "Vanina Vanini" published in *Chroniques Italiennes* (1829). Like *The Ponder Heart*, it deals with a burning contemporary political issue: the Risorgimento, the movement of liberation of Italy from the Austrian and Spanish rule begun in the eighteenth century among liberal and learned aristocrats, then among craftsmen and common people (called carbonari) under the influence of the French Revolution. On the surface, we have a cruel love story between two young people torn between utter commitment to passionate love and to patriotic love, when an aristocratic young woman falls in love with an escaped patriot/carbonaro. Through indiscretion and jealousy, she will cause the ruin of her lover and his group. In reality, it is a disturbing text about civil war and the general chaos it induces, with the confusion of gender (the young man's sexual identity is mistaken for his disguise) as a sign of the confusion of values, with selfish passion as a sign of betrayal and general suspicion. It is a powerful and deep representation not of the thing itself, but of its symbolic value. And its political message is to herald a new progressive order. Yet, we stop on the threshold, just as we stop on the threshold of a new order with Welty (and for that matter with Faulkner too). *The Ponder Heart* presents a similar insistence on love and passion, no longer throbbing with blood and desire as in "Vanina Vanini" but strangely disembodied and confined within language, and a similar play on confusion. The confusion between money and language becomes a sign of the confusion of values in this dangerous period, just as the empty vacuous reiteration of the word love is the sign of betrayal and general suspicion. Both writers have used the same device: displacement and symbolism, and both require the active participation of the reader.

To continue this analogy with other novelists, the essence of the difference between Faulkner and Welty may be more easily grasped when we compare *Intruder in the Dust* with *The Ponder Heart* from a distance. Faulkner presents himself as a historian in a book encompassing past, present, and future; he tells his story against a vast historical and political background, replacing his character's fate within the larger and more easily grasped context of the Civil War and the enduring rivalry between the North and the South, raising the question of the power of a mob and a crowd, and in the last chapter opening up a vista on America's consumer civilization. Welty, on the other hand, presents herself as a thinker of sorts, some kind of philosopher. Just as Stendhal borrowed his material directly from contemporary life, using events and news items which he recreated and sublimated into his unique and long misunderstood dialectics of the contemporary and the universal, so Welty borrowed equally from current events in the world at large and from the incidents of her daily life, and she too recreated and sublimated them into her clear-sighted unique dialectics of the contemporary and the universal.

The second detour will compare Picasso with Matisse. Picasso was the more inventive and powerful artist, painting every subject and situation, constantly reinventing the art of painting and pushing it to its limits for the endless delight, surprise, or scandal of his viewers—comparable to Faulkner's work. And both, I think, created something closed, complete, a world in itself. On the other hand, we have Matisse, equally inventive and forever playing between abstraction and figuration, and from the first, doing away with realism, verisimilitude, and perspective and in so doing placing the viewer's eye right in the middle of the picture to imbibe a pure riot of colors. At the same time, Matisse worked towards pure abstraction with the simplification of shapes and forms as did Welty, preoccupied,

I believe, with the abstract figure which would best represent her text (not her theme). Both artists were trying to reach the essence of things, to find the pure sound of a specific work of art, as Kandinsky advocated.

Matisse never stopped working on the interaction of shape with color, just as Welty never stopped working on the combination of words and phrases. Her fiction is much more difficult to translate into French than Faulkner's. Her brilliantly controlled text is strangely seductive and repulsive, especially in *The Ponder Heart*. Like Matisse, and unlike Picasso, she never fails to touch secret chords, to enchant and disquiet at the same time, to secure loyalties and secret acquiescence, more of the mind than the heart, yet always vibrating with deep empathy. And like Matisse, now recognized as more influential than Picasso, Eudora Welty may be the more influential writer for the twenty-first century, unless you consider that the postmodern generation of writers like Barth, Barthelme, Coover, Josephine Humphreys, and Ellen Gilchrist in the South, Alice Munro in Canada, or Nadine Gordimer in South Africa have already proved it.

NOTES

1. All quotations are taken from William Faulkner, *Intruder in the Dust* (New York: Modern Library, 1948) and Eudora Welty, *The Ponder Heart* (New York: Harbrace Paperback Library, 1954).

2. Sharon Deykin Baris, "Judgments of *The Ponder Heart*: Welty's Trials of the 1950" in *Eudora Welty and Politics*, ed. Harriet Pollack and Suzanne Marrs (Louisiana State University Press, 2001), 179–201. In his 1978 interview of Welty, Jan Nordby Gretlund was the first to link the writing of *The Ponder Heart* with Welty's commitment in favor of Adlai Stevenson (*Conversations* 226). Michael Kreyling expanded more on the subject in *Writer and Agent* (New York: Farrar, Straus, and Giroux, 1991), 161–62.

3. Faulkner was a lifelong reader of Dickens, he owned two sets of his work, and his answer "most of Dickens" to the question: "Sir, What are some of your favorite books?" is well known (*Faulkner in the University* [Vintage, 1965], 150). *Intruder in the Dust* rings with echoes of *A Tale of Two Cities* (1859), especially since the subject matter is fundamentally similar. We note Dickens's choice of the comic mode to stage first the arbitrary power of the dominant group (the French Aristocracy before the Revolution) to decide of the fate of innocents through life's imprisonment in the sinister Bastille dungeons, then the no less sinister power of the mob with its popular tribunals arbitrarily sending innocents or those it had revered but the day before to the guillotine. Dickens's reflection on the passage of a crowd to a mob may have inspired Gavin Stevens's meditation.

4. This entry, for instance, dated 28 August 1944: "Writing for Hawks again, Faulkner begins the adaptation of Raymond Chandler's *The Big Sleep* for Warner Bros." Michel Gresset, *A Faulkner Chronology* (Jackson: University Press of Mississippi, 1985), 66.

5. As an echo of *Intruder in the Dust*, similar confrontation between a racist conservative discourse and an open attitude creates the tension of Carson McCullers's novel *Clock without Hands* (1961), selections of which appeared in magazines as early as 1953.

6. For a study of the clichés in *The Ponder Heart*, see Danièle Pitavy-Souques, *La Mort de Meduse* (Presses Universitaires de Lyon 1991), 214–21 and *Eudora Welty* (Paris: Belin, 1999), 91–96.

7. Interestingly, Arthur Miller chose that period to transpose in a play (*The Crucible*, 1953) his own involvement in the immediate political situation. At a time when writers, film

directors, and performers were hard pressed to confess their political sins and name their fellow sinners, John Proctor, Miller's hero, is the man who could say *no*.

8. In her well-documented essay on *The Ponder Heart*, Sharon Deykin Baris concentrates on the Rosenbergs' trial, its coverage in the press and the way Welty's eye may have caught a good deal of sideline information from the layout of the newspapers she daily read: the *New York Times* and the *Memphis Commercial Appeal*. And as she shows how "Welty . . . locates her novel's action in the culture of its time," Baris suggests that the target of the novella may have been President Eisenhower himself portrayed as Uncle Daniel. "More daringly," writes Baris, "its pages portray the insidious moral and mortal harassments such a favorite imposed, seemingly in the name of public good will" (198).

9. *Author and Agent*, 167.

10. Paul Ricoeur, *Lectures on Ideology and Utopia* (New York: Columbia University, 1986).

11. Welty's opinion of the first version: "it lacked texture, made the characters much too calculating and too self-explanatory (Uncle Daniel couldn't say he's an innocent), and didn't make the town love Uncle Daniel—they were sort of cynical instead" (Kreyling, 174–75). Or again, "I felt upset on seeing my little story turned into a sort of bedroom dilemma with gags and no characterization remaining; They have removed the very parts I'd have thought were of any dramatic significance—giving away the money, the ball of fire, to name two . . . I am afraid his *simple* character will be lost" (October 22, 1995, quoted by Kreyling, 178).

12. Was Eudora Welty unconsciously reminded of this character when she knew that Steinbeck was among the writers asked, like her, "to contribute to a collection of New Year's greetings to the defeated Democratic candidate, Adlai Stevenson"? (*Writer and Agent*, 161).

13. See Jagna Oltarzewska, "Telling Stories: Resistance to World Reduction in *The Handmaid's Tale*, ed. Martha Dvorak (Paris: Ellipses, 1998), 30–39.

14. *Lion in the Garden*, 251.

Invisible Men: William Faulkner, His Contemporaries, and the Politics of Loving and Hating the South in the Civil Rights Era; or, How Does a Rebel Rebel?

GRACE ELIZABETH HALE

Everybody likes to think of themselves as a rebel.[1]
—Ronnie Van Zant of Lynyrd Skynyrd

In the 1950s, William Faulkner was finally famous. The Noble Prize in 1950 and the National Book Award and Pulitzer several years later had given him a celebrity at home he had long enjoyed abroad. On a State Department trip to Brazil, Faulkner eloquently argued that the world needed to address racial conflict, its most pressing problem. For a moment, that elusive identity, the public man of letters, seemed within his grasp.[2]

Yet Faulkner instead made a fool of himself. When, in 1956, a federal judge ordered the University of Alabama to accept African American student Autherine Lucy, Faulkner sought an interview with London *Sunday Times* correspondent Russell Howe. He pleaded for a middle way, for slowness, for time to let the white South come around. Cornered, he became a rebel. Only violence would result from forcing integration on white Southerners. The student would be killed, he insisted, "the government will send its troops, and we'll be back at 1860. . . . As long as there's a middle road, all right, I'll be on it. But if it came to fighting, I'd fight for Mississippi against the United States even if it meant going out into the street and shooting Negroes."[3]

Although Faulkner had allegedly been drinking when he made this infamous statement, his confusion did not just flow from the bottle. Drunkenness aside (and many of them were drunk), Southern white men appeared confused in the late 1950s, and the craziness lasted, often turning into caricature, through the 1970s. The problem became critical for those with artistic pretensions whose professions placed them in the public eye, writers like Faulkner, Shelby Foote, and James Dickey and musicians from Elvis Presley to Southern rockers like Duane Allman and Ronnie Van Zant. Two distinct groups of Southern white men faced this problem as they self-consciously promoted their Southernness in the civil rights era—the Southern writers of what scholars call the Southern Renaissance and the Southern musicians of that 1970s rock genre the music industry calls Southern rock. The problem, of course, was how did a Rebel rebel?[4]

In the civil rights era South, white Southern masculinity still depended upon a celebration of rebellion. Southern white men had spent almost a century perfecting a contradictory image of alienation and strength. While posing as outsiders within the larger currents of American culture, they enjoyed the power of gender and racial privilege at home and not inconsiderable authority within the federal government as well. But rebellion proved promiscuous in the postwar era. Led by artists, writers, and civil rights activists, beatniks, Jews, and jazz musicians, the ranks of rebellion swelled. Soon young Americans everywhere, with or without a cause, signed on, including women and African American men and then Native Americans, Latinos, and gays. And these rebels challenged both the outsider image and the underlying authority of the original Rebels.[5]

For white Southern men in particular, civil rights' successes meant the end of an old self-image. As truly marginalized black Southerners dramatized their own blatant and often violent exclusion on streets and buses and at lunch counters across the region, white Southern men found it difficult to hold on to power and yet project a public identity as outsiders. When black male writers like James Baldwin, Richard Wright, and Ralph Ellison wrote for little reviews and even more broadly circulated magazines like *Harper's* and *Esquire*, they seized the mantle of the moral rebel from white Southern writers. Baldwin's "Faulkner and Desegregation," for example, a piece originally published in *Partisan Review* in 1956, is well known for its moral power. "Why—and how—" Baldwin asks, "does one move from the middle of the road where one was aiding Negroes into the streets—to shoot them?" Faulkner, Baldwin insisted, "has never before more concretely expressed what it means to be a Southerner." Ellison too blasted Faulkner in a March 1956 letter written to his friend and fellow writer Albert Murray:

> Bill Faulkner can write a million as he did recently in *Life*, but he forgets . . . that *Mose* isn't in the market for his advice, because he's been knowing how to 'wait-a-while'—Faulkner advice—for over three hunderd years, only he's never been simply waiting, he's been probing for a soft spot . . . Faulkner has delusions of grandeur because he really believes that he invented these characteristics which he ascribes to Negroes in his fiction. . . .

The civil rights movement made it impossible to be both a Rebel in the Confederate sense, someone who defied his nation to defend his region, and a rebel in the romantic sense, a seer who defies his society to defend a greater truth. No matter how many Confederate flags they waved, the white Southern rockers who resurrected the image in the 1970s ironically owed more to a blues' image of black masculinity than to an earlier tradition of rebel Rebels.[6]

It's My Party: White Southern Writers as Rebel Rebels

There was never a better time to be a white Southern man. In the years before *Brown* and the Montgomery Bus Boycott, Southern whites who wanted to could still ignore the civil rights movement. Sure, their culture of segregation sometimes seemed threatened—most powerfully in the political arena with Truman's integration of the armed forces and his civil rights plan that sparked the Dixiecrat revolt. But many Southern whites saw African American activism as isolated and easily put down. Local NAACP leader Harry T. Moore's boldness in northern Florida in the early 1950s was attacked not only by Southern whites but by the national NAACP as well. A bomb placed under his house killed him in 1951. Periodic voter registration drives in cities like Atlanta, on the other hand, succeeded in adding a few black voters to the rolls without substantially challenging white Southern political power.

More troubling for whites perhaps were signs of national homogenization and the explosive growth of popular culture. Chain stores and other branches of national businesses, provoked both by protest and by the difficulty of devising different rules of operation for different localities, increasingly standardized their practices. In very visible contradiction to the segregation signs, for colored and for white, scattered throughout Southern commercial districts, these businesses offered some services—bagging groceries, accepting returns, and in the case of gas stations, allowing the use of a single set of bathrooms—for both their black and white customers. When white adults expressed anxiety about their teenagers' interest in Elvis Presley and the new rock music, they focused on the explicit sexuality and transgression of gender conventions. Left implicit were the ways rock and roll challenged segregation by combining both rhythm and blues or black music and country and western or white music and by appealing to an integrated audience. And critics only hinted at Elvis's most disturbing quality, what radio listeners noticed immediately, that he sang and performed like a black man.

It was just this kind of blindness that made plausible some white Southern men's continuing conception of themselves as outsiders. Civil

War veterans, military and otherwise, had nurtured at Confederate reunions and Lost Cause celebrations a sense of white Southern alienation that had its roots in the antebellum era. At the turn of the century, their sons and daughters knit this feeling of distinctiveness into their new segregated social order, modernizing and extending Southern whites' investment in regional as well as racial difference. In the 1930s, the Agrarians provided an intellectual version of Southern white male rebellion, rage against the machine and the greedy, conformist, placeless society it spawned. For white Southern men in the postwar era, alienation paradoxically possessed all the trappings of a tradition.

Yet alienation was complicated in the South's cultural context. Segregation was more than a racial order. Like slavery in the antebellum South, it cemented a distinctive regional culture. As a result, Southerners lived simultaneously two similar and yet different cultural contexts. In a regional version of W. E. B. DuBois's double vision, they were both Southern and American. The racial differences segregation enacted and enforced in turn further blurred an individual's sight, creating in fact a triple vision. What was rebellious for a white Southerner, for example, might not be recognized as rebellious by a white American.[7]

Many white Southern men with artistic and intellectual pretensions followed, with varying degrees of consciousness, the rebellious tradition set up by the Agrarians. In *I'll Take My Stand*, published in 1929, and in their own novels and poems men like Allen Tate, Robert Penn Warren, and John Crowe Ransom created a model for being both modern in a cultural sense—modernist—and yet still being Southern, understood by them as white. White Southerners, they suggested, were not backward or antimodern at all—they were simply alienated from the main currents of American life. Faced with a choice between industrialism or "machine society" and Agrarianism or agricultural society, their modern white Southerner traded the glitter of wealth for the richness of rural society. The South would provide the counterweight to the "eternal flux," the "infinite series," of "our urbanized, antiprovincial, progressive and mobile American life." "The culture of the soil," the Agrarians insisted, was "the best." Still, the life of the land they envisioned was more that of a gentleman farmer who made his money mysteriously elsewhere. At mid-century, small farmers, never mind renters and sharecroppers, had little time to write.[8]

The importance of the Agrarians, then, lay not in any practical application of their ideas but in the model of artistic identity they established for Southern white men. They created a new way of being a Rebel, modern and intellectual and outside of the suspect circles of Lost Cause celebration. This Rebel embraced as "Southern tradition" his alienation from the greedy materialism of the larger American culture. Standing as a lonely voice of conscience for the nation, he made this choice not out of ignorance but out of a sense of moral superiority and strength. White Southern men's sense of this contradictory cultural position—a distance from a larger American culture and yet a rootedness in a distinctive regional culture—generated much of the work later labeled as the Southern Renaissance.[9]

Postwar white Southern male writers as different as James Dickey, Shelby Foote, and William Faulkner were steeped in this tradition as young men. Dickey studied English from 1946 to 1949 at Vanderbilt, a school, he wrote, "where you can't be interested in literature without being made aware of the Vanderbilt literary tradition and the great days of the late 1920s, the days . . . of the manifestos, such as *I'll Take My Stand.*" Dickey retained an agrarian-style opposition to technology, science, and industry all his life. At various times close to both Andrew Lytle and Robert Penn Warren, Dickey also knew Allen Tate, who helped him secure a Sewanee Fellowship to study abroad. His most famous work, his 1970 novel *Deliverance* explores this theme even as it critiques the Agrarians' romanticization of rural life. Shelby Foote did not have this kind of direct experience—he attended Vanderbilt's much more progressive rival, the University of North Carolina at Chapel Hill. Yet by 1951 he sounded like an Agrarian: "I tell you what writing needs, and badly. It absolutely needs a sense of place. And Agrarianism lay at the heart of the 'big novel,'" "Two Gates to the City," that Foote worked on in the early 1950s and again in the mid-1970s after completing his Civil War trilogy. His main character, he writes in letter in 1951, "has a choice (industrialism or agrarianism, spiritualism or materialism, and so forth) and the making of this choice is the novel—all played of course against the background of his heritage. The Delta itself is the 'hero.'" If Foote had ever been able to finish it, "Two Gates" might have been the quintessential Agrarian novel. Like Dickey, he continued to think in part as an Agrarian throughout his life. "Our God isn't Christ," he said, criticizing his fellow white Southerners in 1970. "It's that iron Vulcan over in Birmingham."[10]

Faulkner too, for all the fire of his critique of Southern culture in novels like *Absalom, Absalom!* and *Light in August*, felt something profound was being lost as the South became more integrated into the nation. In his 1929 novel *The Sound and the Fury*, the making of plantation fields into a golf course symbolizes the path of progress swallowing up the old rural life. "The Bear," a short story later incorporated into the 1942 novel *Go Down, Moses*, casts the vanishing wilderness itself as a character in the story which becomes a eulogy to its passing. The South might be fatally flawed, Faulkner's work suggests, but it was better than the North. One romance is critiqued even as another one is created.[11]

The fact that segregation and not rural life grounded both whatever white male freedom existed and the twentieth century Southern social order did not exactly create the ideal foundation for claims of Southern moral superiority. Issues of race, of course, had to be buried to make this version of the Rebel. This absence in turn provided the perfect opportunity for Southern white men with artistic pretensions to join in a more generally American rebellion welling up within the larger American culture in the 1950s. The psychic dislocations of World War II and the postwar expansion of consumer culture, horror and plenty, death and life in massive proportion, marked the uniquely American experience of the postwar period. Levittown and the concentration camp, television and the bomb—the surrealist productions of a modernized world paradoxically raised barely articulated doubts about the survival of American ideals in the midst of American triumph. Artists often self-consciously addressed questions of individual identity and expression in the context of mass production and increasingly anonymous social relations.[12]

Yet attempts to rescue the individual from the deadening weight of mass society were not new. Alienation had deep roots in both European and American culture, from the early nineteenth-century Romantics and the late nineteenth-century revolts of the anti-modernists, decadents, and Impressionists to the attempts of artists and writers to come to terms with the experience of the Great War. What was unique about cold war America, however, was the gradual democratization of romantic alienation, its transformation from an avant-garde stance to, by the end of the 1960s, a central characteristic of American culture. Increasing numbers of Americans imagined the most essential characteristics of identity— their sense of beauty, truth, justice, even reality—as laying outside of and often in opposition to their understanding of American society.[13]

Taking the South's "values" against the nation's materialism had in an odd sense prepared white Southern male artists to embrace an increasingly more general sense of alienation in the 1950s. Being a Rebel, then, helped them to be rebels, to believe in nothing but their own creative acts and pursue their art at the expense of whatever stood in its way. "I have never valued life greatly, since I was in the war so young" wrote Dickey in a 1954 letter to Andrew Lytle. "It seemed then that most of the things that I had been told about human life were false, constructions, rationalizations only, which would not stand up against any kind of forceful reality. But the artist is after another kind of reality: the underlying, the typical, the profound, the symbolic, the substructure of reality, the hidden anatomy." Foote expressed his own sense of alienation a year later in a letter to fellow white Southern writer Walker Percy: "The past fifteen years of my life have been spent discovering that practically 100% of the things told me as indisputably true—the so-called eternal verities—are false." Three years earlier he had written that being a writer in fact depended upon standing outside of society: "A man must write for himself, and then he must accept the penalties—including the possibility of damnation. Youve [sic] got to put it all on the line; anything less than *all* is hedging and your work is weakened at the wellspring, hopelessly flawed, shot through with rot."[14]

For Faulkner in the 1950s, older than these men, a profound sense of alienation flowed both from the larger world and from his failing work and his failing marriage. He wanted "what I have always wanted: to be free; probably until now I have still believed that somehow, in some way, someday I would be free again; now at last I have begun to realize that perhaps I will not. . . . I have already sacrificed too much . . . to try to be a good artist." These white Southern men had, in some strange way, been there—at odds with the region, nation and family—all along.[15]

But the best way to rebel against the South was to refuse to ignore its segregated culture. In his fiction, William Faulkner provided a powerful and yet lonely Southern voice for racial liberalism. Dilsey Gibson, one of the main characters in *The Sound and the Fury*, was at the time one of the most fully realized and yet also admirable black characters in white-authored American literature. She was, however, the white folks' maid. In *Go Down, Moses*, Faulkner created the even less stereotypical character Lucas Beauchamp, the heir to a thousand daguerreotypes of the faces of Confederate soldiers, the embodiment of what had previously been Southern white male valor and courage.[16]

Yet Faulkner made many contradictory statements about race relations in the postwar era. By the early 1950s, he had decided that white Southerners would demonstrate their deep morality and embrace integration if public men like him spoke the words and led the way. The rest of the country, he insisted, must leave the work to white Southerners. In the years after *Brown*, however, it became painfully clear that many white Southerners would never, no matter how slowly, seek desegregation and that blacks would not wait for whites to act. Lost, unable to stop being a Rebel, Faulkner seemed crazed. He talked of taking up guns against Southern blacks and made outrageous statements like "television is for niggers."[17]

Dickey was also contradictory. His poetry manages to pick at white Southern racial pretensions and yet remain racist as well. In "Buckdancer's Choice," for example, a poem from his 1965 collection of the same name, he conflates his sick mother with the figure of an old-time black minstrel, one of the "classic buck-and-wing men." Somehow, he manages to diminish them both, in his equation of her sickness with the burden of slavery: "Proclaiming what choices there are/ For the last dancers of their kind,/ For ill women and for all slaves." His poem "Slave Quarters," from the same collection, also manages to flout white Southern racial conventions by talking about sex between masters and slaves while expressing an even more troubling racism: "I look across at low walls/ Of slave quarters, and feel my imagining loins/ Rise with the madness of owners." Fantasizing about interracial and compulsory sex became a way for Dickey's persona to release his own sexuality: "In that ruined house let me throw/ Obsessive gentility off;/ Let Africa rise upon me like a man/ Whose instincts are delivered from their chains."[18]

The more courageous way, of course, to rebel against the culture of segregation was to attack white Southern racism, as Shelby Foote consistently did during the 1950s and 1960s. In a 1956 letter, he denounced the membership of the Citizen's Council: "it seems to me to be largely recruited from the upper middle class; certainly the ones I know are from it, and they seem to be the leaders. Their claim is that they have taken the lead to offset the violence, which is shit-talk; all they mean is that they are forming the organization; then when violence comes (if it comes) some of them will step aside and watch with horror while the redneck-element starts shooting." Foote lived in Gulf Shores, Alabama, briefly in 1964, where the Klan verbally attacked and threatened him for displaying a Johnson sticker and speaking out for integration.[19]

It was not necessary to be a racial liberal to be a rebel. Flouting white Southern racial laws and conventions took many forms. But all of these rebel Rebels seemed to reach a moment of truth, a point when they had to pick just which kind of rebel they wanted to be. As Faulkner's example illustrates, the results were not pretty. Dickey made his mixed feelings about integration public in his 1961 essay "Notes on the Decline of Outrage." The poet was, he confessed, almost nostalgic for the segregated South now passing. The title mourned both the loss of that segregated world and Dickey's personal loss of his outrage over its loss. In the classes he taught at Reed College during the 1963–1964 academic year, Dickey like Faulkner before him reached his crossroads. Would he continue to be a rebel by poking holes in white racial thinking even if it meant opposing the segregationist stance of many white Southerners? "Slave Quarters," for all its offensiveness, did make visible a miscegenation most white Americans wanted to ignore. Or would Dickey chose to circle his Southern wagons and remain a Rebel? One day in class a student asked him about the Freedom Riders. In an uncanny echo of Faulkner's earlier response, Dickey answered, "if there were a race war, I know which side

I'd be on." By 1972, he boomed, "I am not a Southerner! I'm the Southerner." It had become difficult to tell the difference between the redneck Dickey act and the real Dickey.[20]

Foote did not write about race war or weapons in the streets. In 1963, he went so far as to write Walker Percy that he was "beginning to hate the one thing I really ever loved—the South. No, thats [sic] wrong: not hate—despise. . . . Good Lord, when I think what we could have been, the heritage we perverted!—the misspent courage, the hardcore independence, the way a rich man always had to call a poor man Mister, the niggers who stood up for a century under what would have crumpled the rest of us in a month, the women who never lost the knowledge that their job was to be women." He criticized the Klan, too, less for their violent opposition to integration than for their cowardice and their degradation of the Confederate Flag. The problem with the South, for Foote, was not that African Americans lacked basic rights but that white Southern men had not lived up to some imagined standard of honor. He spent the civil rights era buried in the past where white Southern men, at least in his imagination, acted as he desired. Hard at work on his Civil War trilogy, Foote found that his status as a Rebel was secure.[21]

These men, then, countered a growing civil rights militancy by becoming more militant themselves, by being Rebels. Faulkner talked of guns in the streets. Dickey spoke of race war and collected hunting bows. Foote turned to war too but one safely in the past. "Don't underrate it [the Civil War] as a thing that can claim a man's whole waking mind for years on end," Foote wrote in a letter the year after *Brown*. "It's teaching me to love my country, especially the South." [22]

For white Southern men, then, the civil rights era meant the end of an old image of themselves. As black Southerners dramatized their own blatant and often violent exclusion, white Southern men found it difficult to hold onto power and yet project an identity as outsiders. No longer was it possible to be both a Rebel in that Confederate sense, a white person who defied his nation to defend his region, and a rebel in that romantic sense, a seer who defies his society to defend a greater truth. As Rebels, they could no longer be romanticized outsiders within the larger American culture. Paradoxically, in choosing to support the South, understood as white, in the battle over racial integration, they adopted that most traditional of American male images. Just how alienated, in the sweep of a history that begins with a revolution, was a Southern white man with a weapon? The artist, the man as creator, was an outsider. The white man with a gun in his hand sat at the center. A post-Civil War way of being a Southern white man had reached its end.

No Where to Run To: From Southern Writers to Southern Rock

There had never been a worse time to be a Southern white man. It had been absurd before for people enjoying the privileges of a violently segregated Southern society to claim moral superiority. But after some white Southern men's violent resistance to the civil rights movement, the Agrarian-influenced tradition of being both Rebel and rebel became completely unworkable. The young men who would make Southern rock in the late 1960s and early 1970s heard from outside little but criticism of their native region as they grew up. Instead of the pen, however, these proud Southern white men would pick up the guitar. For them, the choice was easy. They were Rebels. And they resurrected an aspect of this identity neglected by the white Southern male writers who came before them. The Rebel as an old but once again viable image of a white man who had lost some of his privilege had its roots in the sensitive Southern chauvinism of the Civil War veterans and Confederate patriotic societies. As the Charlie Daniels's Band promised in a 1974 song, "Be proud to be a Rebel, cos the South's Gonna Do It Again." The "it" was left open intentionally. Transformed by the Southern rockers, this Rebel in time became less Southern and more an image of injured white men everywhere.[23]

Southern rock, according to guitarist Charlie Daniels, was not a genre of music but "a genre of people that were all basically raised the same way." "None of us were raised with any particular amount of money. Everybody was raised in a blue-collar situation, came up listening to the same music, eating the same food, going to the same type of churches." The Allman Brothers were the first group to play what the industry soon called Southern rock. Along with Lynyrd Skynyrd, the Charlie Daniels Band, and others, the Allman Brothers began attracting a regional white audience of working class youth and college students in the late 1960s and early 1970s. But in 1971, with the release of the double live album *At Fillmore East*, the Allman Brothers developed a national audience. Macon, Georgia, home of Phil Walden's Capricorn Records, quickly became the center of Southern rock. Capricorn recorded the Allman Brothers and most of the other important Southern rock bands, with the exception of Lynyrd Skynyrd whose MCA affiliated *Sounds of the South* label was based in Atlanta.[24]

Southern rockers largely ignored the ongoing conflicts in the region over racial integration. In the late 1960s and 1970s, for example, some school systems in the rural Deep South were just beginning to integrate. An organized attack on integration launched in the wake of *Brown* had fallen apart, but white Southerners individually and, in organizations from the Klan to the segregation academies, collectively continued to insist on racial privilege. Much in the South had changed. Segregation signs had come down, signalling the end of the segregation of public and commercial facilities. Federal programs pushed the integration of employment. And African Americans across the South were able to vote. But it was at best an uneasy peace. George Wallace's three presidential campaigns—in 1964, 1968, and 1972—gave white Southerners upset about their diminished racial privilege a political place to register their anger.[25]

Interestingly, the white Southern supporters of George Wallace and the Southern rockers and many of their fans shared similar class backgrounds. They were lower middle class and working class, struggling financially, attached to white privilege because it often seemed like the only privilege they had. Southern rock provided a safe place outside of politics for white Southern men to express and romanticize their experience of loss. Southern rock made the emotional reaction of these white men left behind by both the civil rights movement and sunbelt success seem acceptable, even fashionable, instead of redneck and retrograde. Even The Band, a group progressive enough to back Bob Dylan, flirted with the Confederate flag in the mid-1970s. The music turned what had seemed like loss of authority over family, African Americans, and local communities into a celebration of the power that flowed from not having to be responsible for any of these individuals or institutions. Ironically, Southern rock accomplished this transformation, this creation and celebration of a different kind of Rebel, by turning to black men, by turning to the blues.[26]

Southern rock bands, as Daniels suggested, did not share a single distinctive sound. Instead, each evolved its own mixture of blues, country, rhythm and blues, rock, and jazz. But the blues was the foundation, the soul of Southern rock. As musicians, these Southern white men were heavily influenced by African American music. The Allman Brothers in particular based their sound on blues rhythms and blues improvisations. Duane Allman and Dickey Betts became legendary for their long, wailing guitar duets, based on the urban blues style of African American musicians like B. B. King. The Allman Brothers, in turn, had a tremendous influence on the Southern rock bands that followed them. Lynryd Skynyrd, for example, adopted the dual guitar format and blistering guitar break style as well. Greg Allman modeled his deep, low, and emotive vocals on the voices of old black bluesmen. The Allman Brothers, Lynyrd Skynyrd, and others filled out their albums and live shows with their own versions of old blues songs. But the song lyrics themselves, often topical and in Lynryd Skynyrd's case overtly political, almost never focused on racial issues or black people. African Americans were also largely absent in the bands themselves and in their audiences. The original Allman Brothers

Band, with their African American drummer Jai Johanny Johanson, were an important exception. It was certainly significant in Georgia in 1969 that five whites and one black formed a band and called themselves brothers. As a whole, however, Southern rock was black-sounding music made for and by white men.[27]

"The Ballad of Curtis Loew" from Lynryd Skynyrd's 1971 album *Second Helping*, the most important exception to the absence of African Americans in Southern rock song lyrics, illustrates the paradoxical expression of white racial loss through the forms of black music. The song tells the story of an old bluesman: "He looked to be sixty and maybe I was ten. Mama used to whoop me—but I'd go see him again. I'd clap my hands, stomp my feet, try to stay in tune. He'd play me a song or two then take another drink of wine." The white boy and old Curtis made a bargain: "drinkin' money" in exchange for music lessons. Lynryd Skynyrd's lead singer Ronnie Van Zant, the coauthor of the song, talked to another musician about "Curtis Loew" in 1974: "Ronnie said that Curtis Loew was a fictional character the idea for which came from Shorty's [Medlocke] front-porch jam sessions and also from a story he'd heard about Hank Williams. Hank always alluded to the fact that it was an old black blues musician who inspired him to pick up the guitar at an early age.... Ronnie explained that 'Curtis' was a combination of characters, that 'Curtis' was every old black blues player who'd ever taught a trick or two to a young white boy trying to learn the blues.[28]

The lyrics of "Curtis Loew" recycle a white fantasy with a long history. White Southerners told tales of old bluesmen teaching white boys about black music much as they told mammy stories celebrating their love for the African American women who had raised them—to relieve white anxiety and guilt about their love for and yet oppression of African Americans. "I am not a racist," these stories implied without ever directly broaching the too dangerous topic, the way both love and theft characterized white musical borrowings. "A black man taught me to play the blues." The tale of the black bluesman also strengthened white claims to their own musical authenticity. This exchange, they shouted, goes back to the source. "We play the blues just like our teachers the old black guys."

Most Southern rockers, however, learned about the blues not from black men but from other whites. Ronnie Van Zant remembered sitting on the front porch and listening to his friend's father, Shorty Medlocke, play. Al Kooper, the man who discovered Lynryd Skynyrd, signed them to his Sounds of the South label, and produced their first three albums, also insisted that Medlocke, a local white Jacksonville blues player, exposed the future members of the band to the blues. Greg Allman remembered learning the blues from a white guitar player named Floyd Miles. "We kind of grew up together, and he pretty much turned me on to black music," Allman said. "Kind of taught me the right people to listen to." But many Southern rock musicians, like white kids across the South, learned about Southern black music when white British bands took up the blues in the mid to late 1960s. Not only did they not learn the blues from African American musicians, they learned it from British musicians who copied the blues styles of American blacks captured on old "race" records. Most Southern rockers, then, were at least two steps removed from the blues as a living music. The mediations made the music safer, muting the troubling fact that these Southern white musicians, like Elvis Presley before them, were copying African American music—its structure, its lyrics, and even its black players' performance style. Southern rockers seemed oblivious to what else their use of the blues implied—that they learned to be Rebels by copying the vision of African American masculinity presented in the blues.[29]

Southern rock musicians, then, adopted a blues-created image of black masculinity as central to their rebellion. Southern rock lyrics, for example, take for their own the blues' image of relationships between men and women as painful and difficult and full of fleeting pleasures that should be valued despite their transience. The Allman Brothers' 1971 song "Whipping Post" bemoans the singer's love for a bad woman: "I've been run down, 'n I been lied to, but I don't know why I let that mean woman make me out a fool. She took all my money, wrecked my new car, yeah, but now she's with one o' my good-time buddies. They're drinkin' in some cross town bar." Southern rockers also copied the blues lyric's love for the road. The Allman Brothers song "Ramblin' Man" valued mobility as an end in itself: "on my way to New Orleans this mornin', leavin' out of Nashville, Tennessee. They're always having a good time down at the bayou, Lord. Them delta women think the world of me." These Delta women may have included black women, as well. The 1973 Lynyrd Skynyrd song "Freebird" summed up Southern rock's celebration of unlimited geographical and emotional travel: "If I leave here tomorrow, would you still remember me? Well, I must be traveling on now, 'cause there's too many places I've got to see. But if I stay here with you girl, things just couldn't be the same. 'Cause I'm as free as a bird now, and this bird you cannot change . . . Lord knows I can't change."[30]

Whether bluesmen lived this image, however, depended upon their individual circumstances. To an important degree the blues was African American's rejection of the white fantasy, on display everywhere from minstrelsy to motion pictures, of the comical, easy-going, and emasculated slave and ex-slave. But Southern rockers collectively tried to live up to their lyrics. And members of the successful bands especially had the money to indulge in endless rounds of drink, drugs, and women. Ironically, then, Southern rockers' version of the Rebel was more than a little indebted to the "white Negro."[31]

The "white Negro" character—white men playing out their fantasies of being black—has a long history in American popular culture, from the blackfaced figure of the antebellum minstrel show to the New York City hipster of Mailer's famous article. Southern rock took the burying of racial borrowings evident in this genealogy one step further. Neither Elvis nor Mailer's urban hipster had needed black face paint. Elvis bought all his clothes on Beale Street, his personal style making plain the African American sources of its inspiration. The hipster demonstrated his "blackness" too in his haunts and his taste in dress. Southern rockers, however, skipped all visual reference to African American performance styles entirely. They cloaked their blues voices and blues-influenced guitars in cowboy hats, boots, and blue jeans, in a funky, outlaw updating of hillbilly style. The Allman Brothers, who called the place where they all lived together "the Big House," had their photograph taken in this kind of dress among the columns of what appears to be an old run-down, antebellum mansion. And Southern rockers also waved Confederate flags. Lynyrd Skynyrd carried a gigantic version from concert to concert, at home and abroad, always playing in front of the Stars and Bars. While Southern rock bands verbally acknowledged their musical debt to black music, in their visual performance they denied the very cultural miscegenation that gave birth to their style.[32]

Lynyrd Skynyrd, more than any other Southern rock band, made it clear just how disturbing this contradictory acknowledgement and denial could be. In the early 1970s, many Americans, white and black, Southern and non-Southern, understood any display of Southern (understood as white) pride as carrying an implicit racial message. By the mid-seventies criticism about its use of the Confederate flag had made the band sensitive. Lead singer Ronnie Van Zant claimed in 1976, "as far as the Confederate flag is concerned, we've carried that with us for a long time before we did anything; it's just part of us. We're from the South, but we're not bigots." That same year, however, he also placed the responsibility for Skynyrd's use of the Confederate flag squarely upon their record company: "It was a gimmick for us, at first, you know, Southern Band, and MCA made that a gimmick, a hype thing, you know, drunken fighters and all. They put out that publicity. Hype, nothing but hype." Other band members and associates have continued over the years to blame the record company. Record company officials disagreed, insisting that they were never involved in the band's stage presentation.[33]

But Lynyrd Skynyrd's second most popular song after "Freebird," "Sweet Home Alabama," off their 1974 album *Second Helping*, suggested that band members, much like those rebel Rebels a decade before them, were trying to have it both ways. The band wrote "Sweet Home Alabama" in response to Neil Young's attacks on the South in his songs "Alabama" and "Southern Man": "Well, I heard Mister Young sing about her. Well I heard old Neil put 'er down. Well, I hope Neil Young will remember, a Southern man don't need him around, anyhow." While the line "In Birmingham they love the gov'nor" was followed by the line "boo boo boo," the end of the song—"Sweet home Alabama, oh sweet home! Where the skies are blue and the gov'nor's true" made no such comment. Too some degree, the strategy must have worked because young men with no sense of the history involved waved small versions of the flag at concerts from England to Japan even as white Southern fans adopted the song as a sort of regional anthem.[34]

Using the blues to reinvent the Rebel created a simultaneous visibility and invisibility, not just for blackness but for Southernness as well. The bands both announced their debt to the blues and yet hid their racial borrowings. They both appealed to an especially white Southern male sense of regional chauvinism and yet managed to symbolize an abstracted sense of lost white male privilege everywhere. In Southern rock, the Rebel and the rebel merged, creating an image specific enough to be appealing and yet vague enough to symbolize whatever kind of rebel a man wanted to be. Southern rock musicians managed to be rebels against conventional middle class American institutions like marriage and the family by adopting their fantasy of African American masculinity. Yet they also succeeded in standing up for their region, understood as white, in displaying their rebellion against a new national consensus on racial liberalism. In the realm of 1970s popular culture, the contradictions that made Southern white men like Dickey and Faulkner and Thompson seem absurd in the 1950s and 1960s coexisted without much comment. Southern rock managed for that 1970s moment to fuse the rebel and the Rebel into one, a white man who wasn't going to take it anymore, whatever that "it" might be. Maybe Faulkner was not so far off the mark with Lucas Beauchamp. In the end, the "white Negro" became a Confederate after all.

NOTES

1. Lee Ballinger, *Lynyrd Skynyrd: An Oral History* (New York: Avon Books, 1999), 67.
2. Joel Williamson, *William Faulkner and Southern History* (New York: Oxford University Press, 1993), 305–7; Joseph Blotner, *William Faulkner: A Biography* (New York: Random House, 1984), 616–18.
3. Russell Warren Howe, *The Reporter* 14 (22 March 1956): 18–20, reprinted in James B. Meriwether and Michael Millgate, eds., *Lion in the Garden: Interviews with William Faulkner, 1926–1962* (New York: Random House, 1968), 262. For other contradictory statements by

Faulkner about race, see James B. Meriwether, ed., *Essays, Speeches, and Public Letters* (New York: Random House, 1966), 87, 225. See also the following letters: William Faulkner (hereafter WF), Oxford, Miss., December 8, 1955, to Bob Flautt, Glendora, Miss.; WF, Oxford, Miss., January 12, 1956, to W. C. Neill, North Carrollton, Miss.; WF, Oxford, Miss., January 18, 1956, to Harold Ober, New York City; WF, Oxford, Miss., March 8, 1956, to David Kirk, University of Alabama; WF, Oxford, Miss., June 23, 1956, to Allan Morrison. See also WF, telegram to W. E. B. DuBois, April 17, 1956. All are reprinted in Joseph Blotner, *Selected Letters of William Faulkner* (New York: Random House, 1977), 389–390, 391, 392–93, 394–96, 397–98, 400–1.

4. On the Southern Renaissance and the cultural context of the 1920s through 1950s South, see Richard H. King, *A Southern Renaissance: The Cultural Awakening of the American South, 1930–1955* (New York: Oxford University Press, 1980); Michael O'Brien, *The Idea of the American South, 1920–1941* (Baltimore: Johns Hopkins Press, 1979); Fred C. Hobson, *Tell about the South: The Southern Rage to Explain* (Baton Rouge: Louisiana State University Press, 1983); John Egerton, *Speak Now against the Day: The Generation before the Civil Rights Movement in the South* (New York: Knopf, 1994); and Daniel Joseph Singal, *The War Within: From Victorian to Modernist Thought in the South, 1919–1945* (Chapel Hill: University of North Carolina Press, 1982). See Michael T. Bertrand, *Race, Rock, and Elvis* (Urbana: University of Illinois Press, 2000) on Southern musicians and fans and the origins of rock. Not much serious work has been done on Southern rock. See Ted Ownby, "Freedom, Manhood, and White Male Tradition in 1970s Southern Rock Music," 369–88, in Anne Goodwyn Jones and Susan V. Donaldson, eds., *Haunted Bodies: Gender and Southern Texts* (Charlottesville: University Press of Virginia, 1997); Paul Wells, "The Last Rebel: Southern Rock and Nostalgic Continuities," 115–29, in Richard H. King and Helen Taylor, eds., *Dixie Debates: Perpsectives on Southern Cultures* (New York: New York University Press, 1996); Reebee Garofalo, *Rockin' Out: Popular Music in the USA* (Boston: Allyn and Bacon, 1997), 283–85; Stephen R. Tucker, "Southern Rock," 328–30, in Charles Reagan Wilson and William Ferris, *Encyclopedia of Southern Culture*, vol. 3 (New York: Anchor Books, 1989); and the not very good Marley Brant, *Southern Rockers: The Roots and Legacy of Southern Rock* (New York: Billboard Books, 1999). Ownby's fine article, although brief, is the best piece on Southern rock available.

5. On rebellion in the 1950s, see Tom Engelhardt, *The End of Victory Culture: Cold War America and the Disillusioning of a Generation* (Amhurst: University of Massachusetts Press, 1998); Stephen J. Whitfield, *The Culture of the Cold War* (Baltimore: Johns Hopkins Press, 1996); Todd Gitlin, *The Sixties: Years of Hope, Days of Rage* (New York: Bantam Books, 1987), 11–44; Daniel Horowitz, *Betty Friedan and the Making of the Feminist Mystique: The American Left, The Cold War, and Modern Feminism* (Amhurst: University of Massachusetts, 1998); Peter J. Kuznick and James Gilbert, *Rethinking Cold War Culture* (Washington, D.C.: Smithsonian Institution Press, 2001); David Halberstam, *The Fifties* (New York: Fawcett Columbine, 1993); Daniel Belgrad, *The Culture of Spontaneity: Improvisation and the Arts in Postwar America* (Chicago: University of Chicago Press, 1998); and on the South in particular, Peter Guralnick, *Last Train to Memphis: The Rise of Elvis Presley* (Boston: Little, Brown and Company, 1994). The romanticization of rebellion in American culture and politics is the subject of my current book project, "Rebel, Rebel: Outsiders in American Culture, 1945–1975."

6. James Baldwin, "Faulkner and Desegregation," *Partisan Review* (Winter 1956), reprinted in *The Price of the Ticket: Collected Nonfiction, 1948–1985* (New York: St. Martin's, 1985), 147–51, quotes, 149; and Ralph Ellison, March 1956, to Albert Murray, in *Trading Twelves: The Selected Letters of Ralph Ellison and Albert Murray* (New York: Modern Library, 2000).

7. Grace Elizabeth Hale, *Making Whiteness: The Cuture of Segregation in the South, 1890–1940* (New York: Pantheon, 1998).

8. Twelve Southerners, *I'll Take My Stand* (1930; Baton Rouge: Louisiana State University Press, 1991), 5.

9. King, *A Southern Renaissance*. I use the term artist in the broadest possible sense to mean novelists, poets, and writers of all kinds as well as musicians and visual artists.

No visual artists are represented here, however, because there has been less of a Southern identity in this area, no school of Southern painting, for example, to rebel against or embrace.

10. James Dickey, *Self-Interviews*, ed. James Reiss (Garden City: Doubleday, 1970), 33; James Dickey, *Deliverance* (Boston: Houghton Mifflin, 1970); and Henry Hart, *James Dickey: The World as a Lie* (New York: Picador USA, 2000). Foote, December 1951, to Percy, 70-72, quote, 71; Foote, April 22, 1951, to Percy, 43; Foote, April 26, 1951, to Percy, 45; Foote, August 22, 1951, to Percy, 52-53, quote, 53; and Foote, August 5, 1970, to Percy, 148-49, quote, 149; in Jay Toleson, ed., *The Correspondence of Shelby Foote and Walker Percy* (New York: Norton, 1997).

11. Faulkner, *Absalom, Absalom!* (1936; New York: Vintage, 1990); *Light in August* (1932; New York: Modern Library, 1968); *The Sound and the Fury* (1929; New York: Modern Library, 1966); "The Bear," in *Collected Stories of William Faulkner* (1950; New York: Vintage, 1977); and *Go Down, Moses* (1942; New York: Vintage, 1990); and Williamson, *Faulkner and Southern History*, 264-65.

12. Engelhardt, *The End of Victory Culture*; Whitfield, *The Culture of the Cold War*; and Gitlin, *The Sixties*.

13. These themes are more fully explored in my forthcoming book, "Rebel, Rebel: Outsiders in American Culture, 1945-1975."

14. James Dickey, November 7, 1954, to Andrew Lytle, James Dickey Collection, Emory University. A slightly different version of this letter appears in Matthew J. Bruccoli and Judith S. Baughman, eds., *Crux: The Letters of James Dickey* (New York: Knopf, 1999), 78-80. Foote, November 8, 1955, to Walker Percy, 104-7, quote, 104; and Foote, February 18, 1952, to Percy, 82-85, quote, 84, in Tolson, ed., *Correspondence of Foote and Percy*.

15. Faulkner, July 30, 1952, to Saxe Commins, as quoted in Williamson, *Faulkner*, 284.

16. Faulkner, *The Sound and the Fury* and *Go Down, Moses*.

17. Faulkner made this comment to Robert Oppenheimer in November 1958. See Blotner, *Faulkner*, 656; and Williamson, *Faulkner*, 310-11.

18. James Dickey, *The Whole Motion: Collected Poems, 1945-1992* (Hanover: University Press of New England, 1992), 202, 235, 237.

19. Foote, August 8, 1956, to Percy, 108-9, and footnote 17, 144, in Tolson, ed., *Correspondence of Foote and Percy*.

20. Dickey, "Notes on the Decline of Outrage," 76-94, in Louis D. Rubin, Jr., and Robert D. Jacobs, eds., *South: Modern Southern Literature in Its Cultural Setting* (Westport, Conn.: Greenwood Press, 1961); Hart, *Dickey*, 254, 290-92, 504-7.

21. Foote, August 13, 1963, to Percy, 124-25, Foote, June 15, 1970, to Percy, 143-44; in Tolson, ed., *Correspondence of Foote and Percy*. See also Helen White and Redding S. Sugg, Jr., *Shelby Foote* (Boston: Twayne Publishers, 1982); Robert L. Phillips, Jr., *Shelby Foote, Novelist and Historian* (Jackson: University Press of Mississippi, 1992).

22. Howe, *The Reporter* 14 (22 March 1956); Hart, *Dickey*; and Foote, April 13, 1955, to Percy, 101-2, in Tolson, ed., *Correspondence of Foote and Percy*.

23. Charlie Daniels Band, "The South's Gonna Do It," on *Fire on the Mountain* (1975). On the South after the civil rights movement, see Dan Carter, *The Politics of Rage: George Wallace, the Origins of the New Conservatism, and the Transformation of American Politics* (Baton Rouge: Louisiana State University Press, 2000); and Numan V. Bartley, *The New South, 1945-1980* (Baton Rouge: Louisiana State University Press, 1995), although neither of these sources pays much attention to youth culture or cultural history in general. On Southern rock, see Ownby, "Freedom, Manhood, and White Male Tradition in 1970s Southern Rock Music"; Wells, "The Last Rebel: Southern Rock and Nostalgic Continuities"; Garofalo, *Rockin' Out*, 283-85; Tucker, "Southern Rock"; and Brant, *Southern Rockers*.

24. Ballinger, *Lynyrd Skynyrd*, 2; and Scott Freeman, *Midnight Riders: The Story of the Allman Brothers Band* (New York: Little, Brown and Company, 1995).

25. Barley, *The New South: The Rise of Massive Resistance: Race and Politics in the South during the 1950's* (1969; Baton Rouge: Louisiana State University Press, 1999); and Carter, *The Politics of Rage*.

26. Chris Charlesworth, "Caught in the Act. Skynyrd: Southern Fried Boogie," *Melody Maker* (December 21, 1974); "The Allman Brothers Story," *Rolling Stone* (December 6,

1973); "Skynyrd's Own Rainbow Show," *New Musical Express* (December 1974); Tom Dupress, "Lynyrd Skynyrd in Sweet Home Alabama," *Rolling Stone* (October 24, 1974); "*Second Helping*—Lynyrd Skynyrd" (album review), *Rolling Stone* (November 7, 1974); Billy Walker and Pete Makowski, "Southern Fried to Roasting," *Sounds* (November 23, 1974); Robert Christgau, "Lynyrd Skynyrd: Not Even a Boogie Band Is As Simple As It Seems," *Creem* (August 1975); Larry Rohter, "Southern Boogie," *Washington Post* (June 21, 1975); and Todd A. Prusin, "Midnight Rider," *Creative Loafing* (March 19, 1994). For descriptions of fans and interviews with band members, see the articles above and Brant, *Southern Rockers*; Ballinger, *Lynyrd Skynyrd*; and entries for the Allman Brothers Band, Lynyrd Skynyrd, and The Marshall Tucker Band at RollingStone.com (http://www.rollingstone.com).

See Martin Scorsese, *The Last Waltz* (1978), a documentary about The Band's last concert in November 1976.

27. Ownby, "Southern Rock," 382. One of the members in the Allman Brothers Band, Berry Oakley, was not from South. Oakley was born in Chicago and grew up in one of its suburbs, Park Forest. See Freeman, *Midnight Riders*. For their music's debt to the blues, see (or hear) *The Allman Brothers Band* (1969), *Idlewild South* (1970), *At Fillmore East* (1971), and *Eat a Peach* (1972), all on Capricorn Records; and *Pronounced Leh-Nerd Skin-Erd* (1973), *Second Helping* (1974), *Nuthin' Fancy* (1975), *Gimme Back My Bullets* (1976), and *One More From the Road* (1976), all on MCA Records. On the blues, see Jeff Todd Titon, *Early Downhome Blues* (1977; Chapel Hill: University of North Carolina Press, 1994), and Robert Palmer, *Deep Blues* (New York: Penguin, 1982).

28. Shorty was Shorty Medlocke, the white father of Rickey Medlocke, a childhood friend of Ronnie Van Zant and a drummer who played for the band's first recording sessions at Muscle Shoals, Alabama. Ballinger, *Lynyrd Skynyrd*, xv, 49, 84–85. In addition to Hank Williams and Ronnie Van Zant, Bob Dylan too claimed to have learned the blues from a blind black Chicago street singer named Arvella Gray. See Carl Benson, ed., *Dylan Companion: Four Decades of Commentary* (New York: Schirmer Books, 1998), 3–10.

29. Ballinger, *Lynryd Skynyrd*, xv, 49, 84–85; Brant, *Southern Rockers*, 30, 71. White men's copying black men's music and black men's style has a long history in America. See for example Eric Lott, *Love and Theft: Blackface Minstrelsy and the American Working Class* (New York: Oxford University Press, 1993); Ann Douglas, *Terrible Honesty: Mongrel Manhattan in the 1920s* (New York: Noonday Press, 1996); Robert Cantwell, *Bluegrass Breakdown: The Making of the Old Southern Sound* (Urbana: University of Illinois Press, 1984), (on blackface performances in country music); Guralnick, *Last Train to Memphis* (on Elvis Presley in particular); and Norman Mailer, "The White Negro," 1957, collected in *Advertisements for Myself* (New York: Putnam, 1959). On British musicians in the 1960s and the blues and other African American music, see Nicholas Knowles Bromell, *Tomorrow Never Knows: Rock and Psychedelics in the 1960s* (Chicago: University of Chicago Press, 2000), which has a chapter on the Beatles and other rock groups and the blues.

30. The Allman Brothers Band, "Whipping Post," on *At Fillmore East* (1971); and "Ramblin' Man," on *Brothers and Sisters* (1973). Lynyrd Skynyrd, "Freebird," on *Pronounced Leh-Nerd Skin-Erd* (1973).

31. I am not arguing that black men really lived this image (although some may have), but that Southern rock musicians tried to copy this bluesman image of black masculinity. Ownby, "Southern Rock," 383–84; Lawrence Levine, *Black Culture and Black Consciousness: Afro-American Folk Thought from Slavery to Freedom* (New York: Oxford University Press, 1977), 190–297; and Mailer, "The White Negro."

32. See the pictures of the bands on their album covers and the photos of the bands that illustrate the articles cited in note 25; Lynyrd Skynyrd, *Freebird*, documentary of a 1976 concert; Freeman, *Midnight Riders*; and Ownby, "Southern Rock."

33. Ballinger, *Lynyrd Skynyrd*, 58–77. In Lynyrd Skynyrd, *Freebird*, the band plays in front of a Confederate flag.

34. Lynyrd Skynyrd, "Sweet Home Alabama," on *Second Helping* (1974). "Sweet Home Alabama," in turn, evokes yet another set of influences that Lynyrd Skynyrd and its fans did not recognize, white men in blackface turning slaves' songs of longing for family left behind—their "sweet Kentucky homes" and "old Virginny"—into the minstrel tradition.

William Faulkner and Guimarães Rosa: A Brazilian Connection

M. THOMAS INGE
AND
DONÁRIA ROMEIRO CARVALHO INGE

Except for James Joyce, few other modern writers have influenced the shape and nature of twentieth-century fiction more profoundly than William Faulkner. It is commonplace to note that nowhere was this influence stronger than in South America, where writer after writer has testified to the power of his example in developing their own voices and artistic visions. Among them were Jorge Luis Borges, Carlos Fuentes, Gabriel García-Márquez, Mario Vargas Llosa, Juan Rulfo, Julio Cortázar, Juan Carlos Onettti, José Donoso, and Isabel Allende, a veritable who's who of Spanish American literature.[1] Less examined, however, has been his presence and influence in Brazil, whose culture and identity differ because of language and social forces that set it apart from the other Hispanic countries.

Nevertheless, some of the same reasons why Faulkner captured the imaginations of the Spanish-speaking writers apply to the world of Portuguese-speaking writers. Deborah Cohn has outlined these reasons as follows:

> [South American writers] ... interpreted the South's experience, its Civil War and resulting sense of regional difference and marginalization, its exclusion from the economic and military successes of the rest of the nation, as well as its problems of underdevelopment in the early decades of this century, as analogous to their own nations' struggles to break the yoke of colonialism and dependency, and to break out of the 'backward' position to which they had been relegated. Carlos Fuentes, who has often acknowledged his debt to Faulkner, once told an American audience that ... "William Faulkner is both yours and ours, and as such, essential to us. For in him we see what has always lived with us and rarely with you: the haunting face of defeat."[2]

Brazil has also shared with the American South "a history of dispossession, of socio-economic hardship, of political and cultural conflict, and of the export of resources to support the development of a 'North'"—that is, the United States.[3] In fact, after 1865, Brazil even provided sanctuary for a group of unreconstructed Confederates who were so unhappy over the outcome of the Civil War that they settled a community a few miles outside

Santa Bárbara near São Paulo called Americana, where they still speak Southern English.[4]

Vargas Llosa also saw direct connections between the social and political histories of the two Souths and the aesthetics of fiction:

> In the Deep South, as in Latin America, two different cultures coexist, two different historical traditions, two different races—all forming a difficult coexistence full of prejudice and violence. There also exists the extraordinary importance of the past, which is always present in contemporary life. . . . Out of all this, Faulkner created a personal world, with a richness of technique and form. It is understandable that to a Latin American who works with such similar sources, the techniques and formal inventions of Faulkner hold strong appeal.[5]

These techniques would include the creation of a fictional community based on reality but designed not to serve as local color but as a microcosm of the entire human society; experiments with language, grammatical structure, and methods of narration and storytelling in an effort to match form and subject matter; and philosophical efforts to address the importance of time and the past in the common history of mankind. The central question Latin Americans posed to Faulkner, according to Tanya T. Fayen, was one of man's freedom in determining his own destiny, "whether or not man's personal destiny is under his creative control or whether it is under the predetermined control of implacable authority which condemns man to a tragic end."[6] All of these same conditions, concerns, and artistic solutions would surface in Brazil, especially with reference to the nation's greatest modern writer João Guimarães Rosa.

Guimarães Rosa was born in the village of Cordisburgo in the state of Minas Gerais on June 27, 1908. He moved to the state capital, Belo Horizonte, for his education, worked for the government, and wrote his first short stories for a local literary magazine. After graduating from medical school at the age of twenty-two, he practiced as a country doctor in the backlands, became involved in the civil war of 1932, and served as a medical officer. An urge to travel led him into the Brazilian foreign service in 1934, which began a distinguished diplomatic career that would place him in a variety of consular capacities in such places as Hamburg, Germany; Bogotá, Colombia; and Paris, France. A volume of poetry, *Magma*, won the poetry prize of the Brazilian Academy of Letters in 1937 but would remain unpublished until 1997. A thousand-page manuscript called "Contos" ("Short Stories") was completed in 1938 but would not be published until 1946 at half its length as *Sagarana*. His reputation as a major writer would be brilliantly established in 1956 with the appearance of two works, *Corpo de Baile* and *Grande sertão: veredas*, to be followed by *Primeiras estórias* in 1962 and *Tutaméia* in 1967. On November 19, 1967, three days after assuming his position as a member of the Brazilian

Academy of Letters, Guimarães Rosa died. Two additional books on which he had been working were published posthumously, *Estas estórias* in 1969 and *Ave, Palavra* in 1970.[7]

In August of 1954, Faulkner came to São Paulo to take part in an international writers conference, two years before Guimarães Rosa would publish his masterwork *Grande sertão: veredas*. While Faulkner toured the city and the countryside, held a press conference, appeared at the Brazil-US Binational Center, and attended one session of the conference,[8] we do not know if he met Guimarães Rosa, then serving his country as Budget Chief of the State Department and deeply engrossed presumably in his own writing.

While it is likely he knew of Faulkner and perhaps even read him, we have no external evidence to prove this. There are records to suggest he was familiar with the poetry of Ezra Pound and T. S. Eliot, and that he admired Homer, Dante, Confucius, Goethe, Melville, Dostoievsky, Tolstoy, Flaubert, Balzac, Kafka, Rilke, Freud, Unamuno, Lorca, Lewis Carroll, Thomas Mann, and Robert Musil. We know too that he spoke six languages fluently (Portuguese, Spanish, French, English, German, and Italian) and read another fourteen.[9] While he need not have depended on translation, there was little available by Faulkner in Portuguese at the time anyway.

According to the best available evidence, two short stories ("Go Down, Moses" and "The Bear"), a collection of stories, and two novels *(Sartoris* and *Intruder in the Dust)* had been published in Portugal by 1954 and almost an equal number in Brazil ("That Evening Sun," "A Rose for Emily," *Light in August*, and *Sanctuary).* A version of *A Fable* would appear in Brazil in 1956. Probably the award of the Nobel Prize for Literature to Faulkner in 1950 would encourage the increasing number of translations that followed after 1956, which by 1999 would total at least thirteen books released in Portugal and another fifteen in Brazil.[10]

The early interest but slow development of translations in Brazil would not appear to suggest a strong desire to make Faulkner available to general readers until the 1980s. Yet according to an unnamed reporter who wrote accounts of two of his appearances for the newspaper *O Estado de São Paulo* in 1954,

> *O Estado de São Paulo* was one of the first newspapers outside the United States to call attention to William Faulkner's work. At a time when in his own country—that is, around fifteen years ago—Faulkner was not yet sufficiently known and appreciated, this newspaper was already publishing articles calling attention to the extraordinary importance of this author, who a decade and a half later would be honored with a Nobel Prize for Literature.[11]

In the course of his articles, the reporter would mention *Sartoris, The Hamlet, Requiem for a Nun, Intruder in the Dust, A Fable, Absalom,*

Absalom!, Sanctuary, As I Lay Dying, Soldiers' Pay, The Wild Palms, Pylon, and *Light in August,* only four of which were available in translation at the time. If the report be true, however, there must have been some discussions going on in the press and among literary people from the time Guimarães Rosa was serving as Vice-Consul in Hamburg, Germany, in the 1940s, over four years before his first book was published.

Proving influence is a difficult if not impossible business at best, short of an outright admission on the part of the author in question, as has been the case with García-Márquez, Fuentes, and many of the South American writers. One would need to examine the library and the papers and correspondence of the writer; study the local reviews of the translations of Faulkner and the criticism with which the writer might have come in contact; and search the work of both for parallels and similarities. Also one should avoid a common conclusion that the influenced writer is somehow less talented or has plagiarized the model writer. All writers borrow from each other, and in the case of Faulkner and Guimarães Rosa, they were both geniuses of an original sort. Both demonstrably changed the shape of fiction in their own countries and will continue to bear influence abroad. Our intention is simply to note some points of similarity and confluence which we have detected in the work of two extremely talented writers facing similar social and cultural circumstances in their respective countries and discovering similar methods and techniques for responding to those circumstances aesthetically. While coincidence may often account for such correspondences, they remain of interest for what they suggest about how two great writers addressed their own times and posterity similarly on the topic of the human condition.

Journalists and critics discussing Guimarães Rosa and seeking parallel talent for points of comparison early on turned naturally to James Joyce, unquestionably the single most influential world writer in modern fiction. The name of Faulkner would inevitably occur next as Joyce's most obvious aesthetic heir and a source of even richer comparative possibilities. In the "Translator's Note" for her 1966 version of *Sagarana,* Harriet de Onís said that Guimarães Rosa was "one of the most skilled practitioners of the art of the short story in the world today—and I am using authors like Catherine Anne Porter, William Faulkner, and Jorge Luis Borges as my basis for comparison."[12] Barbara Shelby in the "Introduction" to her 1968 translation of *The Third Bank of the River and Other Stories* found points of comparison of Guimarães Rosa with Joyce, Thoreau, Emerson, Whitman, Poe, Hawthorne, Melville, and Faulkner, and concluded with regard to the last, "Both authors are preoccupied by the nature of time, and aspects of Rosa's verbal and syntactical manipulation remind one of Faulkner, though Rosa's tendency is toward ellipsis and Faulkner's toward accretion."[13]

Paulo Vizioli's first and only known article to be published in Brazil comparing the two authors appeared in a 1970 issue of the literary supplement to the same newspaper that had declared a continuing interest in Faulkner since the 1940s, *O Estado de São Paulo*.[14] Following a fairly detailed comparison with Joyce, Vizioli provided a well informed and intelligent analysis of both authors in the context of regionalism and the part it plays in their works. He paid attention as well to the presence of moral themes, their use of strong-willed characters, their experimental and difficult prose styles, and their innovations in technique and narrative such as multiple points of view, stream-of-consciousness, and the manipulation of time and plot. This sound and useful beginning has been followed in the United States by a few articles and one dissertation, mostly by Professor Luiz Fernando Valente, who demonstrates a rare command of both languages and a thorough knowledge of both authors.[15] This essay will add some further thoughts to the discussion, limited by the fact that we must deal with Guimarães Rosa through translation, with all the losses in technical virtuosity and stylistic complexity that entails (all quotations will be from the English translations of his works).

Harriet de Onís placed both authors on a level with the best short story writers in world literature. They published their first short stories within four months of each other, Guimarães Rosa contributing "The Mystery of Highmore Hall" to the 7 December 1929 issue of *O Cruzeiro* and Faulkner "A Rose for Emily" to the April 1930 issue of *Forum* magazine, both tales demonstrating a penchant for the mysterious and gothic and the influence of Poe. But their subsequent stories would develop in radically different directions and reflect different dispositions on the art of writing short fiction. Faulkner's stories were well-crafted but mainly traditional in form, being designed to sell to popular American magazines to support the writing of his more radical and experimental novels. Guimarães Rosa wrote stories not for a popular audience but to please himself and in such a different way that critics are not sure what to call them. Ranging in length and complexity, sometimes reading more like essays or character sketches, and often lacking the basic plot structure and conflict of the traditional literary story, they have been referred to as *contos* ("short stories"), *novelas* ("novelettes"), and *romances* ("novels"), and in the case of one critic the coinage *prosoema*, similar to the English "proem," has been used.[16]

The nine stories in his first published collection, *Sagarana* (1946; translated into English in 1966), are written in a thick prose, a richly textured language full of phrases drawn from country wisdom, backwoods folklore, and life lived close to the base line of existence. It is the language of survival and many of the central characters, not always heroes, are involved in finding some sort of meaning and redemption in the brutality, evil, and corruption of life lived outside the norms of law and civilization. Although seldom admirable and usually repellent, they are nearly always fascinating, and we feel compelled to become willing witnesses to their triumphs, tragedies, and often mean deaths. The tales provide deeply felt glimpses into the human condition without recourse to the usual devices of narrative fiction. Like the human heart, they are dense thickets of desire filled with urges to love, consume, and violate the impregnable world around us.

Given their rural settings, it is not surprising to discover numerous analogies in the fiction of Faulkner and Guimarães Rosa on such matters as animals, nature, and folklore. *Sagarana* contains many examples. Faulkner's several comments on the mule,[17] admired for his recalcitrance and independence, find a counterpart in "The Little Dust-Brown Donkey," except rather than describing the mule and telling us his probable thoughts, this story moves inside the donkey and gives us the donkey's point of view. Several of Faulkner's ideas are captured more concisely in passages like the following:

> Though already bridled Seven of Diamonds [the donkey] had no intention of giving in. "He'll go, but it won't be easy," is the motto of an old donkey when he's being annoyed. His ears swiftly assumed a vertical position as he watched the man out of the corner of his eye, taking careful aim to make sure his kick did not miss its mark.[18]

The stampede of wild steers in the same story reminds one of the spotted ponies episode in *The Hamlet*, and Faulkner's Pat Stamper horse-trading stories in the same novel bear interesting comparison with those recounted in a story like "Bulletproof." Rivers, floods, and the forces of nature figure prominently and with symbolic force here as they do in Faulkner and in Mark Twain before him. Guimarães Rosa in fact appears to be borrowing a page from Twain's *Adventures of Huckleberry Finn* when he discusses how the bodies of men drowned in rivers float face up while those of women float face down (55). "Conversation Among Oxen" deals with the transportation of a dead body on an ox cart for burial at a distance as does *As I Lay Dying*, except a second body is added to the funeral progress. The appearance of counterparts to the braggarts and ring-tailed roarers of the American frontier, as in "Bulletproof" and "Augusto Matraga's Hour and Turn" (note especially Juruminho's speech on pages 288–89), and the trickster figure in "The Return of the Prodigal Husband," Lalino, who relates a fable an exact parallel to the story of Bre'r Rabbit in the briar patch by Uncle Remus—these set off cultural resonances of the Twain-Faulkner comic tradition in North American literature. "Mine Own People" contrasts city knowledge with rural folk wisdom, a frequent theme of Faulkner and American humor, and both authors have a penchant for lengthy sentences and catalogues as technical devices (note pages 6–7, 90, and 99–100 for examples).

Guimarães Rosa's second collection of stories, *Primeiras Estórias* (1962; translated into English in 1968 as *The Third Bank of the River and Other Stories*), is unlike his first and anything else the reader is likely to encounter.[19] The twenty-one tales and sketches, between seven and twenty-one pages in length, are mostly told in the first person by a series of narrators about a great variety of characters, the majority of them extreme examples of human behavior (an insane man climbs to the top of a tree and strips naked, or a father goes out in a canoe to the middle of the river and stays there never to return). Faulkner too was fond of idiots and feeble-minded characters, like Benjy Compson and Ike Snopes, usually designed to contrast with the insanity that passes for rationality in the everyday world, but these are in a class by themselves. They are by and large outsiders, deranged and maladjusted people, inhabitants of the backlands who establish their own justice, beggars and thieves, weird and gifted children, loners and foreigners, and even seemingly divine figures who eventually ascend to heaven, as in "A Young Man, Gleaming, White" and "The Girl from Beyond."

Fatal circumstances, violence, fate, and predetermination seem to hedge their lives, and few of them can escape the imprisonment of their bodies. Only a little red cow in "Cause and Effect" seems to exercise total freedom, and even she serves as a pawn in a circumstance that brings two lovers together. One man searches for truth in mirrors only to lose his image altogether in "Mirror," while an Italian keeps a stuffed white horse in his bedroom in "The Horse That Drank Beer."

Many of the titles read like chapters from a philosophical treatise— "The Thin Edge of Happiness," "Nothingness and the Human Condition," or "Cause and Effect"—but they offer no consolation or resolution. The pieces take a variety of forms—narratives, character sketches, contemplative essays, fables, parables, and tall tales. The author has an eye for the bizarre and the unusual and an ear for the speech and dialect of the common people of the backlands of Minas Gerais. Poe and Borges would seem to be his literary masters here, but there is still a good deal of Faulkner in his use of the rural grotesque and his inventiveness in the variety of ways of telling stories.

Nowhere can Faulknerian-style innovation in technique, theme, and sheer brilliance be found in greater evidence than in *Grande sertão: veredas* (1946; translated into English in 1963 as *The Devil to Pay in the Backlands*). Like Faulkner with his Yoknapatawpha County, Guimarães Rosa has created out of his own beloved *sertão*, or backlands, a postage stamp of his native soil, a cosmos of his own which serves at the same time as a microcosm of the larger world and society. The name of his character Riobaldo, which some critics have suggested means a "river" which runs in "vain,"[20] perhaps contains a faint echo of the name Yoknapawtapha, based on a native American word which Faulkner said meant a river or "water that runs slow through flat land."[21] A major theme of Guimarães Rosa is that things are never what they appear to be (like the enigmatic phrase printed on right rear-view mirrors in automobiles, "Objects in mirror are closer than they appear"), a theme that runs throughout the whole of Faulkner's work, especially with regard to narration, history, ethnicity, and gender.

A major ambiguity in the book has to do with the character of Diadorim, to whom Riobaldo is so powerfully attracted emotionally and physically that he is filled with strange desires that cause him to doubt his own sexuality. All the homosexual implications are finally resolved when we learned that Diadorim is a woman, Maria Deodorina da Fé Bettancourt Marins, the daughter of bandit leader Joca Ramiro, raised by him disguised as a boy the better to guarantee her survival in the rough backlands (one is reminded of the country song by Shel Silverstein and Johnny Cash called "A Boy Named Sue" about a boy given a girl's name so he will learn how to defend himself for the sake of survival against taunts and insults in the absence of his father[22]). The disguise also enables her to move more easily in the bandit world of the book to track down and kill the man who murdered her father. She is killed in the effort to revenge her father and maintain his honor.

It is honor too that drives a counterpart to Diadorim in Faulkner's earlier novel *The Unvanquished*. This is Drusilla Hawk, whose fiancé is killed in the Civil War during the battle of Shiloh. Angry over her loss and committed to the cause of the Confederacy, she enters the rebel army disguised as a man and fights throughout the war alongside the soldiers without their knowing her actual gender. Having thus totally compromised herself as a Southern woman in the eyes of the community, the local women assemble to force her to marry Colonel John Sartoris under whom she served during the war. On the way to the ceremony, the couple stops to steal the ballot box to keep the freedmen from voting and to kill two carpetbeggars. The wedding entirely escapes their minds. Later, after Colonel Sartoris is killed in a duel, his son Bayard is required to avenge him according to the Southern code. Drusilla sends him off on his mission after enacting a sexually charged ritual as "the Greek amphora priestess of a succinct and formal violence" by placing in his hands two pistols, "slender and invincible and fatal as the physical shape of love."[23] She tells him, "Sometimes I think the finest thing that can happen to a man is to love something, a woman preferably [note the sexual ambiguity here], well, hard hard hard, then to die young because he believed what he could not help but believe and was what he could not (could not? would not) help but be,"[24] an echo of a phrase later associated with the brief, tragic life of actor James Dean that suggested a man should "live hard, die young, and leave beautiful memories."[25] Realizing that a radical action is required to stop the cycle of violence in the postwar South, Bayard faces his opponent unarmed and drives him from town through shame and loss of honor. Drusilla Hawk and Diadorim would have admired each other as women of independence and courage, and both demonstrated the irrelevance and hypocrisy of culturally imposed gender roles in society. Androgyny can be a powerful and liberating force.

In Faulkner, the truth is seldom clear, certain, ascertainable, or even knowable, and depends on blind biases, imperfect perceptions, and contradictory evidence. We can never be sure what actually happened in many of his novels, given his use of multiple narrators and contradictory versions of events, and readers often have to come to their own conclusions and thus participate in the creative act itself. Faulkner forces us to collaborate in the writing of his novels. So does Guimarães Rosa.

The narrator of *Grande sertão: veredas,* Riobaldo, is sitting in the woods with some of his men, paradoxically near the end of the book and not the beginning, and reports to us, "I had a crazy idea. I would sit in a circle, right there . . ., and relate to them every detail of my life, every foolish thought and feeling, the most unimportant things, early events and recent ones. I would tell them everything, and they would have to listen to me."[26] In essence the author has accomplished just that. The entire book (we hesitate to call it a novel) is a 500-page monologue, without a break or interruption of any kind, a sweeping tall tale or true story (depending on what we can trust or what disbelieve), about everything that has happened to the narrator in the wild hinterland or backlands of the Brazilian northeast, in the northern part of the state of Minas Gerais. But we are not a captive audience without choice. We are rather seduced into listening, drawn into a world of inexhaustible adventure and exotic behavior, and we hang on every word for the surprises and pleasures of each succeeding sentence and paragraph, the author's only concession to traditional story telling in print.

Although Riobaldo says "even a clever storyteller cannot find a way of relating everything at the same time" (340), he seems to succeed in doing just that. Time appears nonexistent as Riobaldo ranges across a lifetime of feelings, events, and travel. We are often not sure where we are in the chronology of things as coincidental associations and unconscious desires dictate what follows upon what. No matter where we touch the narrative, it reflects and influences events elsewhere, vibrating like a vast spider web. We have the impression that the whole narrative is a unitary thing, and we are witnessing an entire lifetime in one not so fleeting instant, as supposedly happens the moment before we drown. Once having finished the book, we feel as if we have embraced a human being who has lived a rich and full life far from our own experience but real nevertheless. Time, language, chronology, and narrative voice collapse into a single fully realized artistic vision unlike anything outside Joyce or Faulkner.

At one point Riobaldo admits, "Ah, but I am not telling the truth. Do you sense it? Telling something is a very, very difficult business. Not because of the years that have gone by, but because certain things of the past have a way of changing about, switching places. Was what I have said true? It was. But did it happen? Now I'm not so sure" (154). It is not that our memories are faulty, or that we intentionally exaggerate, but that the events of our lives actually change and become something else. The present therefore controls the past, and the past controls the present. And when he adds, "everything is merely the past projected into the future" (239), we must conclude that the past, present, and future are ultimately the same thing. This is not unlike Faulkner's belief that the past is never past and remains a presence in the present moment.[27] This also means, however, that the narrator cannot be trusted to tell the truth and any exaggeration then becomes the truth in the telling. Stories can have no conclusion because they are open eternally to revision and rehistoricization. To illustrate the point, Riobaldo tells the story of the two outlaws named Davidão and Faustino (named after the biblical David and the legendary Dr. Faust) who enter into a devilish pact with each other to avoid death. We are given three endings to the story, none of which may be authentic, and the literal minded are given some advice: "In real life, things end less neatly, or don't end at all. To strive for exactitude makes one blunder. One shouldn't seek it. Living is a very dangerous business" (70).

A central concern of the book, as it always was for Faulkner, who structured every novel unlike those that preceded or followed it, is the matter of narrative and point of view: who tells the story and why, where does reality end and fantasy begin, and what is the purpose of fiction? Riobaldo might have agreed with Faulkner who said "those who can, do, those who cannot and suffer enough because they can't, write about it."[28] When Riobaldo's adventures threaten to become a part of the penny press and popular fiction of the day—Zé Bebelo claims, "I want to write up my exploits in the newspapers, with pictures. I'll tell about our battles, the fame that is our due"—Riobaldo promptly responds, "'Not mine, no, sir' I said. He wasn't going to entertain people with my name"(491). This aversion to print and popular fiction privileges the oral tradition over the written word, even though Riobaldo's lengthy monologue ironically has itself been preserved and his wishes betrayed by our author in the book we are reading. In effect we are asked to reconsider the appropriateness and purpose of narratives and stories in our culture, which has been a persistent centuries-long effort to reaffirm our present by establishing and retelling our past. It may be that our archives are not to be controlled and used for political or ideological purposes but rather have their own mission and independent will. Stories tell us, we do not tell them.

Guimarães Rosa not only questions the function and nature of narrative from the perspective of the author but from the other end of the discourse, that of the listener. Throughout the book the listener is given certain attributes by Riobaldo—"My greatest envy is of men like yourself, sir," he tells him, "full of reading and learning" (9), and on other occasions calls him "an unexpected visitor, a man of good sense, faithful as a document" (83) or "a very clever man, of learning and good sense" (398)—and once he is referred to as a writer (380). Perhaps we are to assume the author is functioning in his once real life role as a physician and is thus ministering to Riobaldo's physical as well as psychological needs at the end of his life. Perhaps he is there in his role as a writer and is serving as an amanuensis to Riobaldo by recording for us what the retired bandit chief is telling him. Or perhaps we the readers being addressed directly are meant to be the listener. In any case, because the listener gives himself over to the narrative and comes to grant the narrator a degree of credulity and integrity, the listener is a collaborator in the fictional process. Without us there is no story to tell.

This frame device, of having someone sit around a campfire or a country store and tell a tall tale to the listeners, which includes us the readers, is much the same as that used by the humorists of the Old Southwest in the nineteenth century in the United States. Mark Twain would bring the device into mainstream American literature by having Huck Finn tell his own story in *Adventures of Huckleberry Finn*, except we are also supposed to believe that the practically illiterate fourteen-year-old boy is writing it all down. Faulkner's last novel, *The Reivers* (1962), moved back to the oral tradition by having the narrator relate in a novel-length story what happened to him as a child one summer in Mississippi. In all of these cases, including that of Guimarães Rosa, we must exercise a degree of suspended disbelief in that no one is likely to sit for such lengthy periods of time— Riobaldo tells his in three days (19)—to listen to such stories without breaks for meals, sleep, visiting the toilet, and other obligations of the real world. This is a small concession, however, for such rich returns in reading pleasure, and somehow the discrepancy never bothers us.

The *sertão*, or the backlands, is itself a central character in the book, much as nature and the backwoods of Mississippi served a similar function in Faulkner. It envelops and invades everything and everyone. There is no escaping its presence or denying its influence: "it either helps you, with enormous power, or is treacherously disastrous" (431). We become aware of and intimately associated with the flora and fauna, herbs and insects, ground animals and dangerous beasts, and trees and streams that make up this physical world with a studious care that is almost scientific. Little wonder that those who live with it soon adopt the brutal ways of survival in this chaotic and untamed world. One impulse of the book is to master this wilderness as an essential step in controlling and civilizing man's brutal instincts and tendency towards violence. To master the *sertão* is to save and civilize human nature.

But a greater battle is being waged on the part of Riobaldo in his struggle to deny or believe in Satan. Time and again he returns to the question of his existence and provides at least sixty-six different names for the devil, and sixty of them are retained in the English translation with seven of them in the original Portuguese, a language which has a good many more synonyms and euphemisms for the devil than does English.[29] (In my own second-hand copy of *The Devil to Pay in the Backlands*, the previous owner for reasons unknown took the time carefully to make a full list of them on a page in the back of the book, for other than demonic purposes one hopes.) The book is a veritable catalogue of the names of Satan which in themselves are potent as ways of calling up evil spirits or even the Devil himself, which Riobaldo tries to accomplish one dark and evil night. In theological terms, of course, Riobaldo is attempting to prove the existence of God, because if Satan exists, it would certify the existence of an opposing force, or God. Without the existence of a benign God and the necessity for man to choose between good and evil as a way of proving his faith and goodness, Satan would serve no purpose. Like all doubters, Riobaldo receives no definitive answer to his metaphysical questions and can only conclude in the next to last phrase of the book, "It is man who exists"(492). Which may be a way of saying that Satan exists as a part of man's nature, or we are our own Satans. In that it deals with the eternal struggle over the souls of mankind and the salvation or damnation of the human spirit, the book is on the order of a *Paradise Lost* by John Milton or a *Divine Comedy* by Dante.[30] It also strikes an affirmative note at the end much in accord with Faulkner's conclusion in his Nobel Prize address that man will not merely endure but prevail.

Whether or not Guimarães Rosa ever acknowledged the influence of Faulkner on his work, the number of parallels in theme, technique, and uses of narrative are extensive and suggest familiarity. If he did read Faulkner, like many other South American novelists, he probably felt liberated by the possibility of turning to his own regional world of Minas Gerais as an appropriate fictional matter for fiction, as Faulkner had done in turning to the regional South in his work. He may have learned that one can write universally relevant stories out of local experience, that the nature of time and the influence of history and the past are preoccupations of the modern mind that provide grand themes for the artist, and that the writer can revitalize the language of literature by using an innovative prose style derived from both the oral traditions of the rural backwoods and the carefully crafted styles of world-class authors. In any case, both writers produced complex and difficult novels and stories that have changed the shape of fiction in the United States, Brazil, and the world at large.

NOTES

1. The standard study of the subject is Deborah Cohn, *History and Memory in the Two Souths: Recent Southern and Spanish American Fiction* (Nashville: Vanderbilt University Press, 1999).
2. Ibid., 2.
3. Ibid., 5.
4. Cyrus B. Dawsey and James S. Dawsey, eds., *The Confederados: Old South Immigrants in Brazil* (Tuscaloosa: University of Alabama Press, 1995).
5. Quoted in Cohn, 43.
6. Tanya T. Fayen, *In Search of the Latin American Faulkner* (Lanham Maryland: University Press of America, 1995), 128.
7. No biography has been written. These facts have been gleaned mainly from Jon S. Vincent, *João Guimarães Rosa* (Boston: Twayne Publishers, 1978).
8. George Monteiro, "Faulkner in Brazil," *Southern Literary Journal* 16 (Fall 1983), 96–97.
9. Günter W. Lorenz, "João Guimarães Rosa," *Diálogo com a América Latina: panorama de uma literatura do futuro* (São Paulo: Editora Pedagógica e Universitária Ltda., 1973), 315–55; Kathrin H. Rosenfield, "Devil to Pay in the Backlands and João Guimarães Rosa's Quest for Universality," *Portuguese Literary and Cultural Studies* 4/5 (Spring/Fall 2001), 197–205.
10. See the chronology of Faulkner translations into Portuguese below.
11. Quoted in Monteiro, 98.
12. Harriet de Onís, "Translator's Note," João Guimarães Rosa, *Sagarana* (New York: Alfred A. Knopf, 1966), xv.
13. Barbara Shelby, "Introduction," João Guimarães Rosa, *The Third Bank of the River and Other Stories* (New York: Alfred A. Knopf, 1968), ix–x.
14. Paulo Vizioli, "Guimarães Rosa e William Faulkner," *O Estado de São Paulo*, 11 April 1970, Suplemento Literario, 1.
15. Luiz Fernando Valente, "The Reader in the Work: Fabulation and Affective Response in João Guimarães Rosa and William Faulkner," Ph.D. diss, Brown Univeristy, 1983; "Marriages of Speaking and Hearing: Meditation and Response in *Absalom, Absalom!* and *Grande Sertão: Veredas*," *Faulkner Journal* 11 (Fall 1995/Spring 1996), 149–63.
16. Vincent, 41–42.
17. An early passage in praise of the mule appeared in Faulkner's *Sartoris* (New York: Harcourt, 1929), 226–27.
18. João Guimarães Rosa, *Sagarana*, tr. Harriet de Onís (New York: Alfred A. Knopf, 1966), 14. Subsequent references appear in the text.
19. João Guimarães Rosa, *The Third Bank of the River and Other Stories*, trans. Barbara Shelby (New York: Alfred A. Knopf), 1968.
20. Vincent, 80.
21. Robert W. Hamblin and Charles A. Peek, eds., *A William Faulkner Encyclopedia* (Westport, Connecticut: Greenwood Press, 1999), 446.
22. Recorded by Johnny Cash on February 24, 1969, for his album *Live from Folsom Prison*.
23. William Faulkner, *The Unvanquished* (New York: Random House, 1938), 273.

24. *The Unvanquished*, 261.

25. The origin of the phrase is unknown. The application to James Dean may have derived from a line spoken by actor John Derek in the 1949 film version of Williard Motley's 1947 novel *Knock on Any Door*: "Live fast, die young and have a good-looking corpse." A 1977 documentary by John Gilmore was called *James Dean: Live Fast, Die Young* and was released on videotape in 1999 by Thunder's Mouth Press.

26. João Guimarães Rosa, *The Devil to Pay in the Backlands* [*Grande sertão: veredas*], trans. James L. Taylor and Harriet de Onís (New York: Alfred A. Knopf, 1963), 462. Subsequent references appear in the text.

27. As Gavin Stevens put it in its most frequently quoted form, "The past is never dead, it's not even past." William Faulkner, *Requiem for a Nun* (New York: Random House, 1951), 285.

28. Faulkner, *The Unvanquished*, 262.

29. Nilce S. Martins, *O Léxico de Giumarães Rosa* (São Paulo: Editora de Universidade de São Paulo, 2001), 169. Vincent, 75, 166.

30. Faulkner parodies the tradition in one of his few fantasy passages when Flem Snopes shows up in Hell to confront Satan in *The Hamlet* (New York: Random House, 1940), 149–53.

Chronology of Faulkner Translations into Portuguese

YEAR	PORTUGAL	BRAZIL
c. 1943	"O funeral dum negro" ("Go Down, Moses")	
1945		"Desceu o Sol" ("That Evening Sun") "Uma rosa para Emily" ("A Rose for Emily")
1946	*Contos* (selected short stories)	
1948	*Sartoris*	*Luz de agôsto* (*Light in August*) *Santuário* (*Sanctuary*)
c. 1950	"O urso" ("The Bear")	
1954	*O mundo não perdoa* (*Intruder in the Dust*)	
1956		*Uma fábula* (*A Fable*)
1958	"Folhas vermelhas" ("Red Leaves") *Santuário* (*Sanctuary*)	
1959	*Réquiem por uma freira* (*Requiem for a Nun*)	
1960	*O som e a fúria* (*The Sound and the Fury*) *Os invencidos* (*The Unvanquished*) *As palmeiras bravas* (*The Wild Palms* without "Old Man") *O homen e o rio* (*The Wild Palms* without "The Wild Palms")	
c. 1961	*Luz de agôsto* (*Light in August*)	
1963		*Os desgarrados* (*The Reivers*) "Uma rosa para Emily" ("A Rose for Emily" reprint from 1945)
1964	*Os ratoneiros* (*The Reivers*) *Na minha morte* (*As I Lay Dying*)	
1965	*A aldeia* (*The Hamlet*)	
1970		*Paga de soldado* (*Soldiers' Pay*)
1972	*O Solar* (*The Mansion*)	

1978	*Enquanto agonizo* (*As I Lay Dying*)
1981	*Os invencidos* (*The Unvanquished*)
	Desça Moisés (*Go Down, Moses*)
1982	*Santuário* (*Sanctuary*)
1983	*O som e a fúria* (*The Sound and the Fury*)
1984	*Palmeiras selvagens* (*The Wild Palms*)
1994	*Três novelas famosas* (*Three Famous Novels: "Spotted Horses," "Old Man," "The Bear"*)
1995	*O intruso* (*Intruder in the Dust*)
1997	*O Povoado* (*The Hamlet*)
	A Cidade (*The Town*)
1999	*A Mansão* (*The Mansion*)

Sources: Linton R. Massey, "Man Working," 1919–1962 *William Faulkner* (1968); Theodore Hornberger, "Faulkner's Reputation in Brazil," *Faulkner Studies* 2.1 (Spring 1953), 9–10; Tanya T. Fayen, *In Search of the Latin American Faulkner* (1995); and the authors' collection.

Contributors

Houston A. Baker, Jr., professor of English at Duke University, is the author and editor of more than twenty-five volumes of criticism and poetry, including *The Journey Back: Issues in Black Literature and Criticism*; *Blues, Ideology, and Afro-American Literature: A Vernacular Theory*; *Modernism and the Harlem Renaissance*; *Workings of the Spirit: A Poetics of Afro-American Women's Writing*; and, most recently, *Turning South Again: Re-Thinking Modernism, Re-Reading Booker T.* He is also the editor of the journal *American Literature*.

Deborah Clarke, associate professor of English at Pennsylvania State University, is the author of *Robbing the Mother: Women in Faulkner* and essays and lectures on Camus, Faulkner, Hurston, Morrison, and automobile culture in America.

Grace Elizabeth Hale is associate professor of history at the University of Virginia. She is the author of *Making Whiteness: The Culture of Segregation in the South, 1890–1940* and the forthcoming book "Rebel, Rebel: Outsiders in America, 1945–2000." She has also served as a consultant and commentator for several television documentaries on lynching and the struggle for civil rights.

W. Kenneth Holditch is Research Professor Emeritus from the University of New Orleans, where he taught for thirty-two years. He is the founding editor of the *Tennessee Williams Journal*; the author of a monograph on Williams, *The Last Frontier of Bohemia*; coauthor, with Richard Freeman Leavitt, of *Tennessee Williams and the South*; and coeditor, with Mel Gussow, of the Library of America's two-volume collection of the works of Tennessee Williams. In 2001 he was awarded the Louisiana Endowment for the Humanities Lifetime Achievement Award.

M. Thomas Inge is Robert Emory Blackwell Professor of Humanities at Randolph-Macon College in Ashland, Virginia. He has taught or lectured in over two dozen countries, including Spain, France, Italy, Denmark, Russia, the Czech Republic Argentina, New Zealand, Japan, and China. He is the author or editor over sixty volumes, including *William Faulkner: The Contemporary Reviews* (Cambridge) and *Conversations with*

William Faulkner (Mississippi), and he is writing a compact biography of Faulkner for Overlook Press.

Donária Romeiro Carvalho Inge is professor of English at the Federal University of Espirito Santo in Vitoria, Brazil, where she teaches courses in British and American literature. She is working on a comparative study of magical feminism and Virginia Woolf and Clarice Lispector.

Donald M. Kartiganer holds the Howry Chair in Faulkner Studies at the University of Mississippi and is director of the Faulkner Conference. He is the author of *The Fragile Thread: The Meaning of Form in Faulkner's Novels* and coeditor, with Malcolm Griffith, of *Theories of American Literature*, and with Ann J. Abadie, of seven volumes of proceedings of the Faulkner and Yoknapatawpha Conference. He is near completion of a book-length study, "Repetition Forward: A Theory of Modernist Reading."

George Monteiro, professor emeritus of English and Portuguese and Brazilian Studies at Brown University, is the author, editor, and translator of twenty-five books, including *Robert Frost and the New England Renaissance*, *The Correspondence of Henry James and Henry Adams*, *Fernando Pessoa and Nineteenth-Century Anglo-American Literature*, and *Stephen Crane's Blue Badge of Courage*.

Danièle Pitavy-Souques is professor in the Department of English and director of the Centre for Canadian Studies at the University of Burgundy in Dijon, France. She is the author of numerous essays and of two books on Eudora Welty and another on Canadian women writers. She has lectured widely in Europe, Canada, and the United States, especially on Canadian and Southern American writers.

Peggy Whitman Prenshaw holds the 2003–2004 Eudora Welty Chair in Literature at Millsaps College. Recently retired as Fred C. Frey Chair of Southern Studies at Louisiana State University in Baton Rouge, she is author and editor of volumes on Eudora Welty, Elizabeth Spencer, contemporary Southern women writers, and Southern cultural history. She is a former editor of the *Southern Quarterly* and general editor of the Literary Conversations series published by the University Press of Mississippi. She has also been awarded special recognition for her contribution to the public humanities by the National Endowment for the Humanities, the Mississippi Humanities Council, and the Louisiana Endowment for the Humanities.

Merrill Maguire Skaggs is Baldwin Professor of the Humanities at Drew University. She is the author of *The Folk of Southern Fiction*, *After the World Broke in Two: The Later Novels of Willa Cather*, and *Willa Cather's New York: New Essays on Cather and the City*. Her current research project is a study of "literary conversations and mutual thefts" between Willa Cather and William Faulkner, Ellen Glasgow, and Mark Twain.

Joseph R. Urgo chairs the Department of English at the University of Mississippi. He is the author of *Faulkner's Apocrypha: "A Fable," Snopes, and the Spirit of Human Rebellion*; *Willa Cather and the Myth of American Migration*; *Novel Frames: Literature as Guide to Race, Sex, and History in American Culture*; and, most recently, *In the Age of Distraction*.

Index

Absalom, Absalom! (Faulkner), xv, 14–15, 17, 56–57, 62, 113, 159
Allman Brothers, 164–65, 167–68
Anderson, Elizabeth, 31
Anderson, Sherwood, 3, 24–28, 30–37
Aristotle, 43
As I Lay Dying (Faulkner), 178

Baird, Helen, 30, 33
Bakhtin, Mikhail Mikhailovich, 123
Baldwin, James, 156
Band, The, 165
Barr, Caroline (Mammy), 124–25
Basso, Hamilton, 25, 30–31
Bataille, Georges, 144
"Bear, The" (Faulkner), 5–6, 9–11, 19, 67–68, 85, 159
Beauchamp, Lucas, 100, 133, 136–38, 144, 147, 161, 169
Beauchamp, Terrel (Tomey's Turl), 11
Beckett, Samuel, 122
Benbow, Narcissa, 105
Bible, xiv
"Big Two-Hearted River" (Hemingway), 58
Big Woods (Faulkner), 79
Blake, William, 4
Blotner, Joseph, 114
Bon, Charles, 17
Borges, Jorge Luis, 179
Bradford, Roark, 25, 27, 34
Brooks, Cleanth, 38
Burden, Joanna, 49

Campbell, Harry Modean, 21
Cash, W. J., 95
Cather, Willa, ix, 40–52, 77, 151
Christmas, Joe, 17–18
Clay, Cassius, 9
Compson, Benjy (Benjamin), 7–8, 109, 179
Compson, Caddy, 95
Compson, Jason Lycurgus, III, 95, 104, 106–7
Compson, Quentin, xxv, 66–67, 103, 105

Coughlan, Robert, x–xi
Cowley, Malcolm, 113–15, 119

Daniels, Charlie, 164
de Spain, Major, 170–78
Death in the Afternoon (Hemingway), 64–65, 70, 75–77, 88
Degas, Edgar, 24
"Delta Autumn" (Faulkner), 102
Dickey, James, 155, 159–63, 169
Dos Passos, John, 21–22, 28–29, 77–80, 145
Douglas, Ellen, 113, 116–18, 121–22, 127–30
Douglas, Norman, 32
Doyle, Don, 114
Du Bois, W. E. B., 15, 158

Eliot, T. S., 4–5, 118
Ellison, Ralph, 156

Fable, A (Faulkner), 68, 76
Falkner, Maud Butler, 124–25
Falkner, William Clark, 113
Fathers, Sam (Old Sam), 10
Faulkner, Jimmy, xxxi–xxxii
Feibleman, James K., 26, 33, 47
Fitzgerald, F. Scott, 77, 151
Flags in the Dust (Faulkner), 103–5, 107
Foote, Shelby, 155, 159–63
Ford, Henry, 93–110
Ford, Model T, 94–95, 104
Foster, Ruel, 21
Frankl, Paul, 104–5
Fuentes, Carlos, 173, 176

García Márquez, Gabriel, 176
Gibson, Dilsey, 7, 161
Go Down, Moses (Faulkner), 67–68, 99–102, 159, 161
Gramsci, Antonio, 96
Grove, Lena, 18, 97
Guimarães Rosa, João, 173–85

INDEX

Hamlet, The (Faulkner), 178
Hammett, Dashiell, ix
Hawk, Drusilla, 180–81
Hemingway, Ernest, ix, 21, 54–73, 74–91
Hönnighausen, Lothar, 115
Hurston, Zora Neale, 8

I'll Take My Stand, 98–99, 158–59
"In Another Country" (Hemingway), 55–56
In Our Time (Hemingway), 58–59
Intruder in the Dust (Faulkner), 97, 132–33, 135–38, 140–41, 144–48, 152

Jackson, Andrew and Rachel, 23–24
Jones, Milly, 14
Jones, Wash, 12–15
Joyce, James, 4–5, 173, 176

Kafka, Franz, 142, 144–46
King, Martin Luther, Jr., 7, 9–10

Lacan, Jacques, 122
LaFarge, Oliver, 33, 36
Leibling, A. J., 23
Light in August (Faulkner), 16–18, 50, 69–71, 97, 121, 159
Loos, Anita, 31
Lynyrd Skynyrd, 164–69
Lytle, Andrew Nelson, 98–99, 159–60

Mahon, Donald, Lt., 42–46
Mansion, The (Faulkner), 107
Matisse, Henri, 152–53
McCaslin, Isaac (Ike), 10–11, 19, 67–68, 102–3
"Mississippi" (Faulkner), 114–15, 123–25
Montagu, Ashley, 16–17
Morrison, Toni, 9–11, 19
Mosquitoes (Faulkner), 34–35, 40

NAACP, 157
New Orleans, 22–38, 47
Nobel Prize Acceptance Speech (Faulkner), 83, 184

O'Connor, Flannery, 113, 151
Old Man and the Sea, The (Hemingway), 80–82
Old Sam. *See* Fathers, Sam
One of Ours (Cather), 40–51

Percy, Walker, 37, 160
Perkins, Maxwell, 75
Picasso, Pablo, 152–53
Pilkington, John, 22
Piper, Louis, 32
Pitot, Genevieve, 34–35
Plimpton, George, 63
Poe, Edgar Allan, 179
Polk, Noel, 114
Ponder Heart, The (Welty), 132–36, 138–53
Portable Faulkner, The (Cowley), 119
Presley, Elvis, 156, 157, 167–68
Private World of William Faulkner, The (Coughlan), x–xi
Proust, Marcel, 87

RAF, 46, 72, 100
Ransom, John Crowe, 99
Reivers, The (Faulkner), 104, 183
Reynolds, Michael, 85–88
Ricœur, Paul, 147
Robber Bridegroom, The (Welty), 119–20, 126, 151
"Rose for Emily, A" (Faulkner), 177

Sanctuary (Faulkner), 75
Sartoris, Bayard, 49, 102–6, 180
Sartoris (Faulkner), 49–50
Sartre, Jean Paul, 142
Saxon, Lyle, 27–28
Shakespeare, William, xiv, 33
Sherwood Anderson and Other Creoles (Faulkner and Spratling), 34
"Short Happy Life of Francis Macomber, The" (Hemingway), 59–60
Smyth, Joseph Hilton, 24, 32
Snopes, Ike, 179
Snopes, Linda, 107
"Snows of Kilimanjaro, The" (Hemingway), 60–62
Soldiers' Pay (Faulkner), 41–46, 50
Souls of Black Folk, The (Du Bois), 15
Sound and the Fury, The (Faulkner), xiii, 6–8, 40, 66–67, 106–7, 120, 159, 161
South Wind (Douglas), 32
Spencer, Elizabeth, 113, 116, 118, 121–22, 126–27, 130
Spratling, William, 32–34
Stein, Jean, xi
Stevens, Gavin, 97, 140–41, 145, 147–48

Stone, Phil, 3
Sun Also Rises, The (Hemingway), 58–59
Sutpen, Henry, 30
Sutpen, Judith, xv
Sutpen, Thomas, 4, 12–15, 127

Tate, Allen, 159
Tennie, 11
Tennie's Turl. *See* Beauchamp, Terrel
Todorov, Tzvetan, 122–23
Tomey's Turl. *See* Beauchamp, Terrel
Town, The (Faulkner), 107–8
Twain, Mark, 96, 178, 183

Ulysses (Joyce), 4–5, 35
Uncle Buddy, 11, 99–102
University of Mississippi, The (Ole Miss), 21–22, 30
Unvanquished, The (Faulkner), 180–81
USA (Dos Passos), 28–29

Valery, Paul, 63
Vargas Llosa, Mario, 174

Wallace, George, 165
"Wash" (Faulkner), 12–15
Wasteland, The (Eliot), 5
Watson, James G., 115–16
Welty, Eudora, 113, 118–20, 122–23, 125–26, 130, 132–53
Wild Palms, The (Faulkner), 36–37, 76–77
William Faulkner in Oxford (Webb and Green), x
Williams, Tennessee, 23, 28, 36–37
Wilson, Edmund, 24, 31
Winesburg, Ohio (Anderson), 3
Wolfe, Thomas, 77–78, 90
Wright, Richard, 6, 19, 116, 156

Yaeger, Patricia, 123

www.ingramcontent.com/pod-product-compliance
Lightning Source LLC
Chambersburg PA
CBHW030343240426
43661CB00052B/1723